MOTHER MARY TERESA
OF ST. JOSEPH

THE SERVANT OF GOD,
MOTHER MARY TERESA OF ST. JOSEPH

THE SERVANT OF GOD

MOTHER MARY TERESA OF ST. JOSEPH

(Anna Maria Tauscher van den Bosch)

FOUNDRESS OF THE CARMEL OF THE DIVINE HEART OF JESUS

An Autobiography

TRANSLATED BY
REV. BERCHMANS BITTLE, O.F.M.Cap.

CARMELITE SISTERS, D.C.J.
1230 KAVANAUGH PLACE
WAUWATOSA, WISCONSIN 53213

NIHIL OBSTAT:
MSGR. JOHN F. MURPHY
Censor Librorum
IMPRIMATUR:
REMBERT G. WEAKLAND
Archbishop of Milwaukee
February 14, 2000

FOREWORD
TO THE 3RD EDITION OF THE AUTOBIOGRAPHY OF OUR MOTHER MARY TERESA

After nearly 50 years this edition appears in the English language.

New zeal and new love to work for the salvation of souls, in the old as well as the new world, comes from the Autobiography of our Mother Foundress as from a fountain.

In the last decades there have been great revolutionary changes in the world and in Church history, and also in the history of our Carmel, D.C.J.

But Mother Mary Teresa had strongly emphasized that this foundation is "God's work." And that has become obvious through God's protection in so many dangers that have poured over the people in different lands. Our Sisters have even been able to alleviate the needs of others.

God wants to use us as instruments of His merciful love. And so the spirit of our Foundress remains active in the Carmel of the Divine Heart of Jesus. In her time Mother Mary Teresa cared for the poor, and especially the children in Berlin and other localities. So in these years, in the times of war, in the needs resulting from natural catastrophes and in the many sufferings that are so manifest, our Sisters have cared for the poor and neglected and those who have become homeless.

Although our Congregation has become smaller in numbers it is seen that God's strength works in the weak. With special gratitude we acknowledge the numerous vocations that God's love is sending us in Latin America and Croatia. But the vocations also in our other Provinces clearly show us God's love and that He continues "His work" also today.

Through repeated reading and pondering on this Autobiography may new hope and firm confidence be awakened in all.

Many people, who come to the grave of our dear Mother Mary Teresa of St. Joseph here in our General Motherhouse, receive strength and patience to endure their various sufferings.

In this way what our Foundress once said is fulfilled, that from Heaven she would dry tears and heal the wounds of souls.

We continue to pray that God will allow that soon a miracle, through the intercession of our dear Mother, can be accepted by the Church and that we will receive the grace that Mother Mary Teresa will be raised to the honor of the altar, for the greater honor of God and as a sign of encouragement for many.

Mother M. Katharina of the Immaculate Heart of Mary,
Superior General
Sittard, April 25, 1999

September 8, 1999

Some years ago I attended a reception at the Carmelite Day Nursery in Toronto on the occasion of a Sister's jubilee. During the reception I met, after some thirty years, some of the women whom I had known, in the early 50's, as young mischievous inhabitants of the Carmelite Girls' Home. There was one in particular (I will not mention her name) who had been, seemingly forever, conjuring a prank or two. Now she was a serious, mature woman, a wife and mother, showing by her very presence her gratitude for what she had been given by the Carmelite Sisters. She is one of the many beneficiaries and success stories of Mother Mary Teresa and her Sisters.

Mother Mary Teresa's autobiography is an extraordinary document. It describes her way from the Lutheran into the Catholic Church, her arrow-like, at least in retrospect, way to found a religious community, and her success after many difficulties and uncertainties.

The autobiography is puzzling as well, because it does not, and is not meant to reply to questions which rise unbidden in connection with what we are told. She tells us how God had led her from the earliest years of her life. We wish to be given something which would allow us to discern the psychological source and growth of her almost instinctive Catholicity, which was perceived by her own family. Likewise we would wish to know the concept and concrete image of what she felt called to by God at various stages of her progress towards creating a religious community devoted to the poor. One cannot help but be amazed at her genuine humility and respect for Church authorities and equally firm will to follow what she knew God expected of her. Of the fact of His plans for her personally she obviously never had any doubt.

Mother Mary Teresa must have been a very attractive person, and very strong and persuasive at the same time. Above all, however, she was a woman who obeyed God's will and served His poor.

Aloysius Cardinal Ambrozic,
Archbishop of Toronto

vii

Rome, January 6, 1999

With great joy we greet and bless the 3rd edition of the Autobiography of Mother Mary Teresa Tauscher van den Bosch, whose cause is in Rome in the process of beatification.

In 1897, Mother Foundress, on her first trip to Rome, received assistance and encouragement from our Carmelite Fathers, especially from Fr. Benedikt Herzog, OCD, an Austrian, who was Definitor General at the time. It is here she became more strengthened in her resolve to remain faithful to the Carmel, come what may.

Some years later, in 1904, again in Rome, the name of the Congregation was given: "Carmelite Sisters of the Divine Heart of Jesus" and it remains this today. The Congregation was aggregated, the same year, to our Carmel OCD, and in this we rejoice, because Mother Mary Teresa was not only a Carmelite Sister in the depths of her heart, she was also open to the needs of her time. In the fifty-eight "St. Joseph's Homes" she founded during her lifetime, she endeavored to alleviate the suffering of so many children, who were in need of motherly care. One hundred years ago she introduced into her Homes the family system, and practiced what we call today the "New Evangelization" by sending out her Sisters to bring the people back to the Church. Her primary intention was to found "Homes for the Homeless", not only to care for the physical needs, but also for the spiritual needs - which are even more important.

We consider Mother Mary Teresa worthy of being elevated to the honor of the altars, because her exemplary life and her message are pertinent for today, now more than ever. Even in the difficult years of foundation her heart was always in close union with God, and the last years of her life, she led a more contemplative life in accordance with the Rule of Carmel. She offered all her physical pains for the Church. Today we hear so many critical voices, but we need souls who will offer themselves for the Church, as did Mother Mary Teresa. And there have never been so many children waiting for someone to give them a "Home". Last, but not least, there are so many souls away from the Church in search of a spiritual home.

May our Dear Lord bless the work initiated by Mother Mary Teresa and impart his spirit among many young women to continue her work with renewed zeal in the new millennium.

Fr. Camilo Maccise OCD,
General of the Order of the
Discalced Carmelites

LETTER OF
FATHER SIMEONE OF THE HOLY FAMILY, OCD

Rome, January 21, 1977

This book is truly soul stirring.

Mary Teresa of St. Joseph, Foundress of the Carmel of the Divine Heart of Jesus, has written these accounts for her daughters so that they "will see God's guidance, and the individual blessings of God" in the foundation of her Congregation. She was convinced that her daughters had a right to know all this, and that she would have done them an injustice if she had withheld from them a faithful and accurate record of the mercies of the Heart of Christ in "her work." Without doubt the Mother had no idea of its being published; at least she had no dream that far beyond her religious community the mystery of the merciful workings of Divine Love would become known, the Love which "wounds and soothes the sore, which hurts and heals with the same hand" (cf. Job 5:18). For on these simple and unadorned, yet honest and true-to-life pages, we meet with a succession of pain and persecutions, of misunderstandings and martyrdom, all accepted, borne with and cherished like a present or a favor. The more this person's suffering increases in depth and in breadth, the more her ability grows to participate in Christ's suffering and love, until it becomes almost second nature. Thus we can understand her words:

"I have but one wish: to suffer as much as possible for this short while. It does not matter what kind of suffering, as long as it is suffering, and from my heart I bless and thank all who have caused me suffering. To be able to suffer for God is the only joy which heaven does not have."

These are terrific expressions, and they are frightening. We could hardly understand them if we did not find familiar words in them, spoken by Teresa of Avila and Therese of Lisieux, and if we did not know that the great lovers of God do not succeed in drawing nearer to God, in feeling the pulsation of His Heart and in contemplating the mystery of His suffering, without feeling the necessity to love as He loved, which means through

x

the cross, and thereby making up for all that still has to be undergone in the Passion of Christ for the sake of His Body, the Church (cf. Col. 1:24).

The pages of this book reveal that Mary Teresa Tauscher belongs to this host of lovers of God. She knows that the history of Redemption is as much a permanent gift of the joy of the Resurrection, as it is the representation of the Easter mystery of death and life, which Christ has consummated on the Cross and which will continue in His friends. How striking are the words coming from the Mother's lips shortly before her death: "I am firmly convinced that all the sacrifices were necessary." No complaint, no bitterness about the painful way she had to go. Nothing but patience, gratitude and devotion. A word, stammered in her last days reveals this to us: "All-that-God-does-is-good! Always-praise-and-glorify-God!" One could call it the last testament of Mary Teresa. It could also be considered the most beautiful summary of her life, her desires, her ideals, and her entire manifold activities in favor of the little and lowly.

A true autobiography, this is what this book has become, exactly because it was never intended to be an autobiography. Above all, the reader is impressed by the writer's sense of reality, when she observes what is happening in and around her; also by her fortitude, when she, leaning on God, pursues the goals she has recognized as God's Will. Her composure gives her calm even in the midst of the "thicket of the cross."

These are truly outstanding characteristics in her which can be explained only in the light of tremendous faith, unwavering hope and immense love. From the day she encountered Christ anew and, though still obscure, discovered His loving Providence for her, there was no more wavering. She had experienced Divine Love in its complete fullness, and had her heart opened wide for the stream flowing from the Heart of Christ Himself. Therefore, without fail, she had to pass the overflowing fullness of the love of Christ on to the Church and there, within the Church, especially to the littlest and most forsaken, the children and later, also the aged. And so, the "St. Joseph's Homes" come into existence. Through an ever increasing interior clarity and vigor, her beloved child, "the Carmel of the Divine Heart of Jesus," fruit of a painful and, at the same time, joyful birth, begins to bloom. She planted the seed of her labor with fortitude, fidelity and love. These seem to be also the most outstanding pillars of the ideal and the work of the Servant of God. However, one must be cautious when typecasting her this way. In the course of her life, filled with long, restless years of activity and toil, all facets of Christian holiness gradually unfold, each according to the grace of the moment, or more correctly, depending on what response the love of Christ demanded of her.

In telling us about the beginning and the difficult upholding of her work, Mary Teresa Tauscher unknowingly reveals to us, in simple words, some of the deepest secrets of her soul. She does not write any learned treatises, she does not spend time on extensive analysis of her spiritual life, and does not explore and investigate the secret of her prayer life. Even in such instances where she has no choice but to indicate the extraordinary interventions of Divine Love in her life, she exposes them timidly, almost fearfully. Apparently she intends to trace out only the simple and yet luminous way of Divine Mercy which "accomplishes all."

It is in this way that the book is a true autobiography, a work, which combined with her letters, reveals the story of her soul better than any literary reconstruction could do. At a given time, Mary Teresa Tauscher will without doubt incite a good historian to study her complete life in its various aspects. We wish that we will soon have a complete biography in our hands, which will give us more than the Mother has told us with so much reticence.

One quality of the Servant of God we wish to underline is her deep devotedness to the Carmel, and her desire to be a Carmelite at all costs. At the beginning of this century she was in communication with several of the most distinguished men of the Order. We meet with their names in this book; Cardinal Gotti, Father Rinaldus a S. Justo, Father Benedikt Zimmermann, and above all, the Servant of God, Father Antonius a Jesu Intreccialagli, Provincial in Rome and later Archbishop of

Montreal. It was he who supported the Mother in difficult negotiations in Rome. He was her inspiration and guide, and he was also accredited with having decided the final name of the Congregation, "Carmel of the Divine Heart of Jesus."

Mary Teresa wholly believed herself to be a Carmelite. She had inherited from Teresa of Avila the unbounded love for Christ and the Church, the spirit of prayer, the joy of the cross, and devotion to St. Joseph. From Teresa of Avila she also had the luminous faith, the unshakable hope and the consuming love. Like Teresa of Avila she does not mind difficulties, trials, persecutions, and extensive travels, if the glory of God, the honor of the Church and the salvation of souls were at stake.

These pages acquaint us with Mary Teresa Tauscher by plunging us into the stream of love that consumed her. They urge us to praise God, who again and again lets the flowers of grace blossom in His Church. They encourage us to live our Christian calling with fidelity and magnanimity, which means to follow Christ in truth by spending ourselves for others, especially for the littlest, the poorest and the most forsaken. True to her talent, the Mother brought her love to life by placing herself in the service of Divine Love, a service in the way of poverty, simplicity and prudence from which no one could ever dissuade her. She had understood that Christ wanted to be loved precisely in the orphans and forsaken; that He wanted to be served particularly in the aged. While others have different missions in the Mystical Body of Christ, this is what Jesus wanted from her and her family. And He wanted it to be lived with the sensitivity of His Heart, with the loving attentiveness of His Spirit and with total availability. Mary Teresa was faithful to this calling, and she wanted her daughters to be faithful to it also.

For the Carmelite Sisters of the Divine Heart of Jesus, these pages are a reminder of their vocation and mission in the Church, after the example of their Foundress. For all of us, they are a lesson on how we must love Christ in works and in truth, and love our brethren with the Heart of Jesus Himself.

L.S.
Fr. Simeone della S. Famiglia, O.C.D.

LETTER OF
THE PASTOR OF HOLY APOSTLES CHURCH

Cologne, February 7, 1977

The hour had a catacomb-like atmosphere. The sacristan at Holy Apostles had just rung the Angelus. Then he went hurriedly to lock the portals of his 1000 year-old Church. He looked once more in all directions to ensure no one had remained in the Church. Now he placed a priedieu in front of the altar of the Blessed Virgin on the epistle side, and went into the sacristy. Here Chaplain Heinrich Esser, administrator at Holy Apostles, was waiting for him. There was a lady with him whose joyful excitement was obvious at first sight. The longing for many years was to be fulfilled on this Anna Maria Tauscher. At the same time all parties concerned were nervous and fearful as though something illicit was going on.

The "Kulturkampf" had reached its climax. For years, the Church of the Holy Apostles had been without a pastor, as were so many other parishes in the surrounding area. The Chancery, the Seminary and the Residence Hall had been closed by the government. Archbishop Melchers had been expelled from the country – accused of treason. The director of the large municipal Lindenburg clinic had simply forbidden the superior of the psychiatric ward, Maria Tauscher, to follow her own conscience and join the Catholic Church. Maria Tauscher went "underground." Instead of the Chaplain of Lindenburg Hospital, it would be Chaplain Esser to admit her into the Church. Before the large Madonna painted by Johann Huelsmann, disciple of Ruebens, the simple rite was now enacted.

Something greater than an evasion of the Kulturkampf is taking place here: The Kulturkampf is being overcome. The Catholic Christian, Maria Tauscher, penetrates into the essence of being Christian. In an environment filled with rejection, she lays the foundation of a community of love. Into the mental image of a government, possessed by power and force, she re-establishes the importance of the heart. Modern society is oppressed by social questions, but does not know how to master them. Maria Tauscher makes a practical contribution to the solving of the social question by her foundations in favor of the children and the poor. Behind the locked doors of Holy Apostles, undercover of fear, a seed starts to germinate and to grow, promising a rich harvest.

This Autobiography is, therefore, not just any kind of reading. It is rather a reading which opens a door, a door of hope for the years to come:

Through this door may many go in and out, to serve the heart!

Prelate D. Dr. Th. Schnitzler
Pastor at Holy Apostles

Einst nahm Gott ein wenig Erde in Seine Hände und schuf daraus den ersten Menschen. Am 17 Juni 1887 nahm Es mir ein wenig Sand, ein Stäublein, das die göttliche Vorsehung schon vom Osten in den Westen des Reiches getragen hatte, zur Hand und durchglühte dies arme Staub- oder Sand-Körnlein mit Seines Herzens Liebesglut um aus ihm ein Werkzeug Seiner göttlichen Majestät zu bilden. — Wunderbar ist Gottes Walten und Gottes Schaffen! Ja, für unser menschliches Fassungs-Vermögen oft völlig unbegreiflich! —

Viele Male im Laufe der Jahre wurde ich von meinem Gewissen gemahnt, meinen lieben Müttern und Schwestern, die Stiftung des Carmel vom göttlichen Herzen Jesu mit den göttlichen Gnadenerweisen, die nicht mich rein persönlich sondern dies „Werk Gottes" betreffen, aufzuzeichnen.

Handwriting of the Foundress

This is actually the first page of Dear Mother's Autobiography. The first paragraph was never translated into English.

DAS WALTEN GOTTES
ODER
DIE GESCHICHTE DES KARMELS
VOM GÖTTLICHEN HERZEN JESU

Einst nahm Gott ein wenig Erde in seine Hände und schuf daraus den ersten Menschen, Am 17, Juni 1887 nahm er nur ein wenig Sand, ein Stäublein, das die göttliche Vorsehung schon vom Osten in den Westen des Reiches getragen hatte, zur Hand und durchglühte dies arme Staub-oder Sandkörnlein mit seines Herzens Liebesglut, um aus ihm ein Werkzeug seiner göttlichen Majestüt zu bilden. – Wunderbar ist Gottes Walten und Gottes Schaffen! Ja, für unser menschliches Fassungsvermögen oft völlig unbegreiflich! –

Viele Male im Laufe der Jahre wurde ich von meinem Gewissen gemahnt, meinen lieben Müttern und Schwestern die Stiftung des Karmels vom Göttlichen Herzen Jesu mit den göttlichen Gnadenerweisen, die nicht mich rein persönlich, sondern dies "Werk Gottes" betreffen, aufzuzeichnen.

Einzelne außerordentliche Ereignisse hatte ich schon in Amerika niederzuschreiben begonnen, dies waren jedoch nur lose Blätter ohne Zusammenhang. Erst als ich nach Europa zurückgekehrt war und mehrere Hundert, während meiner Abwesenheit aufgenommene Schwestern kennenlernte und bemerkte, daß die Stiftungsgeschichte des Karmels vom Göttlichen Herzen ihnen ziemlicb fremd war, fühlte ich mich veranlaßt, noch einmal und nun der Reihenfolge nach, angefangen mit der Heranbildung des armen Werkzeuges bis zum Jahre 1925, die Geschichte dieses Gotteswerkes niederzuschreiben.

Ich halte dies jetzt, am Schlusse meines Lebens, für meine Pflicht; denn ich bin überzeugt, daß Sie alle mit mehr Eifer oder erneutem Eifer und viel größerem Interesse und mit Liebefürden von Gottselbst gestifteten, neuen Zweig des Karmels erfüllt sein werden, wenn Sie das Walten Gottes, die einzelnen Gnadenerweise Gottes kennen. Es scheint mir sogar, daß Sie ein Recht haben, als treue Glieder des Karmels vom Göttlichen Herzen, diese zu wissen und es wie ein Unrecht meinerseits wäre, falls ich sie Ihnen vorenthalten würde.

GOD'S DISPOSITIONS OR
THE HISTORY OF THE CARMEL
OF THE DIVINE HEART OF JESUS

INTRODUCTION

Once God took a little soil in His Hands and from it He created the first man. On June 17, 1887, He took a small grain, a tiny particle of dust, which Divine Providence had already carried from the east to the west of the empire. He put it in His Hand, and inflamed this poor particle of dust, or sand, with the burning love of His Heart, in order to shape a tool of His Divine Majesty. How wonderful is God in his works and in His creation! Yes, for our limited human understanding it is totally incomprehensible!

In the course of many years my conscience often admonished me to write down the history of the founding of the Carmel of the Divine Heart of Jesus for my dear Mothers and Sisters, together with all the favors which concern this work of God, rather than my own person.

Some extraordinary events I began to record while in America, but they were written only on loose leaves, without connection. After my return to Europe however, I became acquainted with the several hundred Sisters received into the Community during my absence, and I noticed that the history of the Carmel of the Divine Heart of Jesus was rather unknown to them. Thus I felt moved to write the history of this work of God once more, this time in sequence, starting with the development of the poor instrument of this work, up to the year 1925.

Now, at the close of my life, I feel it to be my duty to write this history, for I am convinced that all of you will be filled with greater or renewed zeal, with much greater interest and love for the new branch of the Carmel, founded by God Himself, if you recognize the Hand of God and each one of His single favors. It seems to me that you even have a right, as faithful members of the Carmel of the Divine Heart, to know all of these favors, and it would be an injustice on my part if I withheld these facts from you.

I was always aware that I was an instrument in the hands of God, and that God's favors were not, in the least, meant for me personally, but solely for the work, which His abundant kindness and mercy had entrusted to me.

Manifesting these things to you, I feel deeply humiliated before all of you, who have known and seen me, because, despite all my efforts, I have never become a true religious.

Please remember that the lowliness of the tool heightens the glory of the Master. Quite often this thought filled me with new courage and trust, when I was downhearted or deeply saddened because of my misery and my failure to make progress.

Although I have taken great pains to be exact, some inaccuracies will occur regarding persons and dates, for in the course of years one easily forgets or confuses such things. The major events however, and also God's special favors, I have always noted correctly.

Mother Mary Teresa

CONTENTS

xxii

GOD'S DISPOSITIONS

OR

THE HISTORY OF THE CARMEL
OF THE DIVINE HEART OF JESUS

CHAPTER ONE

IN THE DESERT

Sandow, the place of my birth, is situated in the Mark of Brandenburg, not far from Frankfurt on the Oder. The countryside is most pleasing, with beautiful forests, meadows, and fertile fields. The hilly country, to where the village extends, is covered with forests. But what delighted me more than the hills, the woods, and the meadows was the Muehlenbach Creek with its gushing and glistening waters.

This country parish, together with the outlying villages, was the first assignment of my father as a pastor. The church on the ridge, like the whole village, was poor and without beauty, making a cold impression inside and out. It was a true picture of Protestantism.

A short distance from the church was the school. Somewhat nearer to the main road was the parsonage, which was a one story building with rooms in the attic, a style common to all the homes in the Mark. The front lawn and the two snowball trees by the front door gave the rectory a friendly appearance.

I was born on June 19, 1855, and was not baptized until July 24. My paternal grandfather, who was a minister, as were also all his ancestors without exception since the unfortunate so-called Reformation, was the cause of the delay of my baptism. He personally wished to baptize the first child of his oldest son. I received the name Anna Maria. The name Maria had been given to both my mother and to her mother in baptism. I believe that the Mother of God protected me from childhood in a special manner and that I owe all to her motherly care and intercession.

In this lovely corner of the earth, far from the busy world, I spent the first six years of my life. My mother recorded some incidents of my first years. For example, when I was just about eighteen months old, my father took me into the garden just at the time when the first frost had destroyed all the beauty of the flowers. My mother penned this note, "Maria was very sad when she saw the frozen flowers and said, "Packan bit all the flowers."

This, to my sorrow, appeared to me like an omen. I saw in Packan, our Newfoundland dog, an evil spirit, and in the flowers the immortal souls who became victims of that spirit through the ages. In fact, nothing filled all the days of my life so much so as the desire to regain these victims from the enemy. It became the aim of my prayers and labors.

My aunt, the sister of my mother, in speaking of the time of our stay in Sandow, said, "You have been a very pious child, always quiet and happy. There is not much to say about you other than you were a little angel."

My father was more of an artist than a pastor. During his four years at the University in Berlin he also studied music and painting. He loved to draw and paint nature. The park and the nearby forest with its beautiful groups of trees offered excellent subject matter to him. He often went out into the forest with his pen and note pad to sketch, and at such times I was permitted to go along and play nearby.

My mother, no matter where we moved, acted as the mother of the poor, counselor of the afflicted, and nurse to the sick. When still a young girl, she became president of a society to take care of the poor. She had inherited this benevolence from her father. Once she had told me that on part of their land there had been a home for working people, where they could live rent-free. At Sandow, my mother, to my greatest delight, always took me along when she was visiting the sick. The misery and poverty of the poor aroused in me a deep compassion, so much so, that after so many years, I still remember the names of those families, their homes, their poor beds, and their unsanitary conditions.

Through the grace of God I was not the only child of my parents. Seven other children followed me. Four children were born much later. Three died in infancy. My sister Lisa, who was next to me in age, was a beautiful, lively child. Fortunately, she was very talkative, and when I was only five, she was considerably taller than I, so that I was taken for the younger and could remain unobserved. This pleased me very much. The third child was my sister Magdalena. She was different. Magdalena was talented, vivacious, and more like a boy than a girl. Because of her sweet voice my mother called her "my nightingale." I myself was a quiet, deep child, and showed remarkable endurance at play. For playthings we had toy blocks with which I would build churches and rectories. This was my most enjoyable occupation.

On Sundays and holy days I went to church. I could not follow the sermons, but I loved God, and the Lord in His inscrutable way and fatherly love, graciously looked upon me and blessed me.

My most cherished remembrance of my childhood is that of a great grace bestowed on me when I was about five years old. I was sleeping, but it is unforgettable for me. In the drawing room I saw our Divine Savior surrounded by many children. His countenance, expressing

3

love and kindness, enkindled in me the fire of divine love. From that time on I became more serious, for the picture of our Savior was always before my eyes and filled me with the desire that all children should love God as I did. That there should be grownups who would not love Him I did not even surmise. Due to my reticence one can understand my keeping this experience and my feelings to myself. Not even to my mother did I speak of it.

By this time there were four sisters in our family. In the year 1860 or 1861 my mother became critically ill and her death was expected almost any moment. Great pain filled my heart when a friend of my mother came to tell me that my mother would soon go to heaven. But, if I remember correctly, despite my sorrow, I did not weep.

God be praised! My mother recovered, and I could again sit at her feet and listen to her stories. I never tired of listening to the Bible stories and other anecdotes my mother would tell my sisters and me, in which confidence in God was visibly rewarded. Her stories and her realistic telling of them created in my soul a greater love of God and a firmer trust in Him.

The quiet solitude of our country life was enlivened by the occasional visits of my grandparents or other relatives. Such solitude was also enhanced by trips to Frankfurt on the Oder, when I was permitted to accompany my mother, and by a journey to the seashore, where I made my first boat trip on the Bay of Stettin.

As a rule, we had no playmates outside our family. One time it happened (I do not know how) that my sister Lisa and I visited a family who had two daughters our own age. While we were there we went into the garden to eat grapes. We did not know that these children were forbidden to eat the grapes, for in that case we would not have done so. Alas! Scarcely had we returned home when the father of these children came over to complain to my father that we had seduced his children to eat of the forbidden fruit. My father was deeply offended, and being by nature rather vehement, he came to me in great excitement and asked whether or not I had eaten the grapes. I trembled in great fear, for I had never been punished before, nor had I ever seen anybody look so furious, so I answered, "No." My father became more angry and punished me for lying. Yes, I had told a lie. How many tears did I shed for this dreadful lie! I regretted it and confessed it later. This lie was forever a dark cloud in my childhood. I was then five or six years of age.

I must now mention the indescribable bashfulness which followed me like a shadow from early childhood till now. The distress which bashfulness causes will be understood only by one who is bashful himself. Even birthday celebrations became an agony for me. I am not able to describe my embarrassment when I had to extend congratulations to my parents and sisters. Any recognition given me has always been and still is a mortification for me. Afterwards, when I was alone with my presents, I enjoyed these gifts and rewards. I remember, for instance, the great joy I experienced when I received a large picture of the Good Shepherd on my fifth or sixth birthday. Later I realized what that picture meant for me. Was I not the little lamb entangled in the thorn bush of error? How many years and how much labor and sacrifice has it not cost the Good Shepherd to free the little lamb! Eternal thanks to the divine love, patience, and mercy that did not rest until finally, after thirty-three years, the little lamb was led into the flock. That occurred on October 30, 1888.

We children had to learn to pray as soon as we were able to speak. First we learned short children's prayers. At the age of two my sister already knew the "Our Father," and I am sure I also knew it at that age.

A dear memory of my mother blessing us every night always remains with me. Before retiring she came into our bedroom and went from bed to bed to make the sign of the cross on our foreheads. Most of the time I was asleep and did not notice it, but in later years I was still awake and I was happy to receive her blessing. She also taught us to love and venerate the holy angels. For example, when our toys were not in order she admonished us to put them in order, saying, "At night the angels come to see whether or not all is in order, and they are very sad when they find an untidy child."

To make others happy gave me great pleasure in early childhood. There was an old, feeble-minded woman in Sandow who was avoided by everyone. She often called at our house for alms, and she began to like me. I felt sorry for the poor woman, and because of my compassion, I let her play with me. This made her very happy.

ARNSWALDE – BERLIN

In May 1862 my father was promoted to superintendent, a high position in the Lutheran Church, and we moved to Arnswalde. There a new life began for me. Although Arnswalde was only a small city of 7000 population, life was more active than we had been accustomed to in our little village of a few hundred inhabitants. The rectory was also busier. My father was often engaged in official visits, and my mother, filled with great zeal for souls, founded a society for women to help care for the poor. She also started a mission club for India and Africa. All meetings of the society took place in our house. My father renovated the beautiful old St. Mary's Church. Every Sunday I accompanied him to the services, and they filled me with reverence and devotion.

After a few weeks in Arnswalde my mother again found time to devote more attention to us children, at least on Sundays. She spoke to us of the dear Savior and sang hymns with us. My two sisters, Lisa and Magdalena, joined us, and we listened attentively to the words of our good mother. I was so pleased that I asked if I could invite other children to join us on Sunday afternoons. Mother gave permission, and during the week I went to the market place and the church square and said to every child I met, "Come to us next Sunday afternoon and my mother will tell us of the Savior and of the poor heathen children."

Sunday arrived, and only two children made their appearance. I was not discouraged but went out again with new zeal and invited every child, using the same words I had used the week before. I was not quite seven years of age and very bashful, and therefore I could not say more. But this simple invitation was sufficient. To the great surprise of my mother, over thirty children came the following Sunday. I ushered them into the waiting room and entertained them so successfully that within a few weeks over one hundred children attended. In the weeks that followed there were never less than thirty.

My parents had selected my birthday as the foundation day of our club, and this was celebrated for the first time in 1863 in the nearby woods. Our stay in Arnswalde, to my regret, lasted only three years, but before my parents moved, the children's society was transferred to the church and was called, "The Children's Divine Service." Three hundred children usually attended the meetings. Today, after sixty years, Arnswalde, formerly entirely Protestant, has a Catholic Church and a flourishing parish. I recall my seventh birthday, June 19, 1862. A circuit judge in Arnswalde, a friend of my parents, had two daughters our age, and they soon became our best friends. This gentleman came with his family to congratulate me, and he presented me with a small, gold lapel cross. As soon as I saw the present I became disturbed, saying to myself, "This is a piece of jewelry, and I have resolved never to wear jewelry." Just when I made this resolution I do not remember, but it must have been at Sandow. What could I do now? I bashfully thanked the gentleman, thought it over, and came to the conclusion that maybe the cross is not jewelry. The cross was pinned on me, and then we went into the garden to play. When we were called to dinner after a few hours, the cross had disappeared and was never found again.

Later, when I was grown up, I wore a golden cross on two occasions, excusing myself in the same manner that a cross is not jewelry. Each cross I wore once; one of them disappeared without a trace, and the other was accidentally but completely destroyed. From that time on I considered my resolution as a vow and regarded gold crosses as jewelry.

Besides the promise not to wear jewelry I made the firm resolution never to sin. At what time I made that resolution I do not recall, but it must have been in my sixth or seventh year. The following incident impressed itself indelibly upon my mind. My parents were engaged in a conversation when I interrupted them, asking my mother,

"Is this a sin?"

I do not remember what it was about, but my father said, "Go away with your sins and let mother alone!" Such remarks uttered in a severe tone always demanded strict obedience. I never forgot them, and they had a great influence in forming my character. I was only seven years old, but from that moment on I depended solely on God's guidance for my inner life. Never did I ask my mother or a minister for counsel. It was just God and myself. From then on God alone was my teacher, counselor, and leader. I was always occupied with thoughts or questions, but only such that concerned my inner life, for I did not want to offend God or sin against Him. I still remember how absorbed I was at times, until a redeeming thought came to my mind.

I remember just such an incident concerning a dress made for me. The dress was quite fancy and modern. I did not like it at all. Our seamstress used great eloquence to make me proud of it, but I left her to seek solitude, as I was accustomed to do in such cases. Finally I concluded that if my mother had ordered the dress, it could not be a sin.

Autumn was approaching, the first for me in a city with its fall festivals, their noise and amusements for children. We received an allowance which we could spend in our own way when we attended the festivities accompanied by our chaperon. Never did we see anything like this in our little village of Sandow. I considered it all wrong and, without drawing attention to myself, managed to stay at home.

I would like to mention another incident regarding jewelry. I had received a pair of earrings for my birthday. My sister likewise received a pair for her birthday in August and had them put in her ears immediately. But I did not like them because they were jewelry, and since my mother did not command it, I did not wear them.

Arnswalde is situated on a small lake, and we went swimming almost every day in the summertime. The road to the lake led past a very poor home. Near the window sat a young, feeble-minded child whom I pitied very much. I had a great desire to make her happy with something. My mother had taught me to give the thing I treasured the most to the poor. I possessed a doll which I liked very much. I was quite attached to it. I resolved to give this, my most cherished doll, to the poor girl. My mother gave me permission to take her the doll. But a difficulty arose, my indescribable bashfulness. The poor child did not live far away, but it was hard for me to meet a stranger. I asked my girlfriend, three years my senior, to go with me. She agreed, but only on condition that I wear my earrings. After long deliberation I consented. Adorned with the earrings, carrying the doll, and accompanied by my friend, I went to the poor child. I was greatly moved by the great joy the child displayed. Upon my return home I removed the earrings and never wore them again.

The following experience showed me how deeply seated vanity is in children. One time my mother corrected me in the presence of our maid. I do not remember the cause, but I could never forget the humiliation and my hurt feelings. I was so hurt, especially because it was in the presence of the maid, that I could not speak one word. I did not realize at the time that pride was a sin.

On the whole, our education was quite liberal. That is why children of the people who were friendly with our parents came to play with us. Our rooms were large and we had enough toys to accommodate many children.

There were often ten or more children together. I was the natural organizer of the games. Every child was assigned to something, forming one big family. We played tirelessly and very peacefully. There were two children who did not get along with anybody and we called them "Uncle and Aunt." Although they were only little girls, they were looked upon as guests. Despite this arrangement, often a lot of shouting began because "Uncle and Aunt" began to quarrel with each other, then cry, and eventually avoid one another. The next day they were again the best of friends.

The years went by and when May came around the third time in Arnswalde, I received the news that my father was to be transferred to Berlin. On May 25, 1865, many people gathered at the train depot and expressed their love and gratitude toward my parents. We boarded the train and rode to Berlin. Here we rented a house for several months, for the parsonage was too small and had to be enlarged during the summer. A few weeks after moving into the expanded parsonage, I became ill. I felt miserable and lay on the couch tired and lethargic. No one knew what was the matter with me until I developed typhus in January 1866. A few weeks later my sisters and my parents also became ill. Only then did the doctors discover that the dampness of the new house was the cause of our illness, and in April we moved to another house. My parents and sisters recovered, but I was confined to bed again, where I had already been for three months. It was only through good care that I was sufficiently recovered to attend school in the fall, but by the doctors' strict orders I was not allowed to do any strenuous mental work, not even to memorize anything. My health was very precarious, and when the weather turned cold I became ill again. School was now very humiliating for me. How easily I had learned things before my illness, and now I seemed to be the most ignorant of the students. Nevertheless, it seemed as if my classmates had a great respect and showed great consideration for me. I do not know why it was, but it was true that in my presence the professors and teachers were never ridiculed, nor did the pupils make plans to annoy them. They even placed a sentinel at the door to warn those who were mimicking the teachers that I was approaching. But being as bashful as I was, I would not have had the courage to do anything. At school less than a third of the girls had any kind of religion. Two thirds had only ridicule for religion. I heard this from others in whose presence they were not ashamed to reveal their opinions.

I have very little to say about my inner life during these years. It appears to me that the faculties of my soul lay dormant, although I was very zealous when my mother offered me an opportunity to do good to the poor and the suffering. I enjoyed going to church, but more so in the evening than in the morning, for then a minister other than my father conducted the services.

During these years I had some very good friends who were somewhat older than I. Although I often visited them, I still remained shy, and when their parents spoke to me I could utter no more than a timid "Yes" or "No." Once I heard someone say about me, "Still water runs deep."

In those days we often put on tableaux, and I often played the lead role. This did not harm me spiritually since I was not at all vain. In winter, when the skating rink opened and when I was well enough, the doctor advised me to go skating. When I was older and healthy again, I became a passionate ice skater. When I was about twelve, an uncle taught me to play chess, and then I played it with my girlfriend almost all my leisure hours. Later, when the opportunity presented itself, I played it with my uncles and cousins very passionately. We could be found at the chessboard even after midnight. Fortunately such occasions were not too frequent.

During the summer holidays my mother took us children either to our grandparents at Zettemin-Stavenhagen, or at Mecklenburg-Schwerin, or to a summer resort, while my father made a trip to the mountains. Besides these trips with the family, I also visited my grandparents by myself and stayed there for weeks or months at a time. Such vacations were the greatest delight of my childhood.

One day when I was about twelve, we were visiting my grandparents. Grandfather loved nature and was very fond of flowers. As soon as we arrived he took me into the garden, which was in full bloom, and said, "You may pick as many flowers as you like." Next morning I went into the garden to enjoy the flowers. It was a gorgeous sight. The huge garden was blossoming with flowers; the bushes were blooming, and so were the many roses. I strolled from rose to rose, to admire their beauty, and came across one which was especially beautiful. It was a rosebush framed in moss. This flower took my fancy, so I plucked that single bud and took it with me. Several hours later grandfather came to me, his face livid with rage. "Did you pluck the only moss rose in the garden?" he asked. I was frightened, but I did not deny it, as I had done at Sandow. I had had enough sorrow over that lie. I candidly confessed my guilt. When I took my correction with visible sorrow, all was well again. Grandfather must have forgotten that he had given me permission to take any flower without restriction.

Other major events of my youth were the three wars waged by Prussia. The first was against Schleswig-Holstein in 1864. We were still in Arnswalde. We were busy preparing bandages for the wounded soldiers. My parents were full of anxiety because three brothers of my father were on the battlefield; one was adjutant to Prince Frederick Charles. All three returned home safe and sound. Not one was wounded.

In the year 1866 we lived in Berlin on Koeniggraetzer Street, called Hirschel Street at the time. This street was separated from the city by a wall. A railroad ran alongside this wall, encircling the city. It was mostly used for freight trains, but during this war against Austria the soldiers were carried on this spur to Austria, and later the wounded were brought back the same way, passing our house. Most of the trains stopped nearby, and people from all the houses would come and bring gifts for the soldiers and refreshments for the wounded. Again our uncles were in this war, and again they came back safely.

GNADAU

In the year 1870 my sister Lisa and I attended boarding school. My delicate health was the chief reason why we were placed in the Herrnhuter boarding school out in the country. There were ninety-six boarders in this school at Gnadau near Magdeburg. We soon became accustomed to the place and liked it.

I was especially pleased that we were taken to church five times during the week. "Church" is probably not the right term for this praying hall. It had no decorations at all. Nor did it have an altar or crucifix. There was nothing in the room but a table covered by a green cloth, a chair, a podium for the preacher or lector, and benches for the congregation.

Once a month there was a recital of prayers for forty-five minutes, during which the congregation remained kneeling. I can hardly describe the great happiness this prayer period gave me. I did not follow the prayer leader, but I prayed from my own heart and with such recollection that the time passed all too quickly for me.

Brother von Schweidnitz conducted the preparation for Communion. All Herrnhuters were called Brothers and Sisters, whether married or single, whether superior or subjects. This minister was pious, sincere, and recollected, and I believe that his instructions did me a lot of good. Once, however, he made a remark that made me think. He spoke of the true church in such a way as if Herrnhuters were the only true Church, while my father maintained that the Lutheran Church was the true one. Among the young girls were daughters of the Herrnhuter ministers. Some of the Sisters were self-sacrificing and good, and through them I was inspired to become a Sister. I would have liked very much to stay right there, but obedience forced us to return home. On Easter Sunday 1872 we had to leave the peaceful settlement and return home to be confirmed. This thought was dreadful to me because I had a great aversion to "Lutheranism," but it had to be. In obedience I had to be confirmed.

During my stay at the boarding school a census was taken. The teachers had to take a census of the pupils. My teacher took it for granted that I was a Lutheran, but I retorted excitedly, "No, not a Lutheran."

"Well, what are you then?" asked the teacher. When I

didn't answer she said, "Well, then, you are a Uniate."
I thought to myself, "Anything, but not a Lutheran."
I must mention that a certain teacher did me great harm
at Gnadau. The experience may be a warning to my Sisters. I came to school with my hair very plain. Even
before this time my friends in Berlin had tried to get me
to be more modern, but I could not be persuaded. At the
boarding school it was the custom for the teachers to
make up the hair of the pupils at least once a week. My
teacher began immediately to show me how to do braids
in a more flattering way. Through that I learned to use a
mirror, and it didn't take long before I became a vain, little girl. This deviation has cost me many tears of regret.
If the Lord had not added a firm and serious disposition
to my joyousness, what would have become of me? But
all frivolity and carelessness was completely foreign to
my nature.

In the following years I traveled quite a bit, visiting
friends and relatives. In Winter I had to attend social
affairs, but this was contrary to my liking. I pleaded with
bitter tears for my mother to permit me to stay away, but
she insisted on my going with her and my sister Lisa. In
a way it was good for me, for it helped me to overcome
my bashfulness in some measure.

I spent the summer of 1873 with my grandparents. My
grandfather traveled with my father and came back to
Zettemin with a plan to marry me off to a certain young
man. I was completely taken aback, for I had decided to
become a Sister and not to get married. I firmly declined,
and this made my grandfather angry. He immediately
sent me back to my parents, saying that my father would
tell me what to do. To overcome this shock and to gath-

er my wits, I went out into the garden. On the farther side of the premises was a row of poplars, and it was always soothing to me to walk to and fro under the softly lisping leaves. This particular walk stands out in my memory as if it happened only yesterday. For years a picture had been foremost in my mind: a house, a red brick building with the inscription over it: A Home for the Homeless. To build such a home someday in order to help many poor was my heartfelt desire. Absorbed with these thoughts I walked up and down while reconsidering the words of my grandfather.

The young man whom I was to marry was supposed to be rich, and thus I could realize my plans to build such a Home for the Homeless. Resigned and calm I returned to the house, but the next morning I left the cozy home of my grandparents that our dearly loved Grandmother made so beloved. When I arrived home, I asked my mother whether or not I should accept the offer of Dr. X., and my mother said, "No, if you do not want to do so." I felt unburdened, and at once I was as happy as before with my loved ones at home. We were all so carefree and happy because we did not know the future.

In February 1874 our good mother became very ill with pleurisy, and despite all medical care, her life could not be saved. She died at the age of forty-five on May 23, 1874. I was inconsolable. During her illness I did not leave her bedside. And now she was no more. Although God had made it known to me three months before, I was broken up by the shock. Yes, I loved my mother passionately. Even ten years later I shed tears of loneliness. My sorrow was great, but greater was the blessing my soul received through it. It brought me nearer to God, and I learned to recognize the blessing of suffering.

At the age of twenty years I had to take care of the family household. Besides this I had to preside over the different societies, and I had to look after the poor more than before.

I must mention one great sorrow my mother had to endure before she died. This was the enactment of the so-called "May Laws." Mother was proud of father, for he was a deeply believing minister, and he was ridiculed on the stage and in cartoons as the great "zealot" Tauscher. Undaunted, he defended the belief in the Holy Trinity. This doctrine, the foundation of the Christian religion, became to be doubted more and more in the Evangelical Church since Schleiermacher's emergence and was openly denied by a great many professors and ministers. My parents did all they could to keep all loyal preachers united. In our house one conference followed another. Sympathizers with the true faith, among them such laymen as Count Krassow, Count Rotkirch-Trach, Heinz von Kleist-Retzow, Professor Zoeckler, and others, deliberated as to how they could stem the flood of unbelief. My mother attended these conferences regularly, and I think it was due to her great zeal and eloquence that the so-called August Conference of 1873 took place. The purpose of its meetings was to encourage all preachers and professors who still believed in the Holy Trinity to remain loyal. Eighteen hundred Lutheran clergymen from all parts of Germany attended the Conference.

On account of my mother's great interest in all religious and political affairs, my father was accustomed to speak at meals on the topic of the then so exciting development of the *Kulturkampf*. For that reason he was anxious for me to read the speeches of the Parliament. I did so, but very soon I became interested only in the speeches of the members of the Center Party, those of Windthorst, Reichensperger, and the like.

Thanks to Divine Providence I was slowly and unnoticeably imbued with a true Catholic spirit. I don't think any Catholic could have been more provoked than I was when the Catholic bishops, religious, and priests were driven into exile. This injustice, which cried so to heaven, created in me a deep aversion to the Royal Government.

It was either in 1877 or 1879 that an Evangelical Synod was convoked in Berlin. I think it was for the purpose of officially taking a stand against the May Laws. These weeks were rather exciting for my sister and myself, since prominent gentlemen from all parts of the country called at our house. One day we had about thirteen of them for dinner. The guests included supervisors, professors of various universities, and the like. The conversation became quite lively. Finally one of the gentlemen mentioned the dogma of the infallibility of the Pope and said, "How can it be possible for a human being to declare himself infallible!"

I had the courage to say, "It is not meant that way, but *ex cathedra* means the same as when the high priest of the Jews was prophesying only in his capacity as high priest." My simple explanation caused a profound silence at first, and then the conversation turned to something different, without anyone making a remark about the issue.

For some time I attended the services at the Protestant Cathedral in Berlin where the Court Chaplain Stoecker preached on the Old Testament. His eloquence was so forceful and his words so instructive on calling souls to the inner life, that I owe him very much.

Court Chaplain Stoecker introduced the home missions

into Berlin. He appointed missionaries for the city whose duty it was to see to it that the children were baptized and that people were married in the church because ever since the civil marriages were introduced, the Lutheran people thought that baptism and church weddings were abolished.

These missionaries often found over one hundred children unbaptized in a single tenement house. My desire was to get enough money together for at least one such missionary. There were in existence at the time eighteen clubs of women who did needlework, which was sold in the bazaars for the benefit of the home missions.

In 1879 my father married again. Thus I was freed from household duties, and I had more time to realize my desire to found a society for home mission work. It was not so easy to get my father's permission for this. Father was not a friend of Court Chaplain Stoecker, for the latter belonged to the Union. However, after some time I obtained his permission, and in a short time our club numbered forty members. They were all young girls who had plenty of leisure time. The monthly meetings took place at our house, and my father, and occasionally Court Chaplain Stoecker, gave the conferences. God's blessing was with us, for the sale of the needlework netted enough for the salary of the missionary.

For some time my father had desired to get out of Berlin. His position had become very difficult. He was at odds with the officers of the parish, who were mostly without faith, and who had, according to the new law, the decisive voice. Several good parishes were offered to my father, all out in the country, but they all belonged to the Union. The belief in the Holy Sacrament was as firm in my father as it had been in my grandfather. The latter had been sentenced to jail rather that submit to the new "Last Supper Form" which was introduced by King Frederick III. This new form was so dubious that no Lutheran minister who really believed could accept it and administer it the new way.

What a great sacrifice it must have been for my grandfather and his family when the key of the church was taken away from him and when he was threatened with jail if he did not join the Union! There were ten children in his family and no temporal fortune, for the inheritance of my grandmother was used to furnish a small institute where talented boys were educated for the missions in Africa. But God's goodness did not fail my grandfather's trust in the Lord. Count von Voss, Lord von Gerlach, and some other friends procured his acquittal. Lord von Malzahn, a Lutheran, gave him his parish at Zettemin near Stavenhagen on the boundary of Mecklenburg. This was one of the best parishes, and the income made it possible for grandfather to send his four sons to the Granenkloster-Berlin High School and then to the university.

GUSOW

My father had been stationed in Berlin for about nineteen years when he surprised us with the news that he had accepted the Lutheran parish at Gusow, which had been offered him by Count Schoenburg. I was greatly pleased, for I never liked Berlin. From childhood on I had the desire to get out of Berlin and now it seemed my wish would be fulfilled. We moved to Gusow in 1882. Our missionary club was taken over by an older lady, Miss von Liebeherr of Schwerin-Mecklenburg.

I was nearing the twenty-eighth year of my life, and my longing to serve God and to prove my love for Him increased with every year. I had the conviction, I do not know why, that God would call me to His service when I became thirty years of age. The waiting was often very trying. Since my twenty-second year I had been reading Holy Scripture and the *Imitation of Christ* by Thomas a Kempis every day for an hour. A word or a thought of this reading remained outstanding in my mind during the day and united me more and more with God.

In the year 1877 I almost lost my faith. I had heard of a gentleman who enjoyed the reputation of great piety and devotion, and I discovered that he was leading a very sinful life in Berlin. I was so provoked that I threw all faith overboard and wanted to practice virtue in the way of the old Greek philosophers. I stopped praying for about six weeks and tried out my new way, but I could not live without prayer and faith. A deep longing for God took hold of me and brought me back. I began to pray again and to work with renewed zeal. I now worked to please God alone.

At the death of my mother the great value of suffering was revealed to me, and I began to ask God for crosses and sufferings for my whole life. I asked God to lead me on a steep and stony path through life. I promised God to do only His will. When I was twenty-five I began to pray for humility.

I could not ask anyone for advice. God alone was my guide and to Him alone could I reveal my desire for virtue and perfection and my longing to serve Him. My faith, which I guarded zealously, was now my greatest treasure. Lutheran ministers build their faith on St. Paul, St. Augustine, and Luther. These three names I had heard mentioned together from my earliest youth. When I came across the letters of St. Paul, while reading Holy Scripture, I skipped them for fear that some sentences might lead me to Lutheranism. I also avoided Hartmann's book, *Philosophy of the Unknown*. This book created a sensation at the time, and no doubt it sowed the poison of infidelity in the hearts of many young people. My sister Magdalena read it with great interest. We two were very intimate, but I did not disclose my inner life to her.

My father often said to me, "You are more Catholic than Evangelical."

A Minister from Hessen, a friend of the family, once said to my father in my presence, "Just let Miss Maria go to an all Catholic part of the country and she will be cured of her leaning to Catholicism." Yet what were the sources of my Catholic belief? I never associated with Catholics, nor did I ever have a Catholic book in my hand. God, Holy Scripture, the speeches of the members of the Center Party, and the works of art in the museum were the sources of my faith. In these matters did my soul, thirsting for truth, find what it was seeking. I desired to know and to do the will of God and to show Him my love by becoming a Sister. These were the ideas that filled my heart.

I had a special inclination for self-denial. From childhood on I used a hard bed. I mortified my appetite, but in such a way that it did not become conspicuous. For example, I did not eat apples one winter; another time I did not eat grapes, nor did I indulge in sweets during the Christmas season, but afterward treated my Sisters with these things. I worked at controlling my natural inclinations.

A worldly-minded lady brought us romantic novels, and

we devoured them with great eagerness. When I was about twenty it dawned on me that great harm is done by being overpowered by such fancies. I immediately closed the book and resolved never again to read a romance, and I have kept this resolution ever since. Whenever I decided to do something or refrain from something, I carried it out with great faithfulness.

Now, back to my life in Gusow. I benefited greatly from the solitude and quietness, and, because I was less distracted than in Berlin, I became absorbed in Holy Scripture more than ever. The letters of St. Peter and St. John and St. James especially enchanted me. Occasionally I talked to my father on things that interested me most, and when I mentioned St. Peter he said, "Oh, go on with your St. Peter!" When I asked why the Lutherans did not have the anointing (extreme unction), he said that Luther called the Epistle of St. James the "Straw Epistle." I felt a great devotion to the Mother of God, whom I called the Virgin Mary. Wherever I stayed, I wanted a picture of her placed in a conspicuous spot. My associates knew this, and if they wanted to make me happy, they would give me a picture of the Madonna.

We lived a truly happy life in this rather isolated village. Two of my sisters were in boarding school and this made our family circle smaller, except during vacation when we were all together. Toward sundown, as night approached, we children gathered in mother's room, and father joined us too. We entertained one another, or my father played the piano. Sometimes he and mother played a duet. While listening to the music my eyes rested on Murillo's picture of Mary Immaculate, so beautifully tinted by the rays of the setting sun.

One of these evening hours especially is unforgettable.

I asked my father if all Christians believed in the perpetual virginity of Mary. He said, "You can believe it if you want, but it is not necessary, and there are many who do not believe it."

I said, "Even if no one believed it, I, for one, would believe that the Mother of God always remained a virgin." At that time I did not know anything about the Rosary nor did I know the Hail Mary.

I frequently visited the poor and cared for the sick. On Sundays I gathered young girls around me to keep them away from the loose customs so prevalent in the place.

Nearer and nearer I came to my thirtieth birthday, to the year in which, as I was convinced, my desire to serve God would be fulfilled. How and where my wish to become a Sister would be realized I had no idea. I left all to Divine Providence, and God guided me, as later events proved.

Shortly before my thirtieth birthday, June 19, 1885, I received an invitation from Lady von C., who spent the winters in Berlin with her family, to visit her at Godesberg near Bonn. My father not only gave me permission to accept this invitation, but also was delighted that I would have a chance to see the wonderful Rhine country.

The sumptuous home of the family of Lady von C. was situated near the Rhine. There I was surrounded by earthly wealth and glamour in the setting of grand, unsurpassed scenery. This latter had a special attraction for me on account of the open air shrines of the crucifix and of our dear Lady. While we were out riding in the country I viewed them with greatest interest. I liked these sacred sights even better than the Rhine and the romantic hills and ruins. As the fragrance of the vineyards saturates the air, so does the fragrance of piety fill the hearts of the Rhinelanders. It also awakened in my soul a new life, just like the spring air rejuvenates nature. Yes, all of this gave me the first insight into a life which I had experienced only in a dim manner.

I walked into the Cathedral of Cologne for the first time in the summer of 1885, and it was to become a real home to me. There at the feet of our dear Lady I later opened my soul in thanksgiving to God for the great grace of being received into the holy Catholic Church.

I must mention a conversation that took place during one dinner hour. The family of Lady von C. was Protestant, but Catholics, even priests were friends of the family. One day the pastor of Blitersdorf, where the family had an estate, was invited to dinner. Whenever I had a chance to join the conversation, I spoke either of politics, art, or religion. As this was the first Priest I had met, I quickly turned the discussion to religion. At the end of a lively conversation the priest said to me, "You are a Catholic, are you not?"

I answered, "No, I have my own religion."

He replied, "But after all, what you believe is Catholic." At that time I did not think that I would really be a Catholic in less than three years.

CHAPTER TWO

THE SACRIFICE

The time between 1886 and 1888 I could, after a last test, place a nearly three year long sacrifice at the feet of God. For years I had desired to make a real sacrifice for God in order to prove my love for Him. In vain did I search for such an opportunity. Finally the hour arrived.

In February 1886, while visiting a family in Berlin, I was reading in a Cologne newspaper and happened to see the following advertisement, "Wanted: A head nurse for a municipal mental institution." I saw this item in the morning, and it haunted me all the day so that I asked myself, "Is this the great sacrifice I am supposed to make?" It certainly would be a great sacrifice, but I had wanted to make a great sacrifice for God. Before evening arrived, I had made up my mind, and I said the following prayer: "O God, I will apply for that position, and if it is Thy holy will, grant that I am accepted. I will go there to prove my love for Thee, no matter what the cost."

I immediately wrote to the director of the institution, and in order to prevent a change in mind, I called for the butler to post the letter immediately. I spent the next few days in excited expectation until the answer of acceptance arrived. The following day I returned to nearby Gusow to obtain the consent of my parents. I was very much surprised when I received my father's approval without any hesitation on his part. I think he must have overlooked the remark of the director, "The whole institution, patients and personnel, are Catholics with a few exceptions, but I and my family are Lutheran." Perhaps God permitted that my father should overlook this remark, otherwise he certainly would have warned me against socializing with Catholics. Anyway I had his permission, and I wrote that I would report at the institution on March 6.

On March 6th I headed for Cologne, full of confidence and courage. Nevertheless, the nearer I got to my destination, the heavier my heart became. My bashfulness asserted itself when I thought of being alone, and especially when I thought of having to meet so many people. The thought of the mentally ill frightened me. I had never seen such an institution before. I had only briefly visited a hospital, and now with such a future before me, I was completely unnerved.

Fortunately, the train stopped for some time at Elberfeld, and I ordered a good dinner with wine to overcome my fear and to regain my steadfastness. It really did me good. Full of renewed confidence I prayed to God, asking for help, and at the end of my prayer the train pulled into Cologne during a terrific storm. I had regained my courage and determination. Members of the staff had promised to meet me, but the storm must have prevented them from coming. A twenty minute ride on the streetcar brought me to Lindenburg, where the director and his family gave me a friendly welcome. The director took me to the institution and said that he himself would introduce me to the patients.

The head nurse had previously been a member of the Deaconess Community but had severed her connections with it. She was still there. She had a strong physique and was used to the sick and dying. Therefore, she could not understand my trembling when she spoke of the dead or dying. After the director had left, the head nurse took me to the patients. It was evening, and I was tired from the long trip. Here I was suddenly confronted with a dying woman. I had never seen a person die, and here I witnessed the pale, distorted face of one in agony, and heard the ghastly gurgling noise in the throat. I was terrified, but I composed myself and did not show any horror to my companion who took me from room to room. Afterward I was served a small lunch, and then I retired to my room. I was stiff with horror, and the patients appeared indescribable and dreadful to me. I could not go to sleep, and the face of the dying woman was constantly before my eyes. Outside there was a howling wind whistling a terrifying melody around the tower; rain was battering the window. It was a horrible night! I had desired to offer God a great sacrifice. Was this then not the right beginning? But, thank God, that neither that night nor in the following days did it enter my mind to give up or leave. I wanted to show the Lord my true love.

The next day dawned, and I prepared to enter upon my new duties without having slept a wink that night. After breakfast my guide again took me to the patients, this time to the worst cases of the mentally ill. When the director came on his morning rounds. he was extremely irritated because Miss H. had already taken me to the patients. He wanted to do that himself. He noticed immediately that I hadn't slept during the night, and asked why I could not sleep. The next two nights were even worse for me. The patients with their staring, wild eyes were always in my mind and imagination. It was as if I constantly saw them whether I had my eyes open or closed. The director gave me some sleeping pills, and after I had rested two nights, I felt fresh again. I entered upon my new duties with great cheerfulness. I thanked the Lord for guiding me to the poorest of the poor. To bring cheer and happiness to others was what I was looking for, and this was my opportunity. More than one hundred such poor women and girls were entrusted to my care, and I had ample opportunity to lighten their misery. God gave me the grace to bring new life into the institute, so that the visiting doctors remarked that this was not institutional life but real family life. Indeed, all, even the most unfortunate, experienced my motherly care.

At first I did not accept the stipulated salary, for the thought of reward or compensation did not harmonize with my idea of sacrifice. I received what I needed from my parents, but later on I took a salary and used it for the patients. Every few weeks I arranged a little feast and paid for the refreshments out of my own pocket. All the other money I had, I used for burying the dead. Whenever a poor person died who had no relatives to pay for a coffin, the body was sent to the medical school. For those patients who could comprehend it, the thought of this was a terrifying one, and I promised them that if they would die while I was at the institution I would pay for their coffin and their burial.

Spring arrived with the beautiful month of May. Although I had seen this month come thirty times in my life, I now for the first time had the opportunity of witnessing a Catholic month of May. The patients and the nurses were, with one exception, all Catholics, and every day throughout the month they sang hymns in the evening in honor of the Blessed Mother. I can hardly describe my joy when, for the first time in May 1886, I heard the hymn, "Mary Queen of May," and also the other inspiring hymns to the Mother of God.

After 1887 other women, besides the mentally ill, were received in the institution as boarders. One of them told me that she had donated a large candle for the May altar. Rather disappointed, I went to the manager, who also was in charge of the Chapel, and asked why he had not told me of the candles, for I would have liked to pay for them. "Oh, well," he said, "you can get some in honor of the Sacred Heart in the month of June. You ought to buy some larger candlesticks, too, for we always have to borrow them." This proposition pleased me, and I was glad that I could do something for the Chapel.

Two priests, Fr. Wiskirchen and Rector Bong of Cologne, came to visit the manager and the patients. During their visit I became acquainted with them. Fr. Bong gave me Deharbe's large Catechism, which I read with the greatest interest. To my great surprise I found in it what I called "my own religion." There was nothing that was beyond my understanding, with the exception of the teaching about indulgences. But this did not cause me any difficulties, for I understood it after I had studied it a little. Later on I often asked myself why I did not actually enter the Church. The reason was that I thought that Divine Providence would take care of it.

After I had been away from home for over a year and had been day and night with the suffering and unfortunate, my father desired very much for me to come home for a few weeks. The wife of the director volunteered to take my place, and so I decided to go home. My departure was scheduled for early July.

The lady who had donated the May candles was suffering from severe religious delusions. Her suffering reached a high point in June. She believed that if she would be allowed to visit the Chapel of the Good Shepherd at Melaten, she would be cured. Pitying the poor woman, I asked the director to allow her the visit, especially since a nurse and I would accompany her. The request was granted. It was on June 17, 1887, that I went with the lady to the Chapel of the Good Shepherd. It was splendidly adorned, for it was a feast day, but what feast it was I understood only many years later. The lady wanted to go to the first pew where I knelt down with her. Solemn High Mass began, honoring the Sacred Heart of Jesus.

THE GOOD SHEPHERD

God and my love for God were the motives of my sacrifice in going to Lindenburg. Love for suffering humanity led me to the Chapel of the Good Shepherd, where He waited to take the wayward sheep on His shoulder and carry it home. Yes, even more, to embrace it with heavenly sweetness. At the end of the High Mass my patient wanted to leave, but I asked her to wait a little while, as I wanted to speak to the chaplain of the institution.

In the sacristy instead of seeing Fr. Bong, I met with Fr. Wiskirchen, but it made no difference to me as I had great confidence in both of them. After a brief greeting I said, "Father, I want to become a Catholic."

He said simply, "You cannot do this so easily; first, on account of your father, and second, you are going home anyway."

After my vacation great darkness filled my soul. All cheerfulness had vanished. The resolution to enter the Church had also weakened. I had not given up the idea in the least, but my will power seemed paralyzed. This condition lasted about five months until I was filled with new life again. Then I asked Fr. Wiskirchen to start with the instructions. This was in January 1888. The priest's house was near Lindenburg, and for this reason Father advised me to make a little detour so that the director of the institution would not be aware of what I was doing, and thus any eventual unpleasantness could be avoided.

Director L. was anti-Catholic, and it became clear to me that I would have to leave Lindenburg before I could enter the Church. I therefore gave notice to the institution that I intended to leave. Soon a high official of the institution arrived from Cologne and left nothing undone to persuade me to stay. Since he did not succeed, he at least wanted to know the reason for my resignation. I did not reveal my reason, neither did I change my mind.

In May I visited the Chaplain once more. I took the direct route because it was raining very hard, and I did not care if anyone saw me going to the rectory, for I was leaving Lindenburg anyway. My successor had already arrived so that I might have a chance to instruct her in her duties.

A short time after that, while I was walking in the garden with a lady, my father suddenly stood before me. I trembled with fear, for I surmised the reason of his coming. We had barely entered my room when he asked me angrily, "Have you become a Catholic already? I had word from Cologne that you have." I tried to calm my father and assured him that I had not yet become a Catholic. I took him over to visit the director, who received my father with utmost friendliness. We were then invited to dinner.

During my brief absence from my room to tell the director of my father's visit, my father picked up a little booklet written in honor of St. Joseph. A lady who was visiting me had left it in my room. During the dinner my father said, "How can anyone pray to such an outlandish man?" This expression made a deep, indelible impression on me. I thought more and more of St. Joseph, and I conceived such a great, tender devotion to dear Father St. Joseph, as I called him, that I thought I ought to make reparation for the coldness of all unbelievers towards him.

The next morning my father took me back to Gusow. God alone knows what I suffered during these years. God be praised for every hour that brought me new trials.

I was home only a short while when my father received a letter from the director, urging him to allow my return to Lindenburg. He promised my father to do everything possible to prevent me from becoming a Catholic.

God be praised forever that I received permission to return to Cologne. Just at the painful moment of departure from my parents and sisters, my father demanded the promise that I would not become a Catholic. With a trembling heart, for I saw my mother and sisters weeping, I answered, "No, I cannot promise that." All that I could promise was that it would not happen that day nor the next. And thus I left my home forever.

When I reached Cologne, and before I reached Lindenburg, I called on Dr. Lohmer, whose sister-in-law was my personal friend. He said to me, "Since the director has called you back, remain independent, and demand absolute freedom in religious matters."

As soon as I arrived at Lindenburg I called on the director, keeping in mind the advice of Dr. Lohmer. The director became very angry and said, "Are you at it again? I thought you had given up that idea. In that case, it is better if we go our separate ways at once. I think it is better if we come to an understanding immediately. Either you promise not to attend any Catholic Church and to stay away from priests, or you leave Lindenburg."

I was silent at first and pondered what to do, for I did not know where to go. Then I said, "I will not go to a Catholic Church, but if I cannot keep the promise anymore, I will let you know."

On the feast of St. Peter and Paul, when I passed through Berlin on my way from Gusow to Berlin, I had assisted at Holy Mass in St. Hedwig's Church. Now I could no longer attend Mass. On Sundays when I heard the bells of the parish church, together with those of Cologne, my heart ached, and in my room I fell to my knees and wept bitterly! For the first time in my life I experienced what it meant to be forsaken and to be homeless. Now I could not turn back. I longed for the day when I could finally be a member of the Holy Church. But I couldn't see how it would come about. I said to myself, "Only God can do it." He alone had the power to help me, and in Him I put my trust.

Toward the end of October 1888, I met Fr. Bong and Fr. Wiskirchen in the room of the caretaker. We talked of the director's prohibition, which violated my rights and had no legal grounds. I told them of my most fervent desire to enter the Church, but I thought it could not be accomplished here because I was not allowed to go to Mass. Fr. Wiskirchen replied that even if I could not go to Mass, I could still be received into the Church. I could be admitted any time, he said. "Very well," I stated, "please receive me tomorrow." Fr. Bong said that he could not do so on account of the director, but that he would speak to his friend, Fr. Esser, the assistant priest of the Church of the Apostles. Perhaps he would receive me. A few days later Fr. Wiskirchen brought me the good news that on October 30, at noon, when the Church of the Apostles would be closed, Fr. Esser would receive me into the Church. Everything had to be carried out in complete secrecy, so my father would not find out and return to Cologne as he had done the last time. I had taken the direct route to the rectory in Lindenburg because of the rain, and it had been immediately reported to the director, whereupon my father was told to come to Cologne and take me home.

At the appointed time I went to the Church of the Apostles. After the Angelus bells had rung, the doors were locked. I was called into the sacristy and in the presence of two sacristans I signed a document, the contents of which I have completely forgotten. Then I knelt down before the altar of the Blessed Virgin and made my profession of Faith. I was not baptized conditionally, neither did I make an abjuration, as I had never belonged to the Lutheran Church of my own free will.

Afterwards I went to Dr. Lohmer to ask him to advise me how to break the news to the director because I wanted to go to Mass from then on. Dr. Lohmer said he would speak to Counselor von Schwarz; perhaps the latter could speak to the director for me. Time passed, and finally on November 13 they told me that since I had thus far managed my affairs successfully, it would be best if I spoke to the director myself.

ANOTHER SACRIFICE

On November 14 the Feast of All Saints of Carmel is celebrated (a fact which I did not know at the time). That was the day on which I went to see the director and to tell him that I could no longer keep my promise. He became very angry and among other things he said, "If you are a Catholic I no longer have any confidence in you.

I'll consult the superintendent at Cologne and then you will receive an answer." On November 20 he called for me and said that I was to leave Lindenburg on January 1, 1889, and then he added, "I have an excellent and experienced lady to take your place."

This meant that in less than six weeks I would be without a home. Some Catholic women of Cologne, with whom I had become friends, tried to find a home for me. Counselor von Schwarz wanted to obtain a position for me similar to the one I had occupied, but every director of these institutions asked the director of Lindenburg about me, and he gave such bad references that I was refused everywhere. Counselor von Schwarz and Dr. Lohmer made inquiries and found that this was the reason for these refusals.

What was I to do? The weeks that followed were painful for me. I was without a home and without means of support, for I had spent my last wages to buy coffins for the poor. In spite of all this, my trust in God's guidance did not waver. Had I not asked God to lead me on a steep and stony way? Should I not be grateful now to God for answering my prayer?

My confidence in God was rewarded. Shortly before Christmas I received word from Cologne that, upon the recommendation of Counselor von Schwarz, Mother M. had invited me to her convent, to which a home for the aged was connected. I was to remain there until I had found something else.

On January 7, 1889 the gates of the convent opened for me, now the homeless one. Mrs. Ueberweg took me there after I had been a guest of the Lohmer family for the previous week. Dr. Lohmer, her brother-in-law, and Counselor von Schwarz had obtained this shelter for me. I was received very kindly by the Mother Superior. I was first shown the Chapel and it was just at the time when one of the sisters was scrubbing the floor. When I saw that, I felt the desire to do such menial work, and I said to the Superior who accompanied me, "May I help that Sister?"

She replied, "Wait, you will soon receive work."

Miss Ueberweg departed, and Sister H. took me from the main building to an annex. Soon I was in my designated room. Next morning Sister H. gave me the schedule of my duties. I was to clean the corridors and stairways of the annex and wash dishes for sixteen elderly ladies. Some students had done this work before.

I spent many hours in the small dark room assigned to me. This dingy room had one window looking out on the passage, and yet I felt as if I were in paradise. I meditated on the Holy Family of Nazareth, and God, in His unending mercy rewarded me every day with new graces. Happiness, such as I had never experienced, flooded my soul. I had made the resolution always to obey promptly. Despite this firm resolution, it happened one afternoon when I was through with my work, that I felt a desire to go to the Chapel. But first, as always when my duties were finished, I asked the Sister what I should do. She said, "Scrub the floor." Now for the first and last time I spoke back. I replied that I had scrubbed the floor on Tuesday, and this was only Thursday. Quietly the Sister said, "Scrub it again." I was deeply ashamed of my great fault of disobedience. I regretted it for years even to this present day. It was not to shirk work, nor because it was ice-cold in the passage, but because I had such a longing to visit the Chapel during the day. No matter what my intentions had been, I had not been perfectly obedient, since my resolution had been to obey the Sister as I would obey God Himself, blindly, without finding fault with her orders and without remonstrating.

The winter of 1889 was a bitterly cold one in Cologne. One wing of the convent was connected with the main building by an open passageway which I also had to scrub, although it was not very long. One day the water froze right under the mop. I asked the Sister whether I ought to scrub it anyway, and she said, "Yes." When I was finished with the work, the floor was like a sheet of ice. The Superior of the convent happened to come along and, shocked at my stupidity, said, "Get some hot water and mop the floor until it is no longer slippery." Thankful for this order I hurried to the convent and fetched hot water. Then, with very chapped hands, I began the work again with hot water.

There was no resentment; only joy and happiness filled my soul. Not content with the work and the hardships, which I was not used to at all, I looked for other mortifications. The room assigned to me gave me the opportunity for such mortification by overcoming great repugnance. One of the elderly ladies told me that only a short time before I had arrived, an old woman had died in that room and that she had left her furnishings to the convent. Since the room had been kept closed until now, it smelled bad, especially the bed. Now that I knew the cause, I understood why it had that deathlike smell. I found a few boards under the bed. I wanted to sleep on them and so I put them in the bed, as a cross, but I could not sleep at all. I wanted to sleep on the floor, but this did not work either.

Soon enough, the unusual work itself gave me pain. My hands, arms, and back hurt so badly that the pain awakened me as soon as I had dozed off. But these were only bodily pains, and to my soul they caused new joy and happiness. Had the Divine Savior not suffered intense pain especially in His hands, arms, and back? I was happy to suffer something for Him. But this trial did not last very long, for the Lord never left me in the same trial for any length of time. He always had others in store for me.

At the end of February I became very ill. An inflammation of the throat forced me to stay in bed. It was so bad that I could not speak or take any food. One night an abscess opened in my throat. I had nothing with which to rinse my mouth, so I wrapped a blanket around me and ran through the icy-cold passage to the faucet. As a result I suffered a relapse, and the inflammation became worse than before. Weeks passed before I was well again. The good Sisters of Mother Schervier visited me and brought me books as well as wine to strengthen me.

The first months in the convent I had lived an active life in union with the Holy Family. Now I lived a more contemplative life. I regarded all things as coming from God, and, through God's grace, remained calm and happy despite the painful situation. Suffering was no longer suffering for me. I embraced it with love and gratitude, and it was turned into indescribable sweetness. God Himself taught me. He first cleansed me from all earthly and sensible attachment to creatures, no matter how dear they were to me.

During the first days of my stay at the convent, the Forty Hours' adoration was observed. It was the first exposition of the Blessed Sacrament and the first nocturnal adoration I had ever attended. I cannot find words to describe my feelings. I was so filled with holy joy that I knelt before the Blessed Sacrament from nine o'clock in the evening until two o'clock in the morning without realizing the time. God inflamed my heart with such fervor that later on, all the sorrows sent to me, or allowed to happen to me by His grace, seemed to be only a drop of water on a glowing iron. They can only cause a momentary flare, a human twitch of nature, and nothing else. The real fervor stays like the real heat in the iron. When I awoke in the morning, my heart was filled with a burning love for God.

Soon afterwards I became the victim of terrible "temptations". Due to circumstances, a month passed between my first confession and my second. The Sisters and several of the patients received Holy Communion a few times a week. I had a great desire to do likewise. I wanted to go to confession every week. When I made that resolution I asked myself what I could possibly have to confess every week. The hundreds and thousands of confessions of the future rose up before me. I was terrified, but God was my strength, my only Friend and Counselor. I did not know that besides confessing sins, one could ask the confessor for advice in spiritual matters. I no longer remember how long this trial lasted, but I tried to remain calm. The thought came to me, "Why worry about future confessions? Just think of the next one. Any future confessions I need not think or worry about." From then on I went to confession every week.

After a while another "temptation" came to me. My desire to receive Holy Communion more often became stronger every day. I begged permission of my confessor to allow me to receive Holy Communion not only on Sundays, but also on Tuesdays and Fridays. But he was very determined and allowed me Holy Communion only on Sundays. Now followed a painful time for me. When I was in the Chapel a voice sometimes urged me to go to Communion and to confess it afterward. This "temptation" tortured me for weeks until I came up with a solution. I drank a little water before Mass. That settled the matter. The "temptation" ceased, but the longing for Holy Communion increased from month to month until, after ten months, I received permission to receive Holy Communion on Tuesdays and Fridays besides Sundays.

Just as the wonderful season of spring is not without storms and thunderclouds, so too the springtime of my soul was not without tempests. The first "temptations" hardly had been overcome, when soon afterward thoughts would surface in my soul like little clouds. In the beginning I did not even consider them worth mentioning in confession, but then they turned into thunderclouds causing a real thunderstorm within me. The nature of this "temptation" was a sort of pride. For two years I thought it could be nothing else than a "temptation." The thoughts would torture me and followed me like a shadow. I never followed the thoughts voluntarily but tried continuously not to pay attention to them. Every week I confessed that I was troubled by vain thoughts. God permitted that I was never asked about the nature of these thoughts, and I would not have dared to reveal them without being told to do so. Neither confession nor all my prayers could free me from this mental anguish.

One day I was occupied with needlework in a small room in the convent, when I was suddenly urged by a thought, "Do not enter an Order, but found one yourself." To me this seemed to be a painfully torturing temptation. It was so convincing that I could hardly resist and I asked the Blessed Virgin, "What kind of garb shall the Sisters wear?" At that moment I saw to my right a Sister in a heavy brown habit, with a brown scapular, a round white collar, and large white stripes under a brown veil. I was awe struck, and I looked with astonishment on this figure until it disappeared. I could not concentrate and could hardly breathe. I did not want to believe that this vision, in answer to my question to the Blessed Virgin, could be of the devil. Or could it be? How could such a grace be granted to me?

Only God knows the suffering my soul had to endure for two years, until He finally planted the Carmel of the Divine Heart of Jesus in the garden of the Church. I longed for humility, and for years I had begged God to make me sincerely humble, and now I saw myself approaching the abyss of pride. I saw that my only salvation was in entering an Order, and I tried to interpret what I had seen as coming from the Blessed Virgin to show me what Order I should choose.

In Cologne I had the best opportunity to become acquainted with the beauty and the treasures of the Church, and I learned to admire and love her. Devout women, in and outside the convent where I stayed, took the greatest interest in me. Through them I made the acquaintance of Sisters of different Orders, but none of them bore any likeness to the vision I had seen.

Among my friends there was a lady by the name of Teresa, and she spoke of nothing with greater enthusiasm than of her patron, St. Teresa of Jesus. While I was at Lindenburg there was a patient, one of the most mentally ill, who imagined herself to be Lucifer, and in some of her spells she looked like him. This unfortunate woman's name was Teresa. Later, whenever I heard that name, the picture of that woman came to me, with her disheveled hair, rolling her terrifying eyes, gesticulating, and frantically screaming curses. It was not surprising therefore, that whenever my friend began to speak of St. Teresa, I wished she would speak of another saint. To my shame I must confess that I usually followed her long discourses with little interest.

Since my last illness I had not gone to the very early Mass at the convent, but to the parish church nearby. Almost daily I would pray the Stations there. The Stations in the church were artistically carved out of large and beautiful wood. They were located alongside the aisle of the church. At the beginning of the aisle there was an impressive group representing the Agony in the Garden, and a large crucifix at the end. In the seclusion of this cloister I spent many grace-filled hours. From day to day the meditation of the Passion of Christ enkindled in my soul the fire of love and a burning zeal, a burning desire to prove my love for Him. Yes, my soul thirsted for an opportunity to serve Him. I desired to become a holocaust of love for God, and I would conclude my prayers with the following words:

"O Lord, send me wherever You will, to work for the salvation of souls. Fulfill the ardent longing of my soul, O God, to prove my love and gratitude to You. But if it is possible, do not send me to Berlin. However, Your will be done, not mine."

Those ten months in the convent were a grace-filled novitiate for me. Here in the solitude and the greatest, often painful poverty, and the most humiliating circumstances one can imagine, God tried me. I was a poor, homeless creature, tolerated only out of sympathy until I could find employment. However it was impossible for me to find a position because the director at Lindenburg gave such unfavorable references. I was convinced that this was all in God's plan.

In this disconsolate condition I took refuge in the heart of my Heavenly Mother. I often asked our Lady, "Is there really no work for me in this wide world?" And although I did not find employment, daily I received patience and courage and grace to bring this offering to God with my whole will. My real desire was to enter an Order. Archbishop Krementz, who later became Cardinal, said that I should wait for two years. In the meantime I looked around for an Order where the Lord would want me.

During this period I was approached again with an offer of marriage, which would have relieved me of all poverty and humiliation, but I preferred to endure poverty and humiliations a thousand times rather than sacrifice my virginity. Is not this great treasure worth the greatest of sacrifices? Once it is lost, the treasure is lost forever. St. John, the virginal disciple of the Divine Savior, describes how the virgins will be especially distinguished in heaven as well. Oh, may the great and the lowly, the young and the poor learn in our day to esteem virginity. This treasure is exalted even in heaven, and may all realize that its loss is irreparable. There is no compensation on this side of life nor hereafter. Once it is lost, it is lost forever.

My sad position created sympathy and interest in me among my friends in Cologne. The women were very kind to me. I especially loved Mrs. von Schwarz, who was truly spiritual and pious. Another friendly (and rather lively) native of the Rhineland was Miss Kamper. She was anxious to help me and wanted to introduce me to Fr. Augustine Keller, O.P.

On a sunny autumn day we went to Ahrenberg, near Koblenz, to see Father Augustine. When he heard my story of the past few years he was moved to pity and thought of ways he could help me.

Finally, he remembered Louise Hensel, who had been in a similar situation, and she found refuge in the home of Count Friedrich von Stolberg. Then he kept speaking of the granddaughter of this great convert, Mrs. von Savigny, who lived in Berlin. In the end Father Augustine suggested, or rather asked me, if I would object if he wrote to Mrs. von Savigny. "Maybe she will invite you to visit her. I'm not sure, because she has her own ways and ideas. But we could try." What else could I do other than gratefully accept his suggestions.

We returned to Cologne. Miss Kamper was very happy that Father Augustine wanted to help me. I was very grateful for her interest and her love, but I didn't show her the uneasiness in my heart. Berlin! That word made me shiver. But, "Not my will but Yours be done." That firm spirit remains in my soul, cost what it will, and never will I follow my own will, but always strive to know and fulfill God's Will, even in the smallest details!

My suspense and uncertainty did not last long. In a few days I received a very kind letter from Mrs. von Savigny, born Countess von Stolberg, inviting me to come and visit her. It was in the beginning of October 1889. I gratefully accepted her invitation and wrote that I would arrive in Berlin on November 7.

In the meantime, I joined the Confraternity of the Scapular, and I was received into the Third Order of St. Francis.

Finally the hour came to take leave of my friends in Cologne, leave Bonn, the lovely Rhineland and its people. I had come to love this part of the country, which was so full of piety and cheerfulness. Yes, that's what I loved, and here I had found it. Had Cologne not become the city of my "birth"? Was it not here that I was received as a child of the Holy Church and so be counted among the children of Grace? How could I ever forget October 30, 1888 in the Church of the Apostles and the Church of the Assumption, when, on May 31, 1889, I was confirmed, and God shed His blessings upon me?

The past year had gone rather swiftly, but nevertheless time had hung heavy on account of my uncertain future, and even more so on account of my painful poverty. Yes, I was so poor that I could not buy even the smallest of life's necessities. I could not even have my shoes repaired. A piece of strong paper had to serve as a substitute for soles. My sisters, out of compassion for me, sent me some money, but this of course did not last very long. One time when I had only ten pennies left, a poor man asked me for alms. I passed him by, but immediately regretted my lack of charity. I turned around, hurried after him, and gave him my last penny.

Thanks be to God who let me feel poverty which I loved so much and which I desired for life! I had experienced in my own person what it means to be poor. It is true that I had a roof over my head and I had enough to eat; nevertheless my situation was extremely humiliating. But it turned out to be a blessing for me, and it led me nearer to St. Joseph. The recollection of my father asking how anybody could pray to such an "outlandish" man sank deeply into my heart, and out of it came a great, intimate, and trusting love combined with a childlike devotion to his fatherly heart. Thousands of times St. Father Joseph showed me his fatherly love and protection.

While the world seeks no other happiness than wealth, honor, and sensual pleasures, the children of God learn greater happiness through the birth of the Divine Savior.

Mary, our dear Lady, and St. Joseph enjoyed this happiness first in Bethlehem and Nazareth, and we likewise can enjoy it. Such is a life which unites us with God, with the Divine Savior and His Sacred Heart. This is true happiness, and the more sincere this unification is, the greater and more complete this joy will be, finding its consummation in the eternal happiness of Heaven.

We treat children with tenderness and sweets. Was I not a child in the realm of grace while I lived in Cologne? Is it therefore surprising that God took me in His Fatherly arms and overwhelmed me with grace? Let me drink from this nectar of Divine Love? Often such a stream of blessings rushed in upon me that I exclaimed, as on the day of my confirmation, "O God, You are too good to me!" The eternal Father knew what awaited me, and He strengthened my soul. I did not enjoy only sweet blessings but suffering as well. The "temptation" always followed me like a shadow. It assailed me day and night. This "temptation" was that I should found a new religious order.

Did I only have to say farewell to the Rhine, to Cologne, and to dear friends and acquaintances? Oh no, my heart was also tied by a sincere, burning, deep love to the Tabernacle. How happy I had been when evening came. After the evening prayers, the Sisters would file out of the Chapel, and only here and there a Sister would remain on the night watch. The lights were turned off, and only the sanctuary light still illuminated the Chapel. Now I started my audience with my heavenly Spouse. Here I found Him who loves my soul. These were heavenly hours for me. Finally the last evening arrived. I thought my heart would break with pain and sorrow! The thought of being separated from the Blessed Sacrament, perhaps for a long time, overwhelmed me.

BACK TO BERLIN

It might be well to make one more incident known to my Sisters. When the director of Lindenburg made me leave, I noticed especially with what sarcasm he added that he had an "excellent and experienced successor" to take my place. I did not harbor any ill feelings against the director, for I took such statements as answers to my prayers for sufferings and crosses.

It was at the beginning of summer in 1889, if my memory serves me correctly, that Miss Ueberweg, the sister-in-law of Dr. Lohmer, came to me and asked me to see Dr. Lohmer, as he wished to speak to me. Dr. Lohmer was one of the city officials, and he, as well as the other officials, had received a communication, or rather a sheet of calumnies from my successor at the institution, written against the director. The latter was highly incensed when he heard the charges the nurse had made against him, and he considered it impossible to remain any longer in his current position.

I was horrified! Was that the "excellent and experienced head nurse?" Now the list of all the accusations was read to me. Having worked with the director for almost three years, I was able to brand all accusations as obvious lies and malicious inventions. I told Dr. Lohmer to tell the director as well as the city officials that I was willing to defend him should it come to a trial, even though it would be a big sacrifice for me. My defense carried great weight because they all knew how the director had treated me when I had joined the Church. Miss Ueberweg hurried to the director to take him this bit of good news. Deeply moved, the director's wife said, "I always said that Miss Tauscher was of noble character."

After Dr. Lohmer explained to the City Council that I was willing to testify in favor of the director, the case was dropped, and the nurse was dismissed. Was this not an act of Divine Providence, that I had the opportunity of returning good for evil? I was happy that I could do it.

CHAPTER THREE

BERLIN

I arrived at Mrs. von Savigny's home on November 7, 1889. The reception was rather cool because Fr. Augustine Keller had not given them any information about my person nor regarding my predicament, and so it happened that Mrs. von Savigny was somewhat embarrassed when she saw me. When her daughter Miss Anne showed me to my room, she explained the situation. They had expected a rather elderly person and not a young lady. Though I was thirty-four years old, I looked much younger. Therefore no one, at first, believed my age.

The embarrassing coldness did not last very long and Mrs. von Savigny soon showed great trust in me. The whole family treated me very kindly. However, despite the homelike surroundings, for the first few months I felt very lonely and forsaken in Berlin. I missed the Blessed Sacrament, the Chapel, and the entire life at the convent.

Very few evenings passed without me kneeling and weeping bitterly in my room. I wanted to serve God and sacrifice myself totally in serving the poor. That was my passionate desire. Instead, I was once again in more or less worldly surroundings, and for the first few weeks I had no chance to do good to the poor. Oh, I was so sorrowful, and the idea of founding an Order, my old "temptation", plagued me and followed me like a shadow.

From childhood I did not like living in Berlin, and that fact contributed to my unhappiness. Besides, my parent's home was not far away. Gusow was less than one hour's ride by train. There in the quiet countryside, I had spent a happy youth! I had sacrificed everything to God. My sisters also had become estranged from me. It was only years later, when they saw that God was with me, that they became more friendly again to me. They often came to my help and supported me.

During this period I realized that God wanted to be my all, and therefore, I was deprived of even legitimate joys and consolations. The deepest longing of my heart had only one goal: to sacrifice myself entirely to God in a religious Order.

The years of probation are always dark, and dark days often turn into weeks and then years. From the beginning of 1890, visiting the poor became a consolation for me. Fr. Faeh, S.J., gave me addresses of the poor and also money. The poor had always been dear to me, and there was so much misery there to relieve. I pitied the poor children the most. These little ones have hearts as soft as wax, and they are very susceptible to the knowledge and love of God. I often asked myself what would become of them. It would be so easy to mold into these hearts the image of the Divine Savior, and they would be filled with the love of God. There was a Catholic orphanage for school children, but for the children under the age of six there was no Catholic institution in Berlin. These little ones were mostly taken to Protestant institutions and were lost to the Catholic Church. This fact aroused within me the most sincere pity for these poor lost children.

The red house of my youthful dreams was called "Home for the Homeless." By and by it became clear to me that in that "imaginary house" there ought to be children, too.

I must also mention another event of this period. At the suggestion of Fr. Faeh, I visited Court Chaplain Stoecker. I have said before that I owed him very much. Therefore, I visited him.

He received me very kindly and with regard to my conversion to the Catholic Church, added, "I am glad that you have found peace of heart." I was surprised at this remark, and it made me very happy. When did one hear such words, at that time, from an Evangelical minister? These were words worthy of his noble and broad-minded character!

I mentioned that I felt forsaken during my first few months in Berlin, but I should have said that I felt completely useless. The few sporadic visits to the poor did not satisfy my zeal. I had waited thirty years until the anchor of my life's ship had embarked and until the Lord directed this ship into the stream of the Church. I was thirty-three when I was accepted on St. Peter's ship. "O Lord, what do You want me to do?" was the prayer that rose to heaven countless times until the answer was received when God's hour had arrived. What next?

During the night of January 21, 1890, I seemed to see a very touching picture in my sleep. It was a living, life-size crucifix. From the hands to the feet, the body was framed with a wreath of thorns. A wreath of thorns in the shape of a heart was impressed into the left side of the heart. There was no crown of thorns on the head. The arms were not lowered; they were stretched out, as a sign of life. This vision was a shocking and pitiful sight, as well as horrible and jolting. There are no words to describe it. While my eyes rested on it, my heart trembled with pain.

I understood this picture to mean that the Divine Savior is the head in heaven, without pain or thorns. The Body is His holy Church, not only affixed to the cross by earthly powers but also wounded by lukewarm, lapsed Catholics, indicated by the thorns framing the body. The thorns impressed upon the heart are those consecrated to God, who have become the tepid and disloyal priests and members of religious Orders.

That morning I arose quite early and hurried to the church. My heart was profoundly moved by pain and compassion; no, it was wounded. It was clear that God was asking of me prayer and atonement! I was to pray for the conversion of sinners, and to move the mercy of God for the freedom of Holy Church.

From that morning on my heart was filled with a new hunger and thirst, not only for God's pleasure or for perfection, but with a burning hunger and thirst to win souls for the Divine Heart. That crucifix is stamped on my memory, and it not only keeps my zeal for the salvation of souls alive, it increases its fire and creates in me the desire to arrive soon at the throne of God, where my longing for souls may be satisfied.

In March 1890 Mrs. von Savigny asked me to go traveling with her. She intended to visit her daughter who was a Visitation nun. After this visit, she wanted to visit some of her married sisters. Anne, her daughter, had to stay with her brothers.

I accepted the invitation and our traveling started on March 12. First we stopped at Zangberg, in Bavaria, at the Convent of the Visitation. We stayed there from the 15th to the 24th of March. Mrs. von Savigny spent most of her time with her daughter at the grille. I spent my time praying in the convent Chapel, but I could not pray all the time. Besides the mealtimes, which we spent with the Sister in the conversation room at the grille, I was on my own. So I asked Sr. Armella if she would bring me some books to read. She instantly fulfilled my wish, because when I returned from the Chapel, I found two books on the table. One was about the Sacred Heart, and the other was the autobiography of St. Teresa of Jesus, translated by Schwab.

Oh, I thought, why could she not bring me another book, rather than the life of St. Teresa. Instead I became absorbed with the book on the Sacred Heart. But after a few days I desired a change in reading material and with some discomfort I picked up the life of St. Teresa. I leafed back and forth, and as I started to read, I became more and more interested in it and kept reading on and on. What words can describe what I felt? Oh, blessed are the hours and the days I spent at Zangberg! I had found my ideal! My passionate heart was fascinated. Yes, it was fascinated in a glowing love for St. Teresa, whose name up to then I could not even bear to hear!

God is wonderful, and wonderful is Divine Providence! No one in Zangberg knew of my joy. Only God and myself knew of the graces I received in that Chapel. Yes, inscrutable is the love and mercy of God.

It was to be Carmel and only Carmel; to enter Carmel was now my one wish. The humility of St. Teresa and her love of God was what I was looking for; it was what I desired. Everything about this great and holy woman filled me with such enthusiasm that my besetting temptation (to found an Order) was weakened. I did not doubt that I would receive permission from Fr. Faeh, for I felt certain that the Carmel was my real vocation, even if it would only be as a lay Sister. The life of such a Sister appealed to me. I wanted to be the servant of all. During the day I would do housework, as I had done in the convent in Cologne, and spend the nights with my beloved Jesus in the Blessed Sacrament in the Chapel.

Now I wanted to return to Berlin as soon as possible,

but Mrs. von Savigny wanted to visit Fr. Kneipp in Woer-ishofen and then go on to Hildesheim. On March 30th we started from Munich on our northward journey, and we arrived at night at Hanover. After a brief rest we went to St. Clara's Church. It happened to be one of my Communion days. At that time such days were appointed. At Cologne the Sisters received Communion before Mass. Here Holy Communion was not distributed before or after, but during Mass. I thought it might be the custom to receive after Mass because no one received during Mass. During the last prayers I went up to the Communion railing and knelt down. The priest did not pay any attention to my presence there. In a few moments the sacristan informed me that Holy Communion was distributed during Mass.

I returned to my pew and broke into tears. The good lady, Mrs. von Savigny, felt very sorry about my disappointment and drove hurriedly to the Vincentian Sisters and told the superior of my disappointment. To my great happiness the chaplain of the convent gave me Holy Communion. I mention this incident in order that my Sisters may thank God for the privilege of being allowed to receive daily, reminding them of their great responsibility, "to whom much is given, much will be expected."

Special graces always filled me with fear and trembling, and much more so the permission to receive Holy Communion daily. This permission, which was not exactly a permission but rather an admonition, was given me by Fr. Ruetgen, S.J. in Sittard in 1898. All fears, which I experienced in Cologne about Holy Communion, were now dispelled. My longing was satisfied. My heart trembled when I considered this great privilege of which I judged myself unworthy, but I received it with sincere gratitude.

After my return to Berlin I called on Fr. Faeh, S.J. to get his approval of my entering Carmel. In my usual eager manner I said, after a brief greeting, "Now I have found my Order, Carmel. I have read the life of Saint Teresa, and I can't say anything else except that I am so enamored that I want to become one of her daughters." Fr. Faeh listened calmly to me and then said, "This is not your vocation. God Himself trained you for a special purpose. If I knew where you should go I would help you, but I do not know. Let us pray, and God will make known His will. That you have a vocation is certain." Then he added, "Wait and pray. You will be a daughter of Saint Teresa."

Fr. Faeh was transferred to Brazil in October 1890. Later he wrote to me regarding this conversation that at that time he did not want to press the affair, since it was clear to him that I should "found a new Community, and that as a rule God trains the instrument for such work." At the end of the letter he said, "Too bad that you did not express your inner feelings, even though I had encouraged you to do so." But really I could not put my "temptation" into concrete form, since it always appeared to me as a thought of pride. The battle against such a thought seemed to be my greatest trial. It appeared to be a trial, while at the same time the Lord was really training and preparing me. It remained my lot to keep wrestling and struggling. That is how it seemed to me, while God kept working on His tool, unworthy of His Divine Majesty.

The many journeys with Mrs. von Savigny were, in fact, very useful for my future, which to me was still in the dark. Not only did I get to know the country and the people, but more importantly, I also got acquainted with different Orders and religious Communities.

In August 1890 Mrs. von Savigny accepted an invitation

to visit her oldest sister, Countess S. in Innsbruck. On the way there we called on Countess Schmising in Mari-aschein-Teplitz. I cannot forget this visit because during that time we visited the church in Graupen. There the walls were still covered with frescoes from years ago, displaying the life and passion of our Divine Savior in touching scenes.

When we arrived in Innsbruck, I looked for a convent where retreats for women were conducted. At that time it was not as easy to make a retreat in Berlin as it is today. I had heard so much about the retreat movement that I was anxious to attend one. Here, in this thoroughly Catholic city, I hoped that my wish could be fulfilled.

After a long search, I found a large building, which looked like a convent. I had hardly rung the bell when the door opened, and a nun appeared behind the grille. I asked her if she knew of a convent where a retreat for ladies was conducted. "Right here," she said, "but the retreat started last night, and after it starts nobody is admitted.

"Please," I said, "ask if I may have permission to join, since I just arrived from Berlin, and in Berlin I would not have the chance to make a retreat."

The good Sister hurried away, only to return and usher me into the parlor. After I told the Mother Prioress, who was waiting at the grille, of my desire to make a retreat, and that I had arrived only last night, and how Divine Providence had brought me here, I asked whether an exception could be made, so I could make the retreat. The Mother Prioress was so kind and reported my wish to the Retreat Master, Fr. Stentrup, S.J., who allowed me to make the retreat. Mrs. von Savigny gladly consented, and so I made my first retreat at the end of August 1890. How

shall I describe this experience? I was completely overwhelmed and deeply moved, weeping all the time. How
many tears did I shed in the Ursaline Chapel! I paid no
attention to the one hundred ladies around me. There was
only God and myself. Nothing else mattered to me. This
gracious God enlightened, stirred, and ignited my soul to
work and suffer with new zeal for the Holy Church.

There were tears of sorrow for my sins, for having
caused such pain to my Divine Savior, and especially for
having delayed my entrance into the new paradise, the
Church. Why did I not seek the way more diligently?

There were tears of gratitude for God's never-ending
kindness and love, with which He captured the poor wayward sheep, born in the desert of error. He searched until
He found the lamb, freed it from the thorns, and brought
it home to the flock. The heart of God is overflowing with
love and mercy. Oh, if all people would come to know
this, how happy they would be! Let us dive into this
ocean, into this source of Divine love, and we shall shed
tears of remorse and gratitude.

God led me to Innsbruck to purify my soul, but as soon
as the days of remorse and tears were over, Divine Love
shed its graces on me. Indeed, I may say, all the weeks in
Innsbruck I spent in heavenly enjoyment of the Sacred
Heart. Just like in Cologne, I was overflowing with the
nectar of Divine Love and enjoyed heavenly bliss. Did
God want to strengthen me for the future? Did He want to
unite me more intimately to His Divine Heart?

In the late Fall of the same year, after a brief stay in
Berlin, Mrs. von Savigny went to Bonn, on the Rhine, to
visit her married sister, Mrs. V. L. I gladly accepted the
invitation to accompany her, as it meant that I would
again see my beloved Rhineland. In Bonn, we stayed at a

private hotel. I was able to dispose of my time as I pleased because Mrs. von Savigny spent the greater part of the day with her sister. I was with her only during the meals, which were served in a private room of the hotel.

Despite the short retreat in Innsbruck, with all its blessings, I had not been freed from my painful "temptation." Therefore, I decided to make a thirty-day retreat on my own, hoping to be finally rid of these "proud" thoughts. As a retreat master I used the "Book for Retreats of Thirty Days" by Father I. of the Society of Jesus. In the beginning I fared quite well, but as the days went on, my "temptation" increased in violence. But I persevered in silence and patience.

In January 1891 we made a trip to Aachen, which was very enjoyable. My sincere love for St. Teresa made me wish to see one of her daughters. In Innsbruck I had spoken about it to Mrs. von Savigny, but, as soon as my wish passed my lips, she began to weep. Full of anxiety she said, "I see you want to go to the convent, and you are the first ray of sunshine in my life since my husband died." I consoled her as well as I could, but I naturally could not talk about visiting the convent any more because I did not wish to give her any more pain. However, Divine Providence arranged it so that Mrs. von Savigny herself was unwittingly the cause of my wish to come true.

This is what happened. A sister of Mrs. von Savigny had been a Sister of the Sacred Heart at Bl. near Aachen, and she was buried there. Mrs. von Savigny wished to visit her grave, so we stayed in Aachen at a hotel quite close to the Cathedral. It was Sunday, and just like every morning, I went to early Mass, came back, had breakfast with Mrs. von Savigny, and we became so engrossed in our conversation that we did not realize how the time was passing until we heard the Cathedral bells announcing the last Mass. As Mrs. von Savigny had not been to Mass, she was afraid she would be late. We hurried to the Cathedral, but there was a crowd of people standing before the entrance. Because of her anxiety in not being able to attend Mass, she elbowed her way through the crowd. Within seconds I lost track of her. A thought flashed through my mind, and I acted immediately.

I inquired of some people passing by where Lousberg was, and I hurried there. I rang the bell, and when the portress opened the door, I said, "I am from Berlin, a great admirer of St. Teresa, and I am very anxious to see a daughter of hers, but I have only a little time." A few minutes later I was ushered to the grille, and in the bright sunlight, a daughter of my beloved St. Teresa stood before me. She was wearing the brown habit, Carmel's own brown, as I had seen in the vision. Indescribable joy filled my heart. In that moment I remembered that Fr. Faeh had said that Carmel was not my vocation. I said to myself that perhaps he had meant not as a choir Sister, but that I could become a lay Sister. Keeping this possibility in mind, I thanked the good Carmelite Nun and hurried back to the hotel. Everything went well, and my visit to Carmel remained completely unnoticed.

After a few days we returned to Bonn, but I remained greatly disturbed. I did not know what to do. Only those who have had mental trials will understand what I underwent during those two years. Since my great retreat I could not become master of those thoughts. The fear of having consented worried me, and I thought it was a serious sin. Under no condition did I want to commit even a venial sin, nor even a deliberate fault.

When my need was the greatest, help drew near. I had

a friend in Bonn, Miss von Dircking. She told me that she had a good confessor and advised me to go to him. He was a parish priest in the suburb of Bonn. I agreed, and one day we went to the countryside, and in that little village church I found the physician of my soul in the person of Fr. Westenberg. Had my agony reached the threshold, or did God give him the key to my soul? Anyway, I poured my heart out to him about my years of anxiety, misery, struggles, and efforts to free myself of these proud thoughts. When I was finished, I was told, to my greatest surprise, that these were not temptations and that I should no longer "resist this Grace." I felt like an eagle released from its chains. Like a free bird, I soared up on my wings of love, until I found rest high up in the cliffs of the Sacred Heart. The measure of my happiness was as the measure of my former suffering. "To serve God in love and suffering," and that in an Order! Here I am, O Lord, what will you have me do? My heart is willing. These and similar aspirations rose from my heart to the throne of God.

Lenten season was at hand. To fast and to pray more was my delight. Nothing seemed too hard for me. I went to early Mass and then had breakfast with Mrs. von Savigny, but I took only one cup of black coffee. Afterward I went with Mrs. von Savigny to a later Mass. Between twelve and one o'clock I made a meditation in the church of the Sacred Heart. At half-past one we had dinner, followed by a period of recreation. After that I either visited with Miss von Dircking, or she came to see me. Often we both visited the shrine of our Blessed Lady. Now I could talk freely of my plans, but I spoke of a home for children only. I hoped confidentially that Miss von Dircking would become my partner, but her delicate constitution made that impossible.

One day in April 1891 I was standing by the window admiring the sunset, when suddenly the purpose and name of the new foundation came to my mind. I feared that I might forget it, and therefore, I jotted it down immediately. This is exactly what I wrote:

THE SERVANTS OF THE DIVINE HEART OF JESUS
Consecrate themselves to the Divine Heart:

I.   For atonement.
II.   For their own sanctification.
III. For the salvation of souls.

FIRST: For atonement, especially for all dishonor and offenses the Divine Heart of Jesus suffers through heresy and unbelief and in particular for the denial of the Divinity of the Son of God made man; that God in His mercy may cease to afflict any longer the children for the sins of their fathers, and that He may send the Holy Spirit, the Light of the Truth, to the souls born in night and darkness.

SECOND: For their own sanctification. Only a soul striving after greater perfection shall be deemed worthy by the Divine Heart to dedicate herself to His service, and only in so far as she walks the way of perfection, which means the way of self-denial, renunciation, of sacrifice and humility, will the blessing of the Divine Heart rest upon her and her work.

THIRD: To work for the salvation of souls: First by visiting families in their homes, the poor, the sick, and the abandoned, and by conducting societies for young girls, women, and children. This shall be accomplished by the education of children; however, always only the children of the common people, and never may the Sisters engage in school teaching. The Servants of the Divine Heart of Jesus shall always strive to provide good home training. Children: orphans, the illegitimately born, the poor, the abandoned, etc. shall be received and shall find "motherly care and love." The training shall meet the natural abilities and tendencies of each individual child.

The Servants of the Divine Heart shall serve children living in their families: 1. In kindergarten, in which children up to six years of age can spend the day from morning to evening. 2. In homes for children (now called day-centers) where girls and boys from six years on, of course completely separated, can spend their school-free time. After the children have done their homework, they are to be kept occupied with play and constructive hobbies.

If possible, a compensation, even though small, shall be charged for both the children who are in full care of the Servants of the Divine Heart as well as for those in day-care only. However, never should children be refused admittance because no one can pay for them.

Where place and circumstances allow, homes for elderly women may be erected, also in which young girls shall be given the opportunity to learn better housekeeping and domestic science.

Bonn, April 1891

Finally, Lent was over, and I was relieved of the tormenting headaches which were caused by my "unreasonable fasting", as I used to call it later. God does not want us who are endowed with reason to act in an unreasonable manner. If one injures her health by unreasonable fasting or renders herself incapable of working, then God is displeased.

It is pleasing to God if we keep ourselves mentally and bodily healthy and fit for work, especially in our time when the harvest is ripe and the laborers are insufficient to gain countless souls for the Divine Heart.

In days past, it was a little different. I think God permitted me to experience this personally in order that I might be able to judge how we, considering our activities, should act regarding fasting.

ST. JOSEPH'S HOME
FOR HOMELESS CHILDREN

My greatest longing at this time was to be able to start the work beginning with a Home for poor children. We finally left Bonn a week before the feast of the Ascension and returned to Berlin by way of Hildesheim.

The very next day, May 27, I went to see Monsignor Jahnel. He received me with the kind words, "I was happy to see you at the Communion rail again this morning!" This reception made it easier for me to ask permission to open a Home for poor children. Monsignor Jahnel listened to me with evident interest and replied that he had considered such a project for some time, but that he knew no one who could carry it out. He said he was really happy that I intended to found such a Home. "First of all you must look for a house," were his final words.

What a task! To look for a house, and then when it is found, determining who is going to pay for it. Mrs. von Savigny had given me 700 marks. She said it was out of gratitude for accompanying her. I sent 100 marks to the convent in Cologne, where I was given hospitality, to show my appreciation, and another 100 marks I used on myself; that left 500 marks. That was hardly enough to buy the most necessary furnishings, even for a small beginning. How then, was I to buy a house or even rent one? But away with worries! God's work was to be called into life, and it was not for me to ask worriedly, "Where will I find the means?" Besides I had placed all my trust in the help of St. Joseph, and up till then he had never let me beg in vain!

It was in the northern part of the city, the section of the poor, where I began to look for a house. Without any experience in purchasing houses, I wandered about day after day; but of course, to no avail whatsoever.

At the same time I was busy getting things ready for the children. I prepared everything for six children, which took almost all my money.

The month of the Sacred Heart passed, and there was still no prospect of finding a suitable house. In fact, neither a house nor helpers were in sight.

The second of July approached, and that day became a day of grace for me and the whole Order. This day was a never-failing source of consolation and confidence for me. Again and again, my heart is kindled with love and gratitude and glows with a new ardor to suffer, struggle, and work so that the task, which by the mercy of God was entrusted to me, for a short time, may grow and develop entirely according to His will!

On the second of July 1912, I wrote the following while in Rocca di Papa: "Today I stand on the hill which I saw on July 2, 1891. Whenever I find myself at the entrance to the upper garden and see above me the Chapel on the top of the hill, I often, yes, nearly always see that vision which I had on that day of grace. In a dream I saw the

Divine Majesty, God the Father in the clouds, in wondrous brilliance, directly above me. The right hand of God rested on the left corner of a large, golden frame which enclosed a large cross on a background of silver. The cross was large, very large, and wrought most artistically in gold and silver. Lowering my eyes from the cross, I saw a great throng of Sisters spread over the entire hill on the top of which I was standing. The Sisters wore our habit, such as I had seen in that vision in Cologne, and they sang the *Te Deum*, after I had become their superior.

Filled with amazement, I looked up to God, and then noticed that He was raising His left arm with the index finger pointing straight out. Following the direction indicated, I saw in the cloud the partly visible figure of the Divine Savior, just as God the Father also appeared, looking down upon me with the expression of heavenly kindness and love. The face of the Savior was very much like that painted by Baroness von Oer according to a vision of a Sister of the Adoration in Innsbruck.

I was all on fire with an indescribable, rapturous ecstasy and filled with amazement. The wordless question arose within me: What does this mean? Without a word, in a moment, the meaning was revealed to me, "If you found this Order for me, if you take these sufferings upon yourself signified by this large cross, then my Son will be your everlasting reward."

One of the Sisters once said to me that if I continued to work as I did, I would soon be dead. I answered, "I will not die until the Servants of the Divine Heart are spread throughout the whole world!"

When I awoke my heart was aflame with the rapture of love, and all day long it seemed to me that I was on earth only with my body. I was filled with such an unending happiness.

I hastened to St. Hedwig's Church. Then I visited my poor. When I returned home Mrs. von Savigny told me that Monsignor Jahnel had been there, but that his visit was not meant for me but for her, but since he had not found me at home I was to go and see him the following morning.

I went the next day, July 3rd, full of expectation. After a friendly greeting Monsignor Jahnel told me that he had a house for a beginning, and even another one, if only I had some helpers. I was given the address of 112 Pappelallee (Poplar Avenue) and went there in haste.

I found a small, old house in which some rough-looking people lived. All the rooms were occupied, with the exception of two rooms and a kitchen. The manager told me that he and all the tenants had long leases and that no one would move out before the lease expired.

Thus, on this July 3rd, the cross began to settle down upon my shoulders. I embraced it with loving gratitude like a friend for whom one has yearned for a long time. Up to this moment my faithful friend has never left me. But neither has this friend ever been unwelcome.

No, the more I felt its presence the more beloved the cross became, for I always regarded it as the highest proof of Divine love, and, I might say, of God's trusting love for my soul.

Wonderfully strengthened and filled with new zeal and confidence by the fact that the vision coincided with Monsignor's offer of a house on the same day, I coura-geously readied myself for the undertaking. All this did I do alone.

I could not speak at all to Mrs. von Savigny about my plans, because of her fear of losing me. I did speak to

Miss Anne about my need of a house and helpers, and we exchanged ideas about how to get the people to move and about other external affairs. The special tokens of grace granted me by Divine Love, I kept in my heart.

After Fr. Faeh had left, Fr. Frins became my confessor. I told him about the permission of Monsignor Jahnel to establish a Home for children, and I asked him to bless the little Home on August 2. The two rooms and kitchen were quickly readied for a nurse, a maid, and the first three children.

On Sunday August 1 or 2, a mother came with three children and called for me at Dorothea Street, the residence of Mrs. von Savigny, and I immediately went with them to the fairly distant Pappelallee. Shortly after our arrival Fr. Frins appeared, blessed the rooms, and prayed the Litany of the Blessed Virgin with us before a small statue of our dear Lady. This was the beginning of the Saint Joseph's Homes, from which the Carmel of the Divine Heart of Jesus developed in 1898.

Several of the families in the house left after receiving some compensation. However the tenants of the best apartments, without which it was impossible to have a Chapel, absolutely refused to leave. Likewise the sinister group of two men and two women who lived in one half of the basement absolutely insisted that they would remain there for another two years.

The many and various sufferings of the past years, interior as well as exterior, combined with my excessive fasting, had so shattered my health that a doctor, whom Mrs. von Savigny consulted, ordered me to take a trip to the Taunus. To my great joy he also recommended that Miss Anne von Savigny take this vacation trip. However, she was to take the cure at Bad Nauheim, while I was merely to rest.

In the meantime, the Home for Children had been increased by the addition of two apartments, and the number of children had increased to fifteen. These I left in the hands of the nurse and under the protection of my beloved Father Saint Joseph.

Joyfully we set out for the Taunus. We secretly cherished the hope to obtain "big money" there for the construction of a children's Home. We had been in Bad Nauheim hardly two days when I began to feel very miserable, and I was glad when a telegram arrived on the third day from Mrs. von Savigny, telling us to go to Koenigstein. Mrs. von Savigny, in her motherly solicitude, had consulted the doctor again, and he advised that we go to Koenigstein, since Miss Anne could take the cure there also. For me Koenigstein would be a better place. A loud roaring tormented me in my head, and so we stayed in rooms near a noisy brook whose noise drowned out the one in my head. I was greatly relieved.

The following days were days of quiet and prayer. They were glorious weeks of relaxation and eminently suited for gathering new strength for the future. That, of course, still lay before me enveloped in a heavy fog.

I must not forget to mention my leave-taking from Monsignor Jahnel. At that time in 1891, Berlin had only a few Catholic Churches. The predecessor of Monsignor Jahnel regarded the five churches, which also included the two garrison churches, as sufficient. All complaints of zealous Catholics that many people needed one to two hours to get to church or to hear Mass on Sundays could not change his opinion. Then God took pity on the poor Catholics who were in danger of losing their faith and sent Monsignor Jahnel to Berlin as delegate to the Prince

Bishop and head of the Cathedral Chapter of St. Hedwig's. Later he was given the title of Domestic Prelate. He was an upright and somewhat gruff man, and his changeable disposition was due to a disease of the liver, which caused him much suffering and brought him to an early grave. I came to know him well and experienced his fatherly love and kindness, as well as his displeasure, which made me suffer very much. Despite this, I have always had the highest esteem for him, and it always hurt me to see him misunderstood so many times. As far as Berlin was concerned, he was an instrument of Divine Providence, and the Catholics of Berlin owe him very much. He came to this city in 1888, and as soon as he saw the conditions of these Catholics and their great need of Churches, he came to their aid with marked prudence and energy. He had inquiries made about halls and workshops, no matter what kind, as long as they were large enough and had them changed into Chapels. He also established mission Chapels, out of which regular parishes developed after a short time. He had but one aim: to gather the Catholics, to revive their faith, and to enable all of them to attend Mass.

Knowing his zeal, therefore, I ventured to ask his permission before taking leave of him, to prepare a Chapel in the Children's Home as soon as the tenants had left, for the nearest Chapel was one half hour away. Besides there were many Italian people in the neighborhood who never went to Mass. What had I done?

In a severe voice he said to me, "I regarded you as a reasonable person and now you come along with such ideas! If you would come after five years with such a plan, it would be different. But now, when you can hardly take care of the children, you want to have a Chapel? And where are you going to get a priest?"

These words strengthened my resolve even more to preserve the deepest silence concerning my plans and about the work of God to which the Heavenly Father Himself had entrusted me.

I was firmly determined never to settle down in the Home without the Blessed Sacrament. My constant and chief prayer in those months was, therefore, "If you come, I will come!" It was a cry of love and longing. The Savior understood these words and graciously listened to this plea of love, rising to Him many hundreds of times!

But now back to Koenigstein. About twenty-five minutes away is Falkenstein and a cozy path through the woods leads to a poor little church with an old statue of our dear Lady. We walked there almost every day while quietly saying the rosary. Naturally my prayer was for the children's home with a Chapel and, above all, the Blessed Sacrament. All of this seemed impossible, but everything is possible to the Queen of Heaven, through her powerful intercession with God!

The "big money" for the Home was expected to have come from a rich lady living in Koenigstein. But, to our disappointment, instead of 10,000 marks, we received 10! We soon got over this failure; though our stay had not brought in any construction money, at least our health had improved greatly during these weeks of rest.

I must also mention a pilgrimage we made to Fischbach, a two-hour journey, where there is a shrine dedicated to the Most Holy Trinity. My very special devotion to the Holy Trinity inspired me to place, with the greatest confidence, all my concern for the work and for Holy Church into the heart of my Lord, God the Father. For I always considered God the Father as the author of the work entrusted to me for the salvation of souls.

We again made the trip to Falkenstein to the shrine of our dear Lady, and then we started out for home. In Trier the Holy Robe of our Lord was being displayed, and so we made a side trip to that city. It was evening when we arrived, and since the Savignys were well acquainted with Fr. Huley, one of the Cathedral capitulars, we went directly to him to find out the best way to get into the Cathedral. Thousands of pilgrims filled the Cathedral Square. It was a most unusual sight in the evening twilight to see the praying masses of people, in perfect order, slowly disappearing through the doors of the Cathedral after walking around it in solemn procession for three to five hours.

Monsignor Huley received us in the most gracious manner. After a brief conversation he invited us to be at the door of the Cathedral at five o'clock in the morning. He had already asked several other ladies to be there, and together with them we could attend his Mass and receive Holy Communion.

As soon as he finished speaking, he picked up his biretta and asked us to follow him. In a few minutes we reached a small hidden door leading into the ancient, venerable Cathedral. Monsignor Huley unlocked it and sooner than we had expected we found ourselves in the dimly lighted Cathedral, which was, however, filled with devout people. A glorious and stirring spectacle presented itself here. High up on a balcony, surrounded by a sea of lights, the Holy Robe was displayed.

My heart trembled with emotion. The Divine Savior wore this garment when He lived, worked, and suffered indescribably on this earth. Yes, the life of our Redeemer, as accounted by the holy Evangelists, filled my soul and my spirit. Our stay at this holy place, on this evening, lasted only a few minutes. Monsignor Huley arose, we followed him, and just as secretly as we had entered the Cathedral we also left it.

We hastened to the convent of St. Joseph, which had been founded recently by Countess Schafgottsch, a cousin of Mrs. von Savigny, now Mother Gertrud. After a cordial reception we were soon deep in conversation. The Venerable Mother told us of her work and plans, and I, on my part, spoke of our little Home for Children in a poor working-class house in the northern part of Berlin, far from a church. I also spoke of my burning desire to have a Chapel in the Home.

As I finished my story Mother Gertrud exclaimed, "That is something for the chaplain, Fr. Dasbach; he is always interested in something new!" She immediately sent him a message, asking him to see us the next day.

The chaplain acceded to the request and showed great interest in my (as yet) insignificant work. At the end of our talk I mentioned my farewell visit to Monsignor Jahnel in Berlin and repeated his final words, "How do you expect to have a Chapel, and where are you going to get a priest?"

The chaplain replied immediately, "I have all the necessary vestments also a missal and a chalice, for during the *Kulturkampf*, I celebrated Mass secretly in my room. My mother will bring everything here tomorrow. As soon as you get to Berlin, go to Monsignor Jahnel again and tell him that you have everything necessary for Mass and priests too. Either some other priest or I will come several times a week to Pappelallee and say Mass." My surprise, astonishment, and joy can be more easily imagined than expressed in words.

Now I must include a few more words about the Holy

Robe. As agreed upon, we all met before the Cathedral at the appointed hour. At five o'clock Monsignor Huley opened the door and led us to an altar. With profound devotion we few privileged ones attended the Mass in the dusky, empty Cathedral.

After our thanksgiving the affable Monsignor led us to the choir stalls, and soon a most moving scene offered itself to our eyes. At exactly eight o'clock the door near the stairway leading to the balcony was opened, and hundreds of the sick and crippled of all kind walked or were carried in. All went up to the stairs on the right side, spent some time before the Holy Robe, where the bishop himself in most cases offered the Robe to be touched, and then came down on the left side.

All of these people were sick or crippled. Some dragged themselves up painfully on crutches, some were carried in the arms of others, and some on stretchers. Elderly persons and children, men and women, young men and ladies all came. Hope and trust had brought them here; for many times miraculous cures had taken place at the moment the Holy Robe was touched. A peculiar excitement filled the hearts of all, ours too, although we were only spectators.

In spirit I saw our Divine Savior, our Model of merciful love, as He once walked this earth surrounded by the poor and the suffering of every kind.

Filled with enthusiasm, I resolved to sacrifice myself with new ardor, love, and trust for the work entrusted to me: to serve the poor and the children with the self-forgetting love of the Divine Savior. My task should be to dry tears, to heal wounded souls, and to lead innocent children to the Heart of Jesus.

These hours came to an end, and we returned to the

convent for a refreshing rest, after which we visited the other ancient churches of Trier. However, I had one more desire. Like the other pilgrims, I wanted to take part in the tiring procession, which took hours, and to do reverence to the Holy Robe. Miss von Savigny agreed, and so we walked for three hours in that long procession, which moved snake-like around the Cathedral square, until finally our turn came, and we entered the Cathedral for the third time. Here we saw the Holy Robe again, picturing to ourselves the merciful Savior, until it was time again to return to St. Joseph's convent, our hearts filled with the most tender love and gratitude. Here new joy awaited us, for during our absence the good Mrs. Dasbach, mother of the chaplain, had brought all the items promised by her son for the celebration of Mass.

The following day we journeyed through the lovely valleys of the Moselle and the Rhine on our way back to Berlin. I could hardly wait for the next morning and the eleventh hour, the time set for my appointment with Monsignor Jahnel. At last the time arrived, and with tense expectation I waited in his room. What would he have to say to all the good news I was bringing?

Monsignor entered the room. After a brief greeting I began, all radiant with happiness, "Please, Monsignor, now be kind enough to grant permission to have a Chapel, for I have everything necessary!"

"What do you have?" he countered.

I told him that I had been in Trier, where I met Fr. Dasbach, who had donated everything necessary for saying Mass, not only the vestments, but also a missal and a chalice. I explained that he had all these items from the time of the *Kulturkampf*, when he had to say Mass secretly.

Monsignor could not conceal his pleasure while listening to me, but he was not won over so easily, "The main principal is still missing, the priest!"

Joyfully, I replied, "I have a priest, too, and not only one. Fr. Dasbach will come on Sundays and preach to the Italian people in Italian, and he is going to ask other priests to say Mass there several times during the week."

"And the house, is it free of tenants now?" asked Monsignor.

"No, not yet, but if I receive permission for a Chapel, I will soon get rid of the tenants. Please grant permission!"

"You will not get permission until the tenants are gone, and before that I will not write to Breslau for an altar stone!"

As happy as I was when I came to the delegature, so disappointed was I when I returned home. I poured out my troubles to Miss Anne and told her that the tenants would not leave the place before I paid them 100 marks as compensation. Hearing this, good Miss Anne laid 100 marks into my hand.

Naturally, I went to Pappelallee the same day and negotiated with the tenants. It was the end of October, and they demanded two weeks time to look for another place, and then they would leave only on a Sunday, since they didn't have time on weekdays. We then made an agreement in writing that they were to receive 100 marks if they left the place in two weeks.

The next day I went to the Monsignor and told him that the people were going to leave the place around the middle of November, and that I was very anxious to have the Home blessed on December 8. I ended by asking him again to write for the altar stone. "Come, when all the people are out of the house, then I will write for the stone!" was his answer.

The first apartment, which had been blessed on August 1 or 2, seemed to be the only suitable place for a Chapel, but the children would have no room until the other apartment was vacant. That was the one for which the 100 marks was demanded.

In the meantime I instructed the builder where and how to make the arch for the sanctuary; I ordered everything necessary, and told all to hurry, since the Chapel was to be dedicated on December 8.

Fr. Augustine Keller, O.P., who had introduced me to Mrs. von Savigny, wanted to donate the altar. People in Cologne had promised to donate the statues of our dear Lady and Saint Joseph, and several young ladies had promised to sing for Holy Mass in order to heighten the solemnity.

Finally the Sunday arrived that the tenants had promised to leave. I was there, and when the rooms were vacant, I gave them the 100 marks and then hurried to Monsignor Jahnel to repeat my plea. It was eight o'clock in the evening.

"Now you may get the Chapel ready," was the answer, "and I will write for the stone, which ought to be here in eight to ten days."

"Please, Monsignor, be so kind as to bless the Chapel yourself, and tell us at what time, so we can announce it."

"At eight o'clock on December 8," he answered!

Thanking God, I brought the good news to Miss Anne, but I had not the least idea of settling down in the Pappelallee as long as the Blessed Sacrament was not reserved there. None of us dared to think of this after all the trouble and begging it had taken to get the approval for the Chapel.

All worked with zeal and interest to get the Chapel

ready, for the few weeks left seemed to fly by.

I think it was on the Friday before the blessing, when our friends, the young ladies arrived, and of course we talked about nothing but the dedication and furnishings of the Chapel. Suddenly one of the ladies asked, "Could all of us go to Holy Communion on this great day? Oh, Miss Tauscher, why can't you go to the Monsignor and ask him."

This request was directed to me, and again, I went to the delegature. After I apologized that I was disturbing Monsignor so often, I presented my wish: "At the first Holy Mass in Pappelallee, we all would like to be allowed to go to Holy Communion."

For a few moments the Monsignor remained silent, then he said, "I had planned to reserve the Blessed Sacrament there."

"Yes," I replied, and added, "Praised be Jesus Christ." I was completely incapable of saying another word. I felt as I were out of my mind since I was so filled with heavenly joy. Was it really possible? Would my most fervent wish be fulfilled? My soul rejoiced, scarcely able to grasp this good fortune.

I hurried back to Dorothea Street and rushed up the stairs. Miss Anne was at home. I embraced her, and in tears of happiness and joy, I could only stammer, "The dear Savior will remain!" Overwhelmed with emotion and gratitude, her tears of joy were mingled with mine!

When we had calmed down a bit, she urged me to see Fr. Augustine Keller, O.P. quickly. I had just told him of my happiness and joy, when he quietly said, "Miss Tauscher, that is impossible."

Once more I firmly told him that Monsignor would leave the Blessed Sacrament there.

Then Fr. Augustine replied, "Yes everything is possible here, but nothing has been arranged for the Blessed Sacrament. I have to order a Tabernacle at once. There are only two days left to complete the work. We have to send telegrams to Cologne, Breslau, and Munster and order everything that is still missing." Arrangements were made and joyfully we hurried away.

Preparations filled the day so completely that I had little time to consider how I could leave Mrs. von Savigny and her hospitable home where I, homeless as I was, had been received and treated like a member of the family. For the time being not a word could be said about a complete separation. Miss Anne thought also that I should ask leave only for a few days. I told Mrs. von Savigny that Monsignor Jahnel was going to bless the Chapel on December 8 and reserve the Blessed Sacrament, and for that reason I would have to be there for a few days. Mrs. von Savigny was too devout not to let me go for a few days for this legitimate reason. She made it very clear that it was to be only for a few days. We waited tensely for the ciborium and the other items to arrive. Nothing was to be had in those days in Berlin. One item after another actually arrived on Monday, and on December 7, late in the evening, the statues of our Blessed Lady and Saint Joseph also arrived.

It was about half past nine when I went to Miss Anne's room to bid farewell. We knew that the hour was near in which the Lord would hear my prayer, "If You come, I will come!" Only a few hours and the long awaited moment would be here. The day of happiness and joy was already dawning.

Suddenly I was seized with a mortal fear, a terror that defied comparison, a horrible dread of the step I was about to take. At that moment death would have been a relief from the torment that held me. I stood there, wrestling and battling against a horrible anguish of soul, a wild revulsion against this sacrifice! Forgetting about Anne's presence I cried out, "O God, have you forgotten that I am only human?" After a few moments I pulled myself together. With a last embrace and a last handshake, I hurried down the stairs, climbed into the wagon, and drove out into the dark night. Alone, all alone, I faced the future, which lay dark before me like the black night that surrounded me.

A half hour later the wagon stopped before the house. My belongings were carried in, and the wagon rolled away. I was in my new Home.

My soul was quiet again; the battle had been fought and won. Yes, the anguish soon turned into joyous longing while I got the Chapel ready and prepared for Mass. It was five o'clock when I retired. After sleeping for an hour I was at work again. The children and the Home had to be given a festive appearance, for it would soon be eight o'clock. The guests arrived before that time, and Monsignor came on the strike of the clock. The little shrine was blessed, Holy Mass began, and the ladies sang. The Sanctus bell rang out, and in only a few minutes the great God would take up His dwelling in this house.

Let me be silent. There are moments and hours in one's life when one is carried away and overpowered by feelings which no words can describe!

Joy filled the hearts of all the guests, especially the young ladies who had become members of the recently founded Sacred Heart Society. The purpose of this Society was to help and support the Children's Home. Each of them had a collection book with the recommendation of Monsignor Jahnel.

At last all were gone, and I was alone No, not alone, and as I believed, I would never again be alone. I was with Him whom I had longed for so ardently, and over whose absence I had shed so many tears since leaving the convent in Cologne twenty-five months ago. He was here now, the great King, hidden in the Most Blessed Sacrament. Oh, I felt unutterable bliss; He was mine, and I was His!

This was the happiest day of my life. After this day and after those hours before the Tabernacle during that quiet night, even the making of my profession was not such a feast for me. No, that was, as far as I was concerned personally, merely an act of obedience. But on December 8, 1891, I had become His. I was His own, wholly, and eternally.

My entire soul was burning with love, and I had but one desire: to prove this love for God by my work and my suffering. Yes, to give God joy was my one desire since I had been twenty-two years old, and now I wanted to make this desire a reality.

Around that time before the Chapel was dedicated and when I was staying with Mrs. von Savigny (I think it was in November), Fritz von Savigny, her nephew, happened to visit her on his way to Saxony. He had been transferred from Catholic Silesia to the Protestant City of Merseburg and was quite upset about it. He spoke to me about his disappointment, and I naturally told him about my troubles and worries. I told him about the founding of a Children's Home, about the preparation of the Chapel, and especially about the need of a new building, and so forth.

He was very devout and very interested in the progress of the Church in Berlin because he had personally come to know its sad condition, having lived there for a long time. After this brief visit he went to Merseburg, and after a few weeks we received the shocking news that he had suffered a sudden hemorrhage and was so ill that his life was threatened. His mother, Mrs. von Savigny, nee Countess Arnim, hastened to see him, and as soon as he could be moved she took him to Falkenstein in the Taunus. Here, across from the little church we had visited so often while staying in Koenigstein, he lay on his sickbed, in a sanatorium for tubercular patients. His illness progressed rapidly. Surrounded by his mother, brothers, and sisters, he expressed the wish that 15,000 marks from his estate be given for the future Children's Home. The family promised this, and shortly afterward he passed into eternity to receive the reward for the confidence he had placed in the work of God. At the time this work appeared very insignificant and hidden, like a seed in its hull.

The family kept the money for some years, but I was given the interest. When I began to build, at the wish of Monsignor Jahnel, I was given the 15,000 marks, and it was enough to pay for the bricks. This was in 1894.

Was this not a miraculous gift from our dear Lady? I have always considered it the fruit of my reciting the rosary on the way from Koenigstein to the shrine in Falkenstein.

CHAPTER FOUR

RAGING WATERS OF AFFLICTION

It was in May of 1892 that I had a dream which I always considered a special grace. I found myself standing in the middle of a large, broad, high cliff, but I was situated more near the top. Suddenly an immense torrent of water poured over this high wall, not evenly and smoothly like Niagara Falls, but roaring down into the depths in wild, surging waves.

In the first moments it seemed as if I would be washed along with the current of waters raging about me. But no, I turned my head a little to the left and turned my eyes upward and there, in the clouds, I beheld a crucifix. In the same moment I stretched out my arms, and all the powers of my soul merged with the suffering Divine Savior. At the same time a flood of strength and confidence in God, yes, of joy in suffering, flowed into my soul.

Soon I heard another tremendous roar, and to my right a torrent of water came raging, two-thirds as high as the one surrounding me, tumbling down wildly and joining the other roaring fall of water, throwing up immense waves, and rolling onward until it finally formed a large sea. It was a horrendous, wildly raging, terrifying torrent of water. It was so incredible and so overwhelming that it made even the Niagara Falls (which I saw in 1913 or 1914) seem quite mild by comparison. I have never forgotten this vision, for it was too horrible. It exceeded everything imaginable, and I will always remember the indescribable terror and deathly anguish which had seized me in this first moment of this dream.

When I awoke I was filled with a great desire for suffering. Yes, a burning thirst for suffering arose in me. I wanted nothing, absolutely nothing, except to suffer in order to prove my love for Him. I was not content with that desire and longing for suffering, so I immediately began a novena to obtain "suffering" from God!

The little house in Pappelallee was damp, and as a result, the children became ill. To my great grief many of the little ones died. Due to the children's illness, the doctor advised me to take them to the suburbs for the summer. I presented the matter to Monsignor Jahnel, and he kindly permitted me to look for a suitable location and a house. Near the woods in Oranienburg, I found a most appropriate building. Again I asked Monsignor's advice, and he completely agreed that I should rent the house. He did not show the least dissatisfaction.

On June 2, 1892, I led the children with the nurses and the maids to their new home in Oranienburg. This was a healthy place near Berlin. I then tried to fix up the house, as far as my poverty would permit, for the dear little family. To my great joy the children perked up wonderfully and recuperated quickly by their stay near the pine woods.

Full of gratitude to God who helped me in my need, I returned to the Pappelallee on July 2 where one of my own sisters had taken my place. After a short greeting, she handed me a letter from Monsignor Jahnel.

According to my custom, I first went to the Chapel to greet my dear Savior in the Blessed Sacrament. I knelt down on my kneeling bench, which stood under the thirteenth station. After a short prayer, I took the letter and opened it. This was the first time I read a letter kneeling before the Blessed Sacrament. I read:

Berlin, July 1, 1892

Esteemed Miss:

Heretofore I have observed your effort and your work with favorable interest. Although some things did not please me, I did not want to disturb you in your plans. On the contrary, I have promoted your work wherever I could. But gradually I have become convinced that your foundation will not survive. I abstain from further explanations because they would serve no purpose. But as for you, I cannot and may not leave any doubts about my position. I withdraw my approval, and I ask, therefore, that the collection books, which I think have not created much revenue, be taken back and submitted to me when convenient. I regret that this institution, in which I had placed such great hopes, does not show itself able to survive.

With respectful greetings,
Jahnel

My novena was heard! My nature did indeed rebel, but my soul drank the chalice of suffering with fervent gratitude and joy. Like standing on the rock with the waters raging and roaring about me, I now felt myself united with my suffering Savior on the cross!

A few days later I went to confession at Saint Mathias Church. Just as I was leaving several ladies rushed up to me and said excitedly, "Miss Tauscher, have you heard that Monsignor Jahnel announced in the Catholic Societies that he has withdrawn his approval from you, and no one may give you further assistance?" I remained calm and even consoled my worried friends. Despite everything they remained faithful to St. Joseph's Home, which had now been placed under condemnation.

One blow followed another. A notice was published in the Catholic papers that no one was to give aid to the institution in Pappelallee and so on.

The eldest child of Herman and Pauline Tauscher was born on June 19, 1855 in Sandow, Germany (now Poland). Little Anna Maria was to become the future Mother Mary Teresa of St. Joseph.

Pastor Tauscher, a descendant from a long line of ministers, was a staunch Lutheran Superintendent and a pious man. But, in Mother Mary Teresa's own words, he was "more of an artist than a Pastor."

The parsonage and church in Sandow

Anna Maria in her younger years… and in her early 30's

Would that all
were children of this most
loving and lovable Mother,
and esteem and love her as such!
I regard everyone, no matter
of what class, or race, or nation,
who does not have the
Mother of God as his Mother,
as being a motherless orphan.

Mother Mary Teresa of St. Joseph

One of the two "little Nazareth cottages" in East Chicago, Indiana, in which Mother Mary Teresa began a new foundation for children in 1913. Today, St. Joseph's Carmelite Home for Girls operates as a Residential Treatment Center.

After 50 years, members of the first novitiate – established in America in East Chicago – gather in Wauwatosa in 1966 to celebrate their Golden Jubilee. Pictured with them are Mother M. Fridolina, Archbishop William E. Cousins and Mother M. Pia.

Carmelite Sisters D. C. J.
Silver Jubilee
Of the first American Sisters

April 23, 1941   Wauwatosa, Wisconsin

The year 1962 was a memorable one indeed for the first American Provincial Motherhouse. On July 2nd – the day this picture of retreatants and visiting Sisters was taken with Archbishop William E. Cousins – five postulants were invested, increasing the number of novices to a grand total of ten. Later on, in the fall of the year, a celebration was held marking the 50th Anniversary of the establishment of Carmel D.C.J. in America, when Mother Foundress was given permission by Archbishop S. G. Messmer to open a Home for Children in Milwaukee.

In 1991, the year that marked the Centennial of Carmel D.C.J., Sisters from many countries, who were attending the General Conference being held at the Motherhouse in Sittard, visited the birthplace of the Congregation – the first St. Joseph's Home at 61 Pappelallee in Berlin. The first little chapel, 100 years later, is pictured above.

Mother Mary Teresa remained the Mother General of the Congregation until her edifying death on September 20, 1938 in Sittard, Netherlands. Since then many have found help in their needs through her intercession. The cause for her beatification is presently being processed in Rome.

I received a formal notice from the delegature, that is, from Monsignor Jahnel, "to leave the little Home by October 1, 1892." That was not all. "By no means go to the pastor, Fr. Alesch. He is so angry with you, that he will throw you down the steps." This was the answer to my inquiry whether or not it was advisable to ask Fr. Alesch for the reason for Monsignor's displeasure.

It was hard to believe, but the Catholics in Berlin were made my enemies, and neither they nor I learned the reasons for Monsignor's changed attitude.

That Fr. Alesch was angry with me really caused me great concern. He was the pastor of the nearest church. This Sacred Heart Church was twenty-five minutes away from the Home. Whenever we had no priest, we took the school children there for Mass because the other Chapels and churches were forty or sixty minutes away. Now I was troubled by the thought that, since the pastor was supposed to be angry with me, he might refuse to give me Holy Communion if I went to Mass in his Church.

The second torrent of tribulation was not long in coming. This was the hardest to bear.

It was the month of August. As resident chaplain, we had a young priest who was studying at the University. It was nearing vacation time when he said to me, "Monsignor has ordered me to consume the Blessed Sacrament this morning!"

A pain pierced my heart like the stab of a dagger. Oh, God alone knows what I suffered at that moment! I drew my strength from the Divine Heart so that I would be able to assist at this last Mass. But when the bell rang for the *Agnus Dei*, tears gushed from my eyes. My God, my God! Deep as the sea was my grief!

Holy Mass was finished, and the empty ciborium stood

on the altar! My Savior, whom my soul loved with a burning love, had been taken from me. How great, how strong, how burning this love was He alone knew. Now He was gone! Gone was the Beloved of my soul! He left me! Oh, my Savior, why have you left me? What have I done to you? In what have I grieved you?

The work called. God gave me the grace to compose myself and attend to my duties. There was plenty of work to sustain me that day, but this day too came to an end. Everyone went to bed. One light after the other went out. I locked all the doors of the little house in which I alone, as guardian of the Blessed Sacrament, lived. I went to the Chapel. I knelt down on the altar step and sank lower and lower until my head rested on the altar step. I then broke out into a flood of tears.

Where was a sorrow like to mine? O my Savior, my Beloved, did You come here, to this poor Bethlehem merely to make me come, too? Now You have left me. What have I done to You? I wanted to give You joy, not sorrow! Oh, forgive my faults; open my blind eyes that I may see them.

Who will bring Him back to me, the Beloved of my soul? For the possession of Him I have renounced all and left all. Had it not cost me the agony of death to come to this Bethlehem? Now I am completely alone on the ocean of sorrow, abandoned by Him who was my strength and my power and on Whose help my complete confidence rested!

The morning dawned. With a little rest I went back to work, which had been interrupted only by the night. When night came, all was quiet. Again I lay, weeping and lamenting before the altar and the empty Tabernacle. Again and again I went to see Monsignor Jahnel, until he finally received me. Then he said to me, "No one knows whether the Home was Catholic or Protestant." He concluded, "You yourself are more Protestant than Catholic, and you have no talent for organization!"

Nothing could have hurt me more; nothing wounded my heart more than the first charge. I accepted this in silence, then bade him farewell and returned home.

From childhood on I relied completely on God and had surrendered myself completely to Him. Had He not guided me miraculously for thirty-seven years until now? I always firmly believed, and still believe to this day, that God saved me from the errors of Protestantism. For six years I had lived among Catholics and never had something such as this been brought to my attention. The reason was perhaps that I had asked my sister Magdalena to come and help me since I could no longer manage the work alone.

I was alone and overburdened with work. I had only kindergarten supervisors and girls to assist me. I had no one to take my place or to assist me in training the children. I had over seventy children at that time. My sister had been educated in a boarding school and had passed her exams for higher studies. Thus she could be of great help to me. In fact she was, for as soon as she came to the home in the beginning of 1892, she took over the supervision and the direction of the help. With the best of intentions, I could not find time for this. She also gave her warmest interest to the children with self-sacrificing devotedness. She was indeed a Protestant, but nobody noticed this, for she taught the children to venerate our Blessed Virgin and St. Father Joseph. She also practiced hymns for Mass and Benediction with the children.

God alone knows how many calumnies were spread to

cause Monsignor to withdraw his approval and which reached all the parishes in Berlin!

Deep down in my heart I thought, "God has heard my novena for suffering." He permitted all this to happen to me, and so I bore it without complaint.

Whenever my grief over losing the Blessed Sacrament threatened to cast me down, I hastened to the Heart of Jesus and drew new strength and courage from this inexhaustible fountain of grace.

To my inner torment was added not only the exhausting labor but also dire poverty, the most bitter need. The children had to be fed. At that time we had seventy-two children. Only about thirty paid anything which was, at the most, five marks a month. I had taken in all the others without payment. A large number of these had been offered for "adoption" in the advertisements of the local paper. I had written for them and thus saved the poor little children for the Divine Heart. To these we added the support of the nurses and aids. They not only expected to be fed, as were the children, but also wanted to be paid.

My beloved St. Father Joseph proved himself a wonderful helper in this time of distressing need!

I have given instances of his help in the letters from St. Joseph's Home. Besides the pecuniary help, which we received through his intercession, I would like to regard it a miracle that, despite the meager food, everybody was healthy, and not only contented, but cheerful and happy.

The Catholics were forbidden to help us. Some of them, who were well disposed toward us, did not heed this prohibition. In this way we received alms now and then, and especially later on when the delegates of the Center Party came to Berlin.

The good Canon Wenzel of Bamberg was a delegate to

the Reichstag and a member of the Party. He was very indignant about Monsignor Jahnel's procedure, for he had been saying Mass two or three times a week for us. At times he paid us a visit in the afternoon with the other members of the Party. He knew the Home and me. He spoke to Monsignor, as did some of the others. They finally succeeded in changing Monsignor's attitude.

We could not leave the place on October 1 as ordered, for no place could be found for ninety people. The Monsignor, therefore, had the lease extended until April 1, 1893.

Times of joy fly, but sad times crawl. I prayed and worked. In memory of the miraculous intervention of our dear Lady in obtaining the Blessed Sacrament for us on December 8, 1892, I began another novena before her feast with all the children, even the smallest. In the middle of the novena, I went to Monsignor and to my great surprise, I was not only received at once but was welcomed in a friendly manner, just as I was a year ago. He said to me, "I had intended to visit you and see how things are going!" He added, "God permitted these things to try your faith!"

Filled with joy and gratitude I hurried to the little Confession Chapel in St. Hedwig's Church. Here the Blessed Sacrament is reserved on the Sorrowful Mother's altar. There I fell on my knees to thank our dear Lady for hearing my prayer, contrary to all expectations. I added the plea that she might bring the Blessed Sacrament back again into our Chapel.

Fr. Wenzel and my friends among the members of the Center Party shared my joy, as did also my other acquaintances.

The storm of slander quieted down. However, who

could wipe or retract the lies that had traveled from mouth to mouth and which were believed by thousands of Catholics? No retraction was made in any society or newspaper. I had lost my good name. Always, year after year, I ran up against mistrust, and I found that many worked against my work and me. Many spoke evil about me, even in the United States.

Personally I was sincerely thankful for this, as long as God's work did not suffer. The humility of St. Francis of Assisi and the love of St. John of the Cross for contempt had awakened in me a great longing to be humiliated and despised, because only thereby can one acquire true humility. I wanted to be a rag under the feet of all people. Therefore, I gladly bore all the injustices and humiliations.

On December 2, 1892, I went to the pastor, Fr. Kappenberg, who was my confessor since Fr. Faeh's transferal to Brazil and Fr. Frin's departure from Berlin and told him about the change of attitude of Monsignor Jahnel. After that I went to confession to him. At the end of the confession, he said to me, or rather commanded me, "From now on you will go to Fr. Alesch to confession!" Fr. Alesch was more angry with me than was the Monsignor and had remained irreconcilable until now. I have never found out the reason for his displeasure. I regarded it as a disposition of Providence. I was silent for a moment, so Fr. Kappenberg continued, "Don't you want to obey?"

"Yes, I will obey and go to confession to Fr. Alesch," was my reply.

Hardly had I returned to my place in the pew, when a veritable revolution broke out within me. God gave me the grace to stand fast against this fierce assault.

Whether the command is just or unjust, I thought, it is

all the same, and I will obey. The choice of a confessor is free to everyone in the world. That thought had caused the storm within me. I had indeed promised our dear Lady, after my first confession, never to choose my own confessor. I was not attached to Fr. Kappenberg, for I always felt that he did not understand me. But to have to confess to a priest who was so bitterly against me seemed impossible!

"I want to obey, and I will obey, no matter what the cost!" With this firm resolution I left the church of Saint Mathias and went home, a distance of about one and a quarter hours. It was my custom to spend this time in meditation and prayer, but on this day I was unable to do so. My soul seemed dead, truly dead. Not even an act of faith, confidence, or love, which always strengthened me before, could be awakened within me. Night had settled in my soul. Darkness had come, paralyzing all spiritual faculties. This condition did not last several days or weeks, but for eight long months.

From the moment of awakening in the morning until I fell asleep at night, all day long there were tormenting temptations against obedience. But God again gave me the grace not to listen to them, much less to consent to them.

Twice during those months of darkness, the Divine Savior had pity on me and strengthened me by special graces. Hardly any winter was more difficult for me to bear than the one of 1892-1893. Outside the weather was bitterly cold. On the inside there was no Blessed Sacrament in the Chapel, and the darkest night was in my soul. Dire poverty, the work, and all the responsibility consumed my soul.

Although several priests, such as Canon Wenzel or

other members of the Center Party, said Mass several times a week, we were still not given permission by Monsignor Jahnel to reserve the Blessed Sacrament. He stuck to his first directives that we had to have a house chaplain before this would be permitted. After many efforts, in March we found a chaplain in Fr. Feldmann (later a professor in Bonn) who came to us in the beginning of April. Our Divine Savior returned to St. Joseph's Home the day on which we had been ordered, according to our second notice, to vacate the building. God's ways are wonderful!

What joy and bliss had filled me when the Blessed Sacrament was reserved in the Chapel on December 8, 1891. Now I was unable to feel any joy. Everything seemed to have died within my soul; my feelings seemed to have left me. I was as a dead person, and yet I continued to work. I performed my duties as a living person, and yet I felt as though I were dead! Only one who has experienced this can know this torture and understand this condition.

Spring came and went; summer was near. But not a ray of sunshine lighted up my soul, until our dear Lady again took pity on me and brought me relief. In August it suddenly became light again within me. I awoke to a new life and was inexpressibly joyful and grateful. My happiness was too great to keep to myself. How I longed to tell someone about the new life granted me, about my joy and happiness, but there was no one to whom I could speak.

Fr. Alesch was my confessor and steadfast in his anger against me. I believe I went to confession to him "in obedience" until the late summer of 1893, when he left on vacation. What a sacrifice this was for me, God only knows. When I went to confession to him the first time in 1892, he spoke as soon as he saw me, "So now you want to gain my favor in this way, but you will never succeed!" I did not use the Sacrament for this purpose, and I never did win his favor. It was only in obedience that I made this sacrifice!

In my loneliness I took courage to write to an old, saintly priest whom I deeply revered, and in whom I had much confidence. I told him about the long period of anguish, the darkness I suffered, and my sudden restored happiness. I received a very kind letter in return but with the friendly admonition, "Keep such affairs of the soul" to myself and remain silent. I have followed this advice even toward my confessor, with the exception of Fr. Ruetgen and two or three others. To these I communicated more or less of my inner life. To other confessors, as far as I remember, I told only my sins.

I lived a lonely life. In those years I often felt terribly alone. Human nature demands that at times we unburden ourselves. It takes a bitter struggle and a strong effort to overcome this natural desire. But this struggle and this self-conquest are very profitable and bring great graces in the end.

As the world became less joyful, as life became more lonely, so the deeper and stronger became my union with God. God was my all, and I was given to rest in Him and enjoy heavenly bliss. And I was allowed to suffer and work for Him, my Heavenly Father.

It may seem peculiar that I speak of loneliness, living as I did with and among so many Sisters. Yet it was, in fact, a lonely life for me. In the beginning of the foundation, I was all alone. After some years the first young women came. Some were twenty years old, whereas I was almost forty. Had I been able to start with friends of my own age, it would have been entirely different. However, God disposed otherwise, and only He knows why.

WEISSENSEE

The children, who had been taken to Oranienburg in June 1892, were still there. The little Home in Pappelallee was overcrowded and so was the house next to it, which we had rented. It had become necessary to find a suitable place for the little family in one of the closer suburbs of Berlin. I asked Monsignor Jahnel for advice, and he recommended Weissensee.

On August 2,1893, I paid a visit to the pastor. At that time there was nothing but a forbidding wasteland between Pappelallee and Weissensee. I found the little Chapel, a miserable shed with a tin roof, and nearby the dwelling of the priest. He was a young man, but very sad and full of worry, sick in body, and hopelessly depressed about his charge in these wretched outskirts of Berlin. Although he did everything he could, he was not able to inject life into the parish. With tears in his eyes, he told me that hardly twenty people came to Mass on Sundays. One could hardly blame the people for not coming, for the Chapel was unbearably hot in the summer and icy cold in the winter. I heard his tale of woe with deep sympathy, and in my heart I was hoping that I would be able to help him.

My plan to establish a home for children in this place gave him great pleasure, and he immediately offered to help. After some thought he remembered a Catholic family in whose house the upper story was vacant. Perhaps we could live there until a suitable house was found. I went to talk to this family, and I rented the place. The transfer from Oranienburg to Weissensee took place in

September.

It was not long before a house was offered for sale on 8 Gurtel Street. It had been a small institute for the blind. Since I could not hope to find anything better in this section, I bought it.

In 1897, after I had received some postulants from Bavaria who had a vocation for parish mission work, we began this apostolate. In the meantime the place of the sick young priest, as well as of his successor, who had died suddenly from a stroke, was taken by the zealous and energetic Father Stephan. With him a new life flowed into the parish. The pastor availed himself of the help of my Sisters, who were really only postulants, for parish visits. He knew how to train them to be zealous missionaries. God blessed the zeal and self-sacrificing work of the priest and of the Sisters in a visible manner. In a few years there was a flourishing parish for which Father Stephan built a beautiful church. On Sundays and Holy days this church was always filled.

In my letters from St. Joseph's Home, there are more particulars about Weissensee and the mission work in the parish.

That these postulants were to become Carmelites one day was unknown even to the pastor. For the Carmel of the Divine Heart was then known only to heaven. In this world I had to proceed, little by little, with utmost caution. Only now and then, here and there, could I reveal a little of my secret. Otherwise the germinating "Carmel of the Divine Heart of Jesus" would have been destroyed with one blow.

Beginning in February 1892, young girls came to us from various parts of the country as volunteers. Some stayed for a few weeks, some a few months, until they saw for themselves that such a life of sacrifice was not their calling, or Fr. Alesch, who was our confessor, told them that if they stayed at the Home they would never become Sisters, and so forth. One would talk the other into going home. For as Father Alesch said, "This will never be a religious community."

I gladly let them go home. Unfortunately, some of the talk kept making the rounds and induced first one, and then the other, to heed the warning of the confessor and leave the Home. Hence, our Home was almost like a pigeon coop! What a sorrow that was for me, everyone will readily understand! I could do nothing against these hostile maneuvers but suffer in silence.

Due to the increasing number of children in the Pappelallee, where we had over one hundred of them, both boys and girls, and in the close quarters of the neighboring house, which we had rented, we were forced to found a second Home. Monsignor Jahnel gave his approval, and the pastor, Fr. Kappenberg, agreed to receive the Sisters into his parish. Vacant quarters were found in a large tenement house on Goltz Street, and we rented this place for the time being, since it was impossible to find a place with a garden. In March 1894, Mother M. Bernardine, the first candidate who had firmly resisted Fr. Alesch's efforts to give up her vocation and who always had shown unusual reliability, moved to the new quarters with some of the girls. The other girls went to Weissensee, the first branch Home. All the boys and all the children under five remained at Pappelallee.

I kept working day and night without rest, and I did not believe that one day my strength could be exhausted. In the first years I found little time during the day for prayer, and so I prayed for one hour every night in the Chapel.

Later the days were not long enough for all the work, so the nights had to furnish time for writing letters and keeping the books.

Many visitors came to inspect the Home. The daughter of the Belgian ambassador, Baron von Greindl, brought most of the Catholic ladies of other embassies to the Pappelallee. Fr. Faber, too, of St. Hedwig's Church, sent many women to help in the work.

Newspapers had made our "Home for Homeless Children" known throughout Germany. In this manner we gained many benefactors. If they happened to come to Berlin, they often visited the Home in order to observe our poverty in person. All were full of admiration at the large number of children, who were so happy and healthy, despite the dire poverty in which we lived.

Thanks be to God for sending us so many faithful benefactors through the intercession of St. Father Joseph. Most of the donations came outside of Berlin, and they had to be acknowledged in writing. There was no one to assist me in this work; therefore, I was forced to use the nights for this purpose.

As long as I could give myself six hours of sleep, all went well. However, when these hours dwindled to four, I suffered so much from lack of sleep that I became more miserable from month to month. With a great deal of worry, Monsignor Jahnel saw my health decline, and he advised me to hurry and find a place where I could rest and recuperate. As he told others, he was afraid that if I died, he would inherit the whole "wretched group in the Pappelallee."

My sister Magdalena was willing to come again and take my place for a few weeks, so that I could rest without having to worry. While I was thinking of a suitable place to go, I remembered that I had spent several days with Mrs. von Savigny in Mariaschein in northern Bohemia. This is where I went in September 1895. Countess S., a relative of Mrs. von Savigny, whom we had visited at that time, was still living there and received me very heartily. I saw her almost every day in her loneliness, and since she was a very devout woman and interested in all works of charity, she became very well disposed toward St. Joseph's Home.

The rest and the invigorating mountain air strengthened my nerves so that I soon recovered my strength. However, I not only took new strength back with me from Mariaschein to Berlin but also a new cross. This cross became so heavy that it finally threatened to crush me. But no, my beloved Heavenly Mother, our dear Lady of Mount Carmel, preserved me from this fate.

True to my resolve never to choose my own confessor, I asked Countess S. to direct me to a good confessor. She immediately recommended Father S. and praised him highly. I went to confession to him, and soon after, he told me to meet him in the parlor of the college. Here I saw him for the first time, and he made an unfavorable impression on me. It seemed to me that I could never have confidence in him. I told him all about Saint Joseph's Home, and he seemed very interested in it.

After returning to Berlin, I did all I could to complete the building of the Chapel, which had been begun in the spring. To my great joy, the Italians living in the neighborhood gladly came to our little Chapel. It was so crowded that the good people had to attend Mass standing in the corridor and on the stairs.

The Chapel was not ready by December 8, as I had hoped. On the day of the octave, December 15, 1895,

Monsignor Jahnel solemnly blessed it. A number of the church societies with their banners had appeared to enhance the solemnity of the occasion, and three representatives of the Center Party also honored the poor Home by their presence. Monsignor Jahnel spoke encouraging words about the name of the Home inscribed in the front:

ST. JOSEPH'S HOME
A Home for Homeless Children

When Monsignor had seen this name for the first time printed on a sign over the door in 1891, he was very displeased and was against calling it "St. Joseph's Home." First of all, he said everyone would think that it was named Joseph after him, and then the word "Home" was a Protestant term. It took many pleas before he gave permission to let the name stand. My last words had been, "Right Reverend Monsignor, what is written is written!" He then had nothing more to say, and the inscription remained over the door!

I caught a severe cold while getting the Chapel ready and supervising the construction, but I paid no attention to it until Sylvester eve when I could no longer continue my work. The doctor diagnosed pleurisy. The good Mrs. von Savigny had sent her own doctor for me. He had contracted this insidious disease himself, a disease that often brings its victims to an early grave. This doctor had not spared himself, and he knew the results of this disease from his own experience. In fact, he was torn from his family by death when he was only forty years old. He admonished me in the strongest terms to take care of myself. He stated that I ought to think of the children, and what would become of them. God be thanked for sending this kind gentleman to me, as well as our own house doctor, Dr. Bertram.

Following the advice of both doctors, I remained in my room for three months until I was entirely cured. Only God knows how painful this time was for me. I remained there ill and all alone without a secretary, assistant, or nurse. Except for the youngest, my natural sisters were not in Berlin at that time. This sister came once in a while to help me with my correspondence, which I took care of while lying in bed.

Mother M. Bernardine was on Goltz Street. It was my responsibility to look after the house, the children, money, and building, despite my illness.

Beginning with the spring of 1896, the good Lord sent candidates to me who had a vocation for the Carmel. Fr. Alesch remained an unbending enemy of our work, telling the candidates, "If you want to be a Sister, then go to some other Congregation and don't stay here at St. Joseph's Home. Miss Tauscher is deceiving you, for you will never become a Sister here." Nevertheless, more and more young women stayed with us and turned a deaf ear to Fr. Alesch.

In the fall of 1896, I went to Mariaschein again for a short rest. Countess S. this time begged me to establish a Home there also, as nobody cared for the poor, neglected children. In the little village of Graupen, near Mariaschein, she knew a real Nazareth house, which would serve as a beginning.

The plight of the poor children awakened in me my deepest compassion. I asked the pastor of Graupen for his permission to establish another home. He gladly gave this permission, as well as that of the Bishop of Leitmeritz. On this occasion I asked His Excellency about Father S. who had been in Berlin to visit us, and of whom I felt an increasing distrust. Nonetheless, the Bishop praised him very highly. I had to force myself to gain confidence in this Priest, who claimed that God had called him to be the director of the work, and accordingly he demanded "absolute obedience" from me.

His direction caused me deep sorrow, but God permitted this great trial. To Him I offer thanks for every occasion of suffering! Heaven has everything but suffering, and therefore, I cannot get enough of it here on earth.

Now back to Berlin! The children moved into the new building in November 1896. The quarters that the children had occupied were made ready for the Sisters. From then on we observed a life of religious observance according to the rule of Carmel and the constitutions of St. Teresa. Instead of fasting, we offered God our work on behalf of the children, and instead of the enclosure, we offered our parish mission work. A life of prayer and the striving for perfection always remained the main goal. It was, indeed, the fuel which kept the fire of our zeal and our love burning ever brighter.

Countless words of advice from well meaning priests tried to drive me away from Carmel and rigorous observance. I always answered them, "Either we are genuine religious according to the original ideals of the founder or none at all." I have no sympathy with half-hearted measures. Had not Divine Providence led me to the Carmel? Had not the Lord God filled my soul with a great love for, and a great confidence in, our holy Mother St. Teresa? I often said, "I will let myself be crucified for the Carmel!"

We were very zealous in our prayer and in observing and performing our duties. However, we still lacked the exercises of penance in the refectory. Due to my painful shyness, I always had to force myself when introducing something new. After table prayers had been said, I knelt down before each postulant and kissed the hem of her dress, just as I do today, saying to myself, "Lord, I am not worthy" with the deepest sense of unworthiness. For who am I but a child in the dessert. These are children born in the bosom of the Church! I have always felt my greatest unworthiness of being a child of the Church.

Let me now return to my practice of penance. I was kneeling down before the postulants, one after the other. Suddenly I felt the hand of God lay on my head in blessing, just as I had experienced before in the little Chapel in the Pappelallee when I prayed for enlightenment concerning the establishment of a Home on Goltz Street.

I understood clearly that our Heavenly Father was showing His good pleasure to me, or rather, to all of us for all the acts of penance we undertake and perform for the salvation and conversion of souls.

I reveal these favors of God only for the reason that my beloved Sisters may never grow weary, but perform these and other penances with great zeal and fidelity, having the above-mentioned intentions, unless hindered by illness.

God's eye penetrates the heart. He never judges according to mere appearance, but according to the spirit which moves the soul, especially according to the humility and the complete surrender to the Divine Will. This is true not only in great matters but also in little matters and the smallest daily occurrences, according to our self-renunciation.

We not only are to be Tabernacles, dwellings of the Most High, but tools or instruments, with which He, the

Divine Savior, the physician of our souls, may use for the
salvation of souls. What God is looking for in our souls is
a striving to reach the most profound humility and the
desire for humiliation. A soul will never be truly humble
without having suffered many humiliations, not just
endured, but borne thankfully and joyfully. This was so
with St. Peter and St. Paul! As the Scripture says, "After
being scourged shamefully, they departed rejoicing."

My last letter to Cardinal Kopp was answered only with
silence. In that letter I had informed him again that by no
means did I want to start something "new" but wished to
live with my Sisters according to the old Rule of Carmel
and the Constitutions adapted to the times. I regarded the
Cardinal's reaction as silent approval. We, therefore, continued to live our secluded cloister life, fully trusting in
the help of our dear Lady of Carmel and our St. Mother
Teresa of Jesus.

In January 1897, I opened a small hospice with a Chapel
on Anhalt Street in West Berlin. This was done at the
urgent request of several priests and devout laymen,
including members of the Center Party in the Reichstag.
Cardinal Kopp gave his approval for this project. Here the
priests could offer Mass without having to walk half an
hour to the nearest church. At times we had ten to twelve
Masses each day, and on Sundays and Holy days the
Chapel was crowded with Catholics from the neighborhood. Without my asking for help, Cardinal Kopp even
sent a donation of 1000 marks for this foundation through
Monsignor Jahnel.

In the past year, several priests, good friends of ours,
had advised me to take steps to obtain ecclesiastical
approbation. This was my duty, they said, for the sake of
the postulants who had joined me with so much confi-

dence. How was I to go about it? I was unsure. I waited for God's guidance. I was corresponding with some Carmelite Fathers and they directed me to the Father General in Rome, for he alone could lead me to the goal.

Father S. came to Berlin in 1896 and was admired by everyone. The priests, who came to know him, became his friends. He cast a spell over most of the people who met him and whom he intended to use for his purposes.

He gave conferences to my companions. He had young women, who were willing to join his proposed Congregation, come to Berlin. Finally he said quite openly in my absence, that he intended to use my foundation, our Carmel, as a start for " his foundation", since God's blessing manifestly rested upon it.

He forgot that God's blessing rests upon a work only as long as it is conducted according to His will. That his plans were not such, the future was soon to reveal.

In the beginning of 1897, Father S. came again to St. Joseph's Home. On the day before the feast of the Holy Name of Jesus, he gave me the formula for Profession. He ordered that all the postulants who had been with me for a year and who were then at the Home, were to pronounce their vows the next morning at Mass. This was to be done after Holy Communion, while he held up the Host.

Besides taking the three vows, the formula contained a special clause, "According to the intention of our Reverend Father for one year." No one was told what that intention was!

Before this I always had to struggle with my reason and my conscience, as long as I was under the direction of Father S. Now this struggle broke into a violent storm, which God alone witnessed. He alone knows what I suf-

fered during those months and years, especially during
the following night, and during that Mass after I had
received Father's command.

Hardly had we finished the formula, when I realized
that I could control myself no longer. I could not remain
until the end of Mass, despite my greatest efforts. I left
the Chapel before the final prayers.

A storm was raging within me. How could I vow something one was not allowed to know or make vows without
any preparation? How could young girls, none of whom
had a religious vocation, as later events proved, make
vows? Why was this? Because Father S. had had a sudden "vision!" Just as I had little confidence in him when
we first met, so little was the confidence I now had in his
"visions."

I wanted to become humble as was St. Father Francis of
Assisi, or to be stepped on like a mat, or be torn to pieces
like a rag, according to the vision of Blessed Henry Suso.
Yes, I wanted to let myself be treated like a rag and a mat.
I was even longing to be treated thus, no matter by whom,
whether superior or subject. I longed for this so that my
ego might be destroyed. I wanted to be nothing, absolutely nothing! I would become a pure vessel, free from all
self-will, self conceit, and self love, so that God could fill
it with His grace.

In indescribable excitement, I left the Chapel before the
end of Mass. I hastened to my cell for I was determined
to break this stubbornness of my nature. I wanted to
learn to obey blindly; I wanted to be a "nothing." I seized
the discipline. The storm raged within me. My conscience writhed in pain, while my heart groaned, and my
reason rose up in high rebellion. In this terrible emotion-
al conflict I threw the discipline from me against the wall,

and when it hit the floor, the noise it made brought me to my senses. I calmed down in a short time, and I was able to continue struggling and wrestling against myself. I suffered in silence until help came.

In March of 1897, I brought dear Mother M. Bernardine to the little house of Nazareth in Graupen. I had rented this house the preceding fall. Here, with the help of several postulants, Mother Bernardine prepared a Home for the poorest abandoned children.

In August of that year, while I was in Berlin, Father S. and Monsignor K. requested that a second Home for children be opened in Marschen. This Home was located about one half hour from Mariaschein. I had to send several postulants, whom Father S. had selected from Berlin, and with them a superior, who also had been chosen by him. The house belonged to the mother of Monsignor K. It was an old mill, over thirty minutes from the nearest church. The building as well as the location was absolutely unsuited, and yet it had to be established "in obedience."

In the meantime fall had arrived, and I went to Vechta with a postulant to open a Home for boys. It was here that I found a kind, benevolent, and prudent counselor in Fr. Grobmeier, the diocesan Officialis.

I told him that I had been urged by a number of priests to take steps to obtain Rome's approbation. I also said that I had written to Cardinal Kopp for a recommendation and that the Cardinal had replied that he would never give his approval to the founding of a new religious Congregation. Nevertheless, Fr. Grobmeier advised me to send a petition to his Eminence, asking for his approval.

I followed Father's advice and wrote to Cardinal Kopp. This is the answer I received:

Breslau, October 29, 1897

In answer to your letter of the 26th of this month I can only repeat my conviction, well known to you, that there is no need to found a new religious Congregation. In order to continue the charitable work performed by you with such a spirit of sacrifice, as is fully recognized, the way is open to join any existing religious Community.

Prince Bishop
G. Cardinal Kopp

To Miss Tauscher
Vechta, St. Joseph's Home,
Oldenburg

G.K. 7031

After Fr. Grobmeier had read the answer of his Eminence, he said, with his incomparable composure and determination, "Nevertheless you will go to Rome."

Filled with the greatest confidence in this worthy priest, I resolved to follow his advice and immediately go to Rome.

First, I had to see how things were going in Graupen and Marschen and get permission from Father S., before I made the journey. Immediately I left Berlin and went straight to Bohemia. Unfortunately, I found my Sisters in disharmony. A strange spirit was dwelling there, and some incorporated it deliberately, especially among the Sisters in Marschen. These Sisters were enthusiastically attached to Father S., but the Sisters in Graupen felt as I did. No one could feel confidence in him except the superior. She was the sister of a priest, who really thought highly of Father S.

What I heard, and what I saw, filled me with growing doubts, anxiety, and worry. I still wanted to force myself to think that everything Father S. demanded, said, and did, was right. Yet my reason and conscience rebelled and rose up like wild waves. Words cannot describe my agony. Only one who has suffered as this can understand the trauma I went through.

When my anguish reached its greatest height, the devil used the moment to cast me into despair. During the night while I was fully awake, he led me in spirit along the broad pathway through the woods to the top of a mountain. There I saw an opening, which existed from the time when copper mines were in operation. A horrible light appeared. The devil told me to throw myself into this opening, so that "then you will have peace and quiet." At that moment I raised my eyes again, and I beheld a crucifix. My soul became united, most intimately with the Divine Savior, and the horrible vision was gone.

On my first visit to the Sisters in the two houses in Bohemia, I found that Father S. had taken over completely. Tormented by my doubts, I went to the pastor and asked about Father S. I inquired if he were qualified to be giving direction to the Sisters. I was told that I could not find a better priest.

Sometime later I wrote to another priest, a dean, who was supposed to know Father Sch. well, and put the same question to him. He wrote that Father S. was an excellent man, "worth 100 priests." Despite all this, my doubts about this Priest grew so strong that I could not get rid of them.

God had again heard my prayer for suffering. I longed for nothing more than to suffer and carry out God's will perfectly.

The morning after the horrible vision I hastened to the church at Mariaschein to ask our dear Lady for help. I begged her to lead me out of this labyrinth of fears and doubts. I pleaded and pleaded, and my Heavenly Mother heard my plea. She obtained new life, power, and courage for me. At her feet I resolved to go to Father S. and to speak to him. I did not speak as before, bound by obedience, for I no longer felt these chains, since God had not imposed them. I no longer felt bound. No, within a moment I had become free. The dear Mother of God had obtained a new spirit for me. In the strength of this spirit, I went to Father S. and said, "I cannot go on like this. I have struggled and suffered, but I cannot go on! I am going to Rome, for I must have certainty!" I added, "May God reward you, Reverend Father, for all you have done for us!"

Then and there the spirit, which I always suspected was in the poor Priest, flashed from his eyes, and with an indescribable look of anger, he said something like, "I will destroy...."

I left Graupen and returned to Berlin. There I looked up my former confessor, Father K., and told him about my doubts regarding the direction of Father S. He was very indignant. I never thought that this calm priest could get so excited. He immediately wrote a letter to a priest friend in Rome and ordered me to go to Rome without delay and deliver this letter personally.

CHAPTER FIVE

THE FIRST JOURNEY TO ROME

We started our journey on November 24, the feast of St. John of the Cross. Sr. Maria Theresia accompanied me. She was from Tyrol and spoke Italian. Divine Providence had sent her to me in the spring of 1897.

Suddenly around midnight, the shout rang out, "Roma, Roma!" My youthful companion awoke from a deep sleep. We hurried to catch a carriage, and since at that late hour of the night no convent door would open for us, we rode to the Hotel Minerva.

This was our first awakening in the Eternal City! The heart beats fast as you hurry along to get to St. Peters. As you enter St. Peter's square and see the giant building, you are seized with amazement. With reverence and in admiration, we slowly ascended the wide steps that lead to the portals. We entered. Overwhelmed by the most profound sentiments of love and gratitude, I was tempted to fall on my knees at the very entrance.

"How did I come here?" This thought made my heart tremble. O God, Your mercy knows no bounds! You, my Redeemer, had pity on the child who, like the lamb in the picture of the Good Shepherd, was caught in the thorn bush. With merciful and bleeding hands You rescued it from the briars of error and carried it home to the flock of Holy Mother Church! Now I, at this moment a poor child of the desert, am in the Eternal City, the Jerusalem of the New Covenant!

We walked up and knelt down at the "Confessio." "I thank you, St. Peter, for you have conducted me as an instrument of God to this place!" How often I had consulted my father about these passages of the letters of St. Peter, for whom I had a special devotion. He told me to "Go away with your Peter!" Thanks be to God that I always held fast to the hand of St. Peter, for his holy hand has guided me to the Holy Church, and now even to the "Confessio", which is the sacred resting place of the "Rock" upon which the Divine Savior has built His Church!

In the afternoon I took the letter of Father K. to a friend of his, Father von Oldenburg. I had to submit my doubts to him concerning the direction of Father S. In the meantime Father M. had joined us. Both were of the same opinion as Father K. They advised me most strongly not to keep any postulants that had come from Father S. but to dismiss them immediately.

In the opinion of both Fathers, my conscience and good judgment had guided me correctly. God had again permitted this trial for the purification of my soul, and the dear Mother of God had protected and watched over me. When danger threatened, her strong hand preserved me from ruin. May she be praised forever!

Fr. M. Meschler, S.J., advised me to approach Monsignor Jacquemin at St. Michael regarding the affairs of our Order. He would be the best advisor for me, since he had displayed great skill in saving a Congregation from ruin and had brought it to a most flourishing condition.

We followed the advice and went to Monsignor Jacquemin. Monsignor was a very pious Priest and asked us to first make a novena in the church of Maria della Scalla, where the foot of St. Mother Teresa is venerated.

Every morning we walked from the Via Olmata, where the Gray Sisters had given us a room, to Maria della Scalla by way of Via Longata, a distance of forty-five minutes. It was in December, and the weather was cold, dreary, and rainy. Whoever has been in Rome in the winter is acquainted with those sudden torrential downpours. At that time they lasted three days. However, this could not prevent us from our daily pilgrimage. Day after day, though soaking wet, we went early in the morning to Maria della Scalla to beg for the help of our dear Lady of Mount Carmel and our Mother St. Teresa of Jesus.

In the first days we visited the Generalate of the Carmelite Fathers. We were told that the Father General was absent and not expected to return until Christmas. When I explained to the Father the purpose of our journey to Rome, namely, to obtain ecclesiastical approbation of our religious family, he replied, "In this matter we can be of little assistance."

What was to be done now? If the Carmel cannot help me, who can? The Sister Superior of the Gray Sisters sent us to Monsignor de Waal as the man best able to advise and help us. I followed her advice, looked up Monsignor de Waal, and acquainted him briefly with our affair. Thereupon I handed him the following letter written by Cardinal Kopp.

Johannesberg,
September 29, 1897

Your Reverence will kindly disclose to Miss Tauscher that I am indeed able and willing to express my warmest appreciation for her self-sacrificing activity in behalf of poor and forsaken children. However, to her efforts of establishing a religious Community, I will neither give my approval nor my support. I again repeat my suggestion that she affiliate her charitable institution with one of the existing religious Communities.

The Prince Bishop

Addressed to:
Rev. Pastor Neuber
Spiritual Council, Berlin

After Monsignor de Waal had read the letter he exclaimed, "How in the world can you be so foolish as to show this letter to anybody here in Rome where you need the very best recommendations to achieve anything from the Cardinals? Let me tell you, do not let anyone see that paper."

After considering my "foolishness," he calmly deliberated how he could be of assistance to us. Then he said, "Tomorrow you go to Monsignor N.N. I will meet you there and see what can be done."

At the appointed time we met the two priests. After Monsignor de Waal had acquainted him with our affairs, Monsignor N.N. asked for the Rule we intended to follow. I handed him the original Rule of Carmel, approved by Pope Innocent in the year 1248 and the Constitutions of St. Mother Teresa of 1581.

He opened the book and when he read 1248 and 1581 he pointed to his forehead and nodded to Monsignor de Waal, as if to say, "She is not very bright." Then he said, "The best thing for you to do is go to Fr. Esser, O.P. He will write the Constitutions for you." Monsignor de Waal agreed with this advice and gave us the address of Fr. Esser.

We went to Fr. Esser and were immediately received by him. I had barely begun to explain my plans when he asked why I did not affiliate myself with the Dominicans, since that was an old Order and the Sisters had experience (which I lacked) in the education of children. Then he continued, "It is pride and vanity that prompts you to found a new Congregation." In this manner he spoke to me for twenty minutes about my project. He used very cutting and humiliating words and all in the presence of the young postulant!

I remained very calm, being convinced that God Himself was the founder of this work and that His Divine Majesty Himself had chosen me to be His instrument. I regretted that the Father opposed it in such a manner. He obviously was convinced that he was correct in leading me down a different road.

Naturally I did not ask him to write our Constitutions, but in a more fervent prayer I turned to God for help. With many tears and profound sorrow I deplored all my sins, every wrong thought, every word, all I had ever said (be it too much or too little), and every act of impatience as well. God demands purity of His instruments, and therefore, I took the blame for these past failures upon myself.

Placing my confidence in our dear Lady of Mount Carmel and my dear St. Mother Teresa, we began a second novena at Maria della Scala. In the course of the week, despite the cool reception we had received the first time, I was encouraged interiorly to visit the Generalate of the Carmelite Fathers once more. This time Fr. Benedict, a Definitor, welcomed us with the words, "I am very glad that you came again. I spoke to the procurator, Father G.R., and he is very anxious to meet you and discuss with you the means of assisting you."

While we were thus conversing, Fr. Raynoldus (the future Archbishop of Reggio) appeared accompanied by Fr. Placidus, a Netherlander who spoke German. My companion (speaking Italian) now explained to the General Procurator our activity in Berlin and the many difficulties we had experienced. He became so interested in our work that he had endeavored to gain the good will of Cardinal Gotti and the Protector of the Carmel, Cardinal Parocchi. A few days later Father Procurator told us to go to Cardinal Gotti and also to the Father Provincial of the Carmelites, Father Antonio, who later on became the Archbishop in Sicily.

A decision, however, could not be made until after the return of the Father General. At last Christmas came, and after we had attended the solemnities in Maria Maggiore, we hastened to the Carmel where we expected to meet the General, Father Bernardin of St. Teresa. He received us very cordially, gave us good advice, and asked us to return the next day when he would bless my scapular and receive me into the Carmelite Order.

This blessing took place in the presence of Father Benedict. Father Raynoldus, Procurator-General, and Father Placido, the Secretary-General, were also present.

Father General advised me that in case Cardinal Kopp would refuse to give his approbation, we should leave Berlin and look for another bishop to receive us into his diocese. Cardinal Gotti, Cardinal Parocchi, and the Fathers were of the same opinion.

I showed the letter of Cardinal Kopp to the Carmelite Fathers. It had been translated for the Italian speaking Fathers.

I would leave Berlin and Germany a thousand times rather than give up my beloved Carmel. When priests advised me to give up Carmel, I had declared more than once that I would rather suffer crucifixion.

We were very happy because of the decisions of our august and excellent counselors and resolved to return without delay. This, however, could not be done, for after we attended Holy Mass the next day and I had given the matter long and serious reflection, it occurred to me that without a writing from some Cardinal, no bishop would grant permission to found a Motherhouse and novitiate.

Instead of going to the train station, we again went to the Generalate once more. Soon Father Benedict and Father Raynoldus appeared, and I asked them to take me to Cardinal Parocchi, as I wished to ask him for a recommendation that I could submit to the Bishops. Without something in writing from Rome, it would be impossible for me to receive permission for a Motherhouse and novitiate. Both Priests shared my opinion and promised to arrange an audience for me.

On the same evening Father Definitor and Father Procurator took us to Cardinal Parocchi. He received us very kindly, and after Father Raynoldus had submitted my request, His Eminence told us to call again on the following evening. Cardinal Parocchi had daily audiences after the "Angelus," at the setting of the sun.

With the setting of the sun on the evening of December 28, and as the sound of the "Ave" bell had died away, Father Procurator was admitted at once. We awaited his return in the waiting room. We not only waited, we prayed. I do not think I ever prayed more fervently in my life than during that hour. I implored my dear St. Mother Teresa of Jesus for her intercession and help. It seemed to me that the future of the work depended on this document, as indeed it did.

After about an hour the door opened at last and Father Raynoldus appeared. His face was beaming with joy. We could read it on his face that he was very happy. He told us that His Eminence had given us a magnificent letter, but as it was written in Latin, he would translate it, and the next day we should call for it at the Generalate. Overwhelmed with gratitude and joy, we returned to the Via Olmata.

On December 29 we received from Father Procurator the Italian version, and from Father Benedict the German translation of the following recommendation:

> Office of the Vicar, Rome
> Feast of the Holy Innocents,
> In the year of our Lord, 1897

Most willingly we accede to the request of the petitioner, for we entertain the hope, and this not without reason, that the work started by her six years ago, with the help of God, will develop to the benefit of both Church and State. And this all the more so for the reason that the foundress and her daughters are determined to follow the Rule of St. Teresa. It is her intention to follow St. Teresa who was always concerned with the spreading of our holy faith and the welfare of souls. She intends to look up to her as a lawgiver and to follow her at a time when the cross of Christ is often devitalized under the pretense of love.

Therefore, in order to do justice to my office as Protector of the Discalced Carmelites, I do not hesitate to bestow due praise upon the work which expresses the spirit and ideal of St. Teresa, to recommend it to those whose duty it is to promote the glory of the Church and the eternal welfare of souls.

> Lucius Maria, Cardinal-Vicar Parocchi,
> *Protector of the Discalced Carmelites*

Regarding our name, I wish to make the following observation. In April 1891 when at Bonn, I had called the future institution, "Servants of the Divine Heart of Jesus." After I had opened the first St. Joseph's Home, and young girls came to my assistance, I had to report and register at the Office of Police. This I did, and I gave the name, "Society of the Servants of the Divine Heart of Jesus."

In Rome my attention was called to the fact that there

existed a French Congregation by that name. This Congregation had many houses in Austria known as "Servants of the Sacred Heart of Jesus." For that reason the Holy See would under no condition give us the approbation under that name. Furthermore, the Carmelite Fathers at Rome, who were well disposed toward us, expressed the wish that our affiliation with the Carmel be expressed in the name. Therefore I decided to prefix "Carmelite Sisters" to "Servants of the Divine Heart of Jesus."

Beginning with 1897 we were called, "Carmelite Sisters, Servants of the Divine Heart of Jesus," until the name was changed once more in Rome. But regardless of the name, we are and ever shall remain "Servants of the Divine Heart of Jesus", our Master and Lord, an ideal of dedicated self-sacrificing love of God and neighbor.

God made man. He did so for love of us poor sinners, making no distinction between rich and poor, high and low. Always and everywhere, He showed preference for the common people. Yes, He Himself chose His disciples from among the common people. It is, therefore, difficult to understand how the poor and the mass of the common people turn away from Him, who on earth lived with and for them.

While busy in Rome with laying the foundation of the institution, I received a peculiar Christmas present on Christmas Eve. It came in the form of a telegram from Cologne on the Rhine and stated as follows:

I AM WITH MY BROTHER IN COLOGNE; WHERE SR. REGINA IS, I DO NOT KNOW.

(Signed) Margaretha

It was from the superior of the St. Joseph's Home at

Graupen. According to the telegram, she had left our Home and returned to her brother, a chaplain, who lived in Cologne.

Sr. M. Regina was the superior of the second Home at Marschen, Bohemia. What had become of the two houses? Where were the Sisters and the children? Since the middle of November, I had been without any news because all my letters had remained unanswered. I had not forgotten those wrathful eyes of Father S. or his clearly expressed design of "destroying" the work and "me and mine as a religious Community." How many times had my sorrowful thoughts wandered to Bohemia and Berlin! How many damaging acts may have been done in my absence by Father S.?

The Divine Child knew that I loved crosses and trials above all else, hence He could not have given me a better Christmas present than that news. It was the work of God, and is God not almighty? Such thoughts dispersed again and again the threatening storm clouds which tried to frighten me.

We left the Eternal City on December 30, 1897, full of gratitude. Fr. Ettl in Innsbruck had promised to give us a monstrance in case we would stop over on our return journey. We did so, and he was overjoyed about the document from Cardinal Parocchi. He too, as well as we ourselves, entertained great hopes for a happy future.

On Sylvester eve we attended the devotions and Benediction in the Church of the Jesuits in Innsbruck. I was very happy that in this place, where some time ago I had spent many weeks of grace, I could express my thanks to God for the help He had given me in the Eternal City. Apparently all our efforts had been in vain for the first few weeks until Divine Providence guided us to the proper counselors whose hearts God filled with interest in our work. The recommendation of Cardinal Parocchi is proof of this. In case Cardinal Kopp would not permit that our house in Berlin become the Motherhouse and novitiate, that would matter little, for I had been told in Rome that a religious Order is bound neither to a certain diocese nor country.

The first thing I did was to go to Bohemia. On our way there we passed through Linz. Father General of the Carmelites had expressed the wish that we call at the monastery of the Carmelite Nuns located there. To my great surprise, I received from the Rev. Mother Prioress the white Carmel mantle. I had never thought that we would be allowed to wear the Elijan mantle. I was full of joy over the goodness and kindness of Father General.

We had arrived in Linz in the morning, and in the evening, I think, we continued our trip. I hastened to Bohemia with a consuming desire for the trials awaiting me there. A real passion for suffering had filled my heart on this return journey from Rome to Berlin.

At last we arrived in Graupen. How many accomplishments had happened in the course of these eight weeks! Father S. had been recalled from Mariaschein. The two St. Joseph's Homes were not only without superiors, but the Sisters in Marschen had completely separated themselves from the Sisters in Graupen and were waiting for news from Father S. in order to enter his new foundation.

At that time we had no Chapels of our own, and that was the reason the Sisters from both Homes attended the services in the church at Mariaschein. Next morning after Holy Mass, none of the Sisters from Marschen came to us, and none of them greeted us. I went to the Bishop of Leitmeritz and reported the results of my trip to Rome as well as the conduct of the Sisters of Marschen. The Bishop promised that he would send them an admonition, and in case this admonition would remain unheeded, I myself should go there and dismiss those who wished to remain faithful to Father S.

The poor Sisters (actually postulants) who had been led astray, received the letter from the Bishop. They read it, and then the leader of the band threw it into the fire saying, "We promised fidelity to Father S., and we will keep our promise."

I sent them notice and demanded that they come and see me, but none of them heeded the summons. Thereupon I went myself, called them together, and told them that this house was my foundation, and if they wished to stay, they would be bound to obey me. In conclusion I said, "You either apologize and then you may stay with us and I will forgive and forget what has happened, or else you will leave the house today."

The reply was, "We have promised fidelity to Father S., and we will keep our promise." With these words they left the room, packed up, and departed that very evening. One of them begged pardon with a contrite heart and became a good and obedient religious Sister.

I now called, by telegram, my most faithful companions from Berlin and handed the two St. Joseph's Homes over to them. In the meantime the Sisters of Graupen told me that all that time they had never received any news from me. The Superior, Margaretha Schweitzer, from Cologne, as I was informed, always took the letters to Father S. and returned with the message that I had had no success in Rome, and that we never would become a Congregation.

As soon as the Sisters from Berlin had made themselves at home, and peace and harmony again reigned in the hearts of those in the two Homes, my little companion, Sr. Maria Theresia and I went to Breslau.

By Divine Providence His Eminence was absent. The priest who received us and to whom I submitted my petition for permission for a Motherhouse and novitiate cut me short with these words, "We have plenty of that kind." From these hard words I made my conclusion as to the sentiments of Cardinal Kopp.

We then returned to Berlin. The chalice of suffering was not yet empty by far, for God allowed that the bitter chalice of slander be offered to me.

At the railroad station of Berlin-Schoeneberg we met, or rather were awaited, by our dear M. Maria Magdalena and dear M. Brigitta. Their surprise and joy in seeing us in the veil was indescribable. We stayed one day in the small St. Joseph's Home in Schoeneberg; after that we invited the Sisters and children for our Thanksgiving celebration on January 18 at the Pappelallee. Then we visited the hospice in Anhalt Street and concluded our visit with the invitation for January 18. We also surprised the Sisters and children in Weissensee, and on January 17 we finally arrived in our first St. Joseph's Home in Pappelallee. Here, too, they were very much surprised, and great was their joy.

January 18 was a day of true joy and jubilation for us all. The girls from Weissensee and Schoeneberg, as well as Pappelallee, were dressed in white as on feast days because the weather was warm and sunny. In the afternoon over two hundred children and forty Sisters, the latter carrying lighted candles, marched in the Thanksgiving procession in the garden. The statue of St. Mother Teresa was carried in front of the procession, and we sang hymn after hymn, thanking and praising God for the favors received in Rome.

The words, "We have plenty of that kind," prepared me for future trials and told me quite plainly that I could not remain in Berlin. I would not spoil the feast day for the Sisters, however, but would rejoice with them.

At the beginning when there seemed to be not the least hope of success, Monsignor Jacquemin in Rome had suggested that we should make some kind of a vow in case we would succeed. For this reason Sr. Maria Theresia promised that later on she would add St. Peter to her name. I promised that as long as our Congregation would exist, we would celebrate a "Thanksgiving Feast in honor of St. Teresa" on the day when all of us would be united in our first St. Joseph's Home. This happened on January 18. For that reason we observe this day as a day of joy and gratitude each year in all our convents.

Immediately after Holy Mass on January 19, I plunged into the work with all the zeal and energy I could command. The first thing I did was to change the small house into a convent for the Sisters. After that I paid my respects to our pastor, Fr. Alesch, who received me with reproaches because I had severed my relations with Father S. It was Father S. who had informed Fr. Alesh that I had been prompted by "vanity and pride".

I knew enough. Had Father S. not told me himself on the occasion of my last visit at Mariaschein of his design to destroy this work? Not only one, but many letters of that kind, had been sent to priests in Berlin, known to him, or with whom he had become acquainted through the postulants. In order to bring about the ruin of our work such letters were sent not only to Berlin but to the provinces as far as Cologne.

If God were not the Founder of the Carmel of the Divine

Heart of Jesus, it would have been an easy matter to destroy us then. For that very reason, however, all efforts of our enemies failed.

Toward noon on January 21, 1898, I received a letter from Cardinal Kopp. At first he expressed his dissatisfaction because I had gone to Rome, and in conclusion, he gave the following command or prohibition: "I hereby forbid you to wear the religious garb both within and outside the institution."

I hastened immediately to Father K., the pastor. I reported on my trip to Rome and handed him the recommendation of Cardinal Parocchi, and he made no secret of his joy. Then I handed him the letter of Cardinal Kopp. When he had read it, he asked, "What are you going to do now?"

"Leave Berlin," I replied, "and look for a Bishop who will grant the permission for a Motherhouse and novitiate."

"And what is to become of the Homes here?"

I answered, "St. Father Joseph will take care of them."

"Now," replied the Pastor, "God can show that it is His work! But who will supply the food for the Sisters and children since you have nothing yourself?" He appeared very concerned.

I went back to Pappelallee as fast as I could. This was a distance of one and a quarter hours, and in those days there were very few streetcar lines in Berlin. I made the necessary arrangements and then was busy packing until morning. After that I took a brief rest which was followed by the very painful parting. Thereafter I was on my way on the early train to Bremen-Vechta.

In the the short time that I had been in possession of the letter from Cardinal Kopp, I had worn the veil undisturbed. It never once occurred to me that I should not be permitted from noon until the next morning to wear the veil while packing. However, in Berlin and Breslau others thought differently, and the rumor was spread abroad that I had been "disobedient" to Cardinal Kopp.

I asked some priests, and later some Cardinals and religious priests in Rome, as to what constituted my disobedience. They all gave me the assurance that my conduct could not be construed as disobedience. In addition Cardinal S. of Rome told me that even if the packing and arranging had taken me eight days, in my position it would not have been disobedience.

The news of this, my latest dreadful deed, spread like wildfire. Even my confessor at Bonn inquired of my deeds and asked for an explanation, as he could not believe what he had heard. God permitted this new persecution. May He be thanked for all eternity! Storms of this nature made the roots of the Carmel of the Divine Heart of Jesus stronger and thus became a source of new blessings.

Our financial condition was extremely precarious. I love poverty, and indeed it was my ideal to live and entirely be supported by Divine Providence. For that reason I was little concerned about payment of board, and even preferred to take very poor or forsaken children for whom no one was able or willing to pay, when the newspaper offered these children up for adoption. I had to support over two hundred children and fifty Sisters in the six St. Joseph's Homes. I was opposed from the start to Sisters going out collecting. Later on I permitted it in the case of foundations. I was forced by necessity, but always was reluctant, and would permit such collecting for a limited time only. Fr. Dasbach, our chaplain, who during the first years showed great interest in the St. Joseph's Home, had instructed me as early as 1892 to collect alms through the mail. I did so very diligently, trusting in St. Father Joseph, our powerful intercessor with God. Through his protection and solicitude I received at that time so many offerings in letters and postal orders that I was able to support all my Homes. Not only this, but with the alms I was able to build a house in Pappelallee for 120,000 marks without taking out a loan.

Of course we lived very economically, in great poverty and simplicity, concerning both furnishings and food. However, all received plenty and healthful food, making our children surpass, by their healthy looks and blooming appearance, other orphaned children, most of whom by comparison looked pale and neglected.

Up to this time I had given no one the right to endorse postal orders and the like in my name. Therefore how could I do so now, when severe storm clouds appeared in the East foreshadowing a new persecution? To whom of my companions could I entrust this power, after I had seen in Graupen that even the oldest had become weak?

Did the conditions in Berlin call for even greater firmness? Ever since the death of Msgr. Jahnel in the spring of 1897, his successor importuned my Sisters at every occasion, urging them to leave me since we could never receive the ecclesiastical approbation for a Congregation. The hospice on Anhalt Street was situated in St. Hedwig's parish and belonged to the district of the Dean. Under these conditions I would not dare empower anyone; therefore, the entire mail was forwarded to me wherever I went. I endorsed it, returned it, and designated in general the distribution of the money.

The Pastor, Father Kappenberg, had this situation in

mind when he spoke about our finances, and for that reason his anxiety was not without foundation. I myself did not share his concern, for I knew that it was the work of God, and therefore God, and not I, would take care of the support. I considered it my duty to do all in my power to generate the income. The success of my effort I always expected from God.

I must mention two genuine friends before I proceed to other experiences. In the fall of 1897, shortly before my journey to Rome, if my memory does not fail me, Fr. Unkraut of Oldenburg paid me a visit in Pappelallee. He made such a favorable impression upon me and gained my confidence so much, that I requested him to be the confessor of my Sisters. In Berlin we were not recognized as Sisters, and therefore, it was my duty to procure a confessor for over twenty postulants who could no longer go to the parish church of Fr. Alesch, since it was quite some distance away.

Father promised to apply for permission at Breslau. Cardinal Kopp granted permission in a gracious letter; this was before my trip to Rome. Fr. Unkraut came every week to St. Joseph's Home, espoused our cause with incomparable loyalty, inspired the postulants who showed signs of a vocation with courage and confidence to such an extent that they remained firm and loyal despite all opposition. Through many years of this caring service, Fr. Unkraut has done great things for the Carmel of the Divine Heart. May God give him his due reward!

Fr. Pluhatsch at St. Hedwig's Hospital was of equal loyalty and solicitude. We, the Carmel of the Divine Heart of Jesus, are profoundly indebted to those two priests. God will reward them for all eternity for what they have done for us.

From Bremen we continued our trip to Vechta. I took Sr. Maria Theresia of St. Peter as my companion. Next morning I called on the Officialis, Fr. Grobmeier, since I had great confidence in him. I told him everything about Rome, Breslau, Berlin, even the recent experience in Bohemia, and asked for his advice. I likewise showed him the recommendation of Cardinal Parocchi and the letter of Cardinal Kopp. The Officialis wanted to think the matter over. It was thought that perhaps the Bishop of Münster (Vechta belonged to his diocese) would grant permission to open the novitiate in Vechta.

I was happy in the hope of achieving my purpose so soon and anxiously awaited the answer from Münster. Before it came, I received a letter from the Spiritual Director K. in Leitmeritz, who had only recently been appointed as our director by the Bishop. This letter included an invitation to come to Leitmeritz and to open the novitiate there. He had, so he said, a suitable place.

Very much surprised, I took the letter to the Officialis. He read the lengthy letter slowly and declared, "You must accept it; you must not refuse this invitation. I have not as yet received the consent from Münster."

A few days later we returned to Leitmeritz in North Bohemia, which is now Czechoslovakia. Father K. led us to the house that he had offered us, but we were little pleased with it. Nevertheless, I thought to myself, "If God has chosen it for us, I will be satisfied." Father K. fixed February 4 as the day of the foundation. In the meantime we went to Graupen to make the necessary arrangements.

At the appointed time, I came with another Sister from Graupen to Leitmeritz, in order to receive the keys of the house from Father K., the Spiritual Director. The other

Sisters were to arrive a few hours later with the necessary equipment. Father received us in a very friendly manner, but instead of giving us the keys, he said, "Now, first of all, you must go to the Bishop and ask for his approbation."

I was petrified. Previously my first concern had always been to ask for the episcopal approbation. Naturally such would not apply in this case, for the Bishop had appointed him as our spiritual director. He had called us here, and in obedience to our newly appointed superior, I had left Vechta and gone to Leitmeritz. What could we do now?

Immediately I went to the Bishop who received us, as was his custom, with fatherly kindness. Yet when I mentioned the project of founding the novitiate in his episcopal city and told him that the Spiritual Director had called us from Oldenburg to this place, he was amazed and said firmly, "How can the Spiritual Director do such a thing? He knows quite well that I will never have two different Congregations in one city." We asked for his blessing and left, but we did not return to the Spiritual Director as our time was limited, and I was not willing to take him that news. We went to the station to send a telegram to Graupen to notify the Sisters not to bring the necessary equipment and that only Sr. Maria Theresia and one other Sister should come. We remained at the station waiting for them, and just before our train left they arrived. I again took my dear travel companion with me while the other two remained in Graupen to tell the Superior and the other Sisters of our misfortune.

Where were we to go now? The approbation of Münster appeared to me to be very uncertain. I learned later that the Bishop would not have given his permission on account of Cardinal Kopp.

Once more we were completely dependent on God's guidance. I decided to go first to Eger and then to Regensburg to the Carmelite Fathers in the hope of obtaining advice.

In sorrow, but not without confidence, we boarded the train. We arrived in Eger at midnight, where we had to wait until morning for the train to Regensburg. The Officials of the station were very kind and allowed us, although we had third class tickets, to go into the waiting room for first class. "There," they said, "you may rest quietly."

My young companion soon fell asleep, but how could I sleep under such conditions? My thoughts wandered from one house of my dear ones to another, as I recommended them all to Divine Providence. Then I prayed and asked, "Lord, what will You have me do? Lord Your will be done. Forget me and think of Thee alone." Then I entreated God to pay no heed to me, as I was willing to suffer joyfully for Him. "Forget me and think of Thee alone."

As was the night outside, the future lay ahead of me shrouded in deepest darkness. Regarding similar cases, my only worry was of doing something contrary to the will of God; therefore, I implored my heavenly Mother for help. When thinking of my forsaken Sisters and children, sorrow would begin to settle upon my heart. Then I recalled the fatherly protection of our Father St. Joseph, and I was filled with new consolation and confidence returned.

In the early morning the long-awaited train approached. We boarded it and within a few hours were in Regensburg. We found a place to stay overnight and then looked for the Carmelite monastery. Since the Prior was absent, I explained our sad case to the Father who received us. I also asked his advice as to where we might obtain the approbation of a bishop for the erection of our Mother-house and novitiate. He replied, "This is quite impossible in Bavaria because of the laws. Go to the Netherlands; we have Fathers there, too. Return here tomorrow after Mass. Then you can speak to Father Prior. He will give you better advice than I."

Next morning we called on Father Prior. His advice was not even to try to get the approbation in Bavaria, for it certainly would be in vain. Then I told him the Father who had received us the day before had advised us to go to the Netherlands, but that we had no address of any of the monasteries there. Father Prior did not want to hear anything of this, and thus we received neither address nor advice.

What now were we to do? We remained a short while before the Tabernacle in the old Carmelite church. Then we went to the station. Fr. Wenzel, a faithful friend of mine, lived in Bamberg, and Bamberg being not far from Regensburg, I decided to ask his advice. This good priest, who had rendered me an incalculable service in Berlin where he stayed as a member of the parliament, received us with his customary kindness. He advised me very definitely to go to the Netherlands. "It will be impossible for you to obtain the approval in Bavaria, and in Prussia [it will be] the same; for every Bishop will first inquire of Cardinal Kopp, and to judge from that letter of January 20, you cannot expect any recommendation from him. Go to the Netherlands; that is the best thing to do. During the *Kulturkampf* the Netherlands was the refuge of many religious. There will be room for you also. I am sorry that

I am not able to give you an address."

I was profoundly grateful for this firm and resolute direction. Without further delay we went to the depot and took the next train to Cologne. How long the trip lasted, I no longer remember, but I will never forget the countless stops we made. It was impossible for me to fall asleep. Like many other times, I spent the night in prayer until we reached Cologne. Whether it was after one day's trip or when it was, I do not remember, but the train was very slow. We had very little money left, and for that reason we could not afford to take the express train or procure refreshments on the way.

From Cologne we went to our dear Lady of Kevelaer, Help of the Afflicted. Indeed, here at the feet of our dear Lady, the best help and advice was to be had. Soon we found gratis lodging with a good woman. Wonderfully consoled and strengthened, we left the shrine the next morning. We had obtained the name of the nearest episcopal city in the Netherlands: Roermond.

After changing trains repeatedly we arrived in Roermond, Netherlands. It was a totally strange country for us, and we were without any address. I was a stranger, although the Netherlands was the fatherland of my ancestors on my mother's side. About the middle of the eighteenth century, the grandfather of my mother, Baumeister van den Bosch, had come to Potsdam where Friederichs II, King of Prussia, had planned to establish a Netherland colony. At that time Limburg did not belong to the Netherlands, and the van den Bosch family came originally from Holland. The inhabitants of Potsdam prevented the execution of the plan since under no circumstances did they want "Netherland houses." Yet my great-grandfather did not return to the Netherlands. I do not know whether the truly royal compensation assigned to him for life or the family which he had founded there had won his heart for the beautiful Potsdam. The descendants remained there until about 1850. When my mother's brothers were about to be drafted for military service, the Netherland spirit awoke in them, and they left Germany one by one. Instead of returning to the Netherlands, all three of them settled down in the United States of America. Two of them died soon after, but the oldest brother of my mother was employed for a number of years as engineer on the large bridge, which connects New York and Brooklyn.

As I was growing up, my father said more than once, "You are all Netherland." At that time I did not understand it, but when I came to the Netherlands I realized that the Netherland nation was closer to me than the German nation.

CHAPTER SIX

A HOME FOUND IN THE NETHERLANDS

We arrived in Roermond on February 7 or 8, and we wandered from convent to convent begging for shelter for the night, but our search was in vain. At last we came to the convent of the Ursuline Sisters in the Brotstraat. Here, at least, we were invited to sit down. Soon a Sister appeared. She expressed her sorrow at being unable to keep us overnight since all the rooms were taken by the sick Sisters, but just across the street we were told that we would find a small family rooming house. If we would go there, we would be well received.

Sincerely we thanked the kind Sister and went to the family that had been recommended to us. A charming Netherland girl received us and called her mother, who shook hands with us most warmly and led us to the vacant guest room.

The good woman scarcely had left us when she returned with a glass of wine for me because I looked so pitiful, and offering me the wine, she added, "It doesn't cost anything." Indeed I not only looked wretched but also felt physically exhausted. A night's rest restored my strength and again gave me confidence in God's help, the assistance of our dear Lady and of St. Joseph. With renewed courage I continued the work that God had entrusted to me.

Dear Sr. Maria Theresia who, to my sorrow, suffered much from stomach trouble, went immediately to buy the necessary provisions. Poverty compelled us to rent the room without board. As we had done in Rome, we prepared our frugal meals with the help of an oil lamp.

As soon as I was alone, I sank to my knees before the small Pieta which I carried with me on all my trips and which I had placed on the table. In most fervent prayer I turned to my heavenly Mother, entreating her to show me the way, and to help me see the will of God. At that time someone knocked on the door, and I arose. The amiable hostess entered and asked me how I felt. Then she began to tell me, with many lamentations, that her husband had died and that she was grief stricken. She concluded her lamentations with these words, "But our good Rector never forsook me; he is a good pious priest."

I asked, "Where does that good Rector live?"

"Don't you know the Church of Our Lady? It is a place of pilgrimage." Pointing to the left, she continued, "Right here, this road flanked with trees on both sides leads to the church and monastery, which are not even two miles distant." Of course, she spoke Dutch all the time.

After I had expressed my thanks to the amiable old lady, she left, and again I knelt down. I felt quite certain that by means of this good woman, the Mother of God had shown me the way I was to follow in order to reach my goal.

My first concern was to establish connections with my dear Sisters. We inquired concerning the nearest German border and then informed the eight Homes to send all mail to "Post Office Dalheim," general delivery.

As soon as these letters had been taken care of, we confidently hurried to the nearby shrine. About twenty-five minutes later we were in the Church of Our Lady of Zand. After we had confided our sorrow and grief to the most compassionate Heart of Mary, our Mother, confidently trusting in her motherly help, we turned our steps to the monastery door. It was not long before Father Rector of the Redemptorist monastery entered. He received us kindly and patiently listened to our tale of misery and woe. Then I told him that I had in mind to try and obtain an episcopal approbation here in the Netherlands. He advised me to call on the Bishop's secretary in Roermond, since the Bishop himself was too old to receive visitors. We expressed out thanks, and the next day called on the secretary. His Reverence, however, firmly and emphatically refused my petition for a foundation since the Cathedral Chapter had decreed to no longer admit any more Congregations. It was clear that that order would be adhered to. It would be useless, as far as this diocese was concerned, to make any further efforts, and that we had better go to Hertogenbosch without delay to obtain the approbation, since that diocese, as well as Utrecht, had German boundaries. I was restricted to the German boundaries on account of the post office address I had given.

We left our belongings with the kind family who had given us a room and continued our trip to Hertogenbosch. The Bishop was full of compassion and kindness. He advised that first of all we should look for a suitable house, and having found one, I should inquire of the pastor of the place whether he would be willing to take us in, and thereafter, we should call on him again.

Now we began our wanderings through all the places along the German border. First we visited the towns which belonged to the Diocese of Hertogenbosch, then farther along, those of the Diocese of Utrecht. We did not spare ourselves any hardship. We were on the road from early morning until late in the evening. All was in vain; we did not find a house.

In the meantime we went twice a week to Dalheim to take care of the mail, and we carried our pen and ink with us. Sitting in the station, we first endorsed the postal money orders, then hastily answered the most urgent letters. Our train would come, and we handed our letters to the depot agent, while hurrying to board the train more than once with pen and ink in hand. The train then took us back to Roermond. All our spare time was used in answering the letters that we did not have time to answer in Dalheim. These letters we took along on our next trip to that city.

By now it was March 10, and still there was not the slightest hope of obtaining the approbation. We did not even find a house in which to make a beginning. In the meantime we had informed the Rector in Zand about our trips. When we poor pilgrims knew not what to do or where to turn, we had refuge in our dear Lady of Zand. Then we called on Fr. Lochmeijer and reported to him about our failures. He thought for a while and then said firmly and emphatically, "You go to Sittard. That is the right place for you."

When I objected that no more religious orders would be admitted in that diocese, he replied that it was always within the power of the Bishop to admit more, and we should just go to Sittard. Taking the advice of Father Rector, we went immediately to Sittard. It was March 10, 1898, when we came to Sittard for the first time. Sittard is about one hour south of Roermond. Up to now we had searched only north of Roermond where the two other dioceses border on Germany.

From the station we went first to the main church, and there, right near the entrance, stood a statue of St. Peter. The sight of this holy Apostle had always filled me with great confidence and so it was at this moment. Great hopes filled our hearts when we came to the rectory and were heartily welcomed by the dean, Father Linders, a kind, fatherly old man. In a few words I acquainted him with our situation, our trips along the German boundaries, and in conclusion, I asked him whether he would accept us in Sittard and whether a large house could be found in this city. His satisfaction was evident. He said a convent and novitiate would undoubtedly be a blessing for the town and that he knew of such a house.

I objected that the secretary of the Bishop had firmly turned us down because religious would not be admitted into the diocese. Some decree forbade it. and for that reason we were not to search for a house in this diocese. The venerable Dean replied, "Don't worry about that; just go to the Vicar General and tell him that I am willing to take you here in Sittard."

The Dean then conducted us to the house that he had in mind. It is the same house that we occupy today. It had been intended for French Sisters, the Dean informed us, but they never had taken possession of it. Six families were occupying the house at the time. The property included a garden, and the entire property was surrounded by a wall. It was very convent-like. It was our good fortune that a small part was vacant, and the renters would soon move in case we should purchase the house.

Full of hope we returned to Roermond. The next day we called on the Vicar General who curtly and emphatically rejected my petition for admittance into the diocese. I thought for a few seconds, and then I asked whether the Chapter would not, in view of our painful situation, be willing to permit us temporarily to occupy the place for two years. Having made the proposition, we were told to call the next day for an answer. The next morning, after we had implored the help of our heavenly Queen, we called on the Vicar General who handed us the permission in writing to stay for two years. I gratefully accepted it and without delay we hurried to the Dean in Sittard. He read the permission but was not at all pleased with it. "That is nothing," he said. "I will go to the Bishop, and you will get the permission to buy the house and open a novitiate." Thus it came to pass, but the good Dean obtained only the oral permission for the foundation and the opening of the novitiate.

Following the advice of the Dean, we bought the house. The necessary finances we obtained quite unexpectedly from Germany. The feast of St. Joseph, March 19, was to be the day of the foundation.

Now it was March 12; we had left Berlin on January 21. How great was the grief I had endured during those weeks. The very thought of it made me tremble, yet I thanked God that He had allowed me to endure those painful days and hours for His work. Now help came unexpectedly, thanks to our dear Lady who had visibly guided us first to her shrine and then through Fr. L.A.J.H. Lochmeijer, C.S.S.R. (who died May 25, 1917) to Sittard.

After our return to Roermond, we informed our Sisters of our new blessing from God and gave them our new address. We had already obtained our mail at the German post office about forty minutes from Sittard. At the same time I designated some of the oldest Sisters to meet us in Roermond on March 19. Others I instructed to come directly to Sittard a few days later.

The Sisters arrived, and in great joy we went to our new house. It was here in our new home where we were welcomed by the holy poverty of Bethlehem. Divine Providence had led us into the land of my forefathers where the cradle of the "Carmel of the Divine Heart of Jesus" was to stand. Here also I was to find the spiritual guide of my soul, for whom I had yearned for so many years.

The enlightened spiritual guide was Fr. Ruetgen, S.J., an elderly, blind Netherland priest. Our entire Community and I are greatly indebted to him. He not only took care of the growth and development of our souls, but no sooner had he been informed of our indescribable poverty than he persuaded some kindhearted people of the town to come to our assistance.

With great zeal we went to work to remodel the house into a convent. This was no easy task, nor did the work progress as fast as we desired. The renters of the small rooms moved out very soon, but the two families occupied the larger rooms until August 1898 and January 1899. The apartment to be vacated in August was designated for the Chapel. We longed for the Blessed Sacrament, but the Chapel and oratory were not finished until the end of October. On October 30, to my great personal joy, Dean Linders blessed our Chapel and the Blessed Sacrament was reserved in the Tabernacle.

For nine long months, filled with trials and hardships, I had been deprived of my best Friend. Divine Providence visibly protected the work and watched over the forsaken Sisters and guided us in a truly wonderful manner. Everything had been permitted by God and redounded to the glory of His Majesty. How else could the Carmel of the Divine Heart of Jesus have survived?

It was most painful for me that I had to leave the five Homes with two hundred children and the hospice in Berlin. I left them alone in the hands of strangers, young postulants, who had only recently entered. It would have been different if the poor Sisters could have found help and advice from the pastor. Such was not the case, since most of the priests in Berlin considered it their duty to show them that I was "disobedient" and that they would never become "religious Sisters" as long as they remained with me. Priests in Silesia sent them letters that contained similar warnings. Thanks be to God, who had provided us with two priest friends, those two whom I mentioned before. They were the pillars and protectors of the work of God, namely, Fr. Unkraut and Fr. Pluhatsch, both of them pastors.

Another difficulty, which Father K. in Berlin had thought of at the very start, was our support. We numbered over three hundred persons. It was a question not only of clothing and food but also of rent, interest, and indebtedness caused by building and maintenance. We had a debt of 20,000 marks which had to be paid off.

Was this not a fine opportunity for St. Joseph to manifest his miraculous powers to the whole world? Thanks to his loving care and intercession at the throne of God, the work grew and struck deeper roots despite storm and persecutions. This was true not only of the work itself but also of our Sisters. All those persecutions, sacrifices, and trials molded these postulants into pillars of the Order. The individual Sisters can tell us better how much they had to suffer during those years of persecutions.

From now on the candidates were received in Sittard. After I had tested and trained them for a few weeks, I sent them to Berlin where there was a shortage of help due to constant defections. Each time it was like "sending them to the front" and exposing them to the fire for testing. How painful it was when news came of one or another who had been persuaded by the Monsignor or the pastor to return home.

Now let us return to Sittard. At last all the rooms had been vacated and everything was ready for the opening of the novitiate. Toward the end of January the retreat began and on February 2 we had our first investiture. Fr. Arnstadt, S.J., a Swiss, conducted the retreat. Fr. Damasus, O.F.M., our confessor, invested the postulants.

FEBRUARY 2, 1899

On the Feast of the Presentation of Jesus, a new sprout of the ancient venerable Carmelite Order under the name of "Society of the Carmelite Sisters, Servants of the Divine Heart of Jesus" (later known as "Carmel of the Divine Heart of Jesus") was planted in the garden chosen by God in Sittard.

Eight years had passed since the foundation of the first St. Joseph's Home in Berlin. Almost seven years ago I stood on the projecting rocks, surrounded by thundering, frightful, surging waves, as I had seen them in a dream in May 1892. Yet it was not I who stood there, immovable, living, like part of the rock. No, it was not I but God within me. The intimate union with the crucified Savior, which in that vision gave me miraculous strength, that same intimate union, again and again, had given me new steadfastness, day and night, during all those years. How else, could I have withstood the trials and sorrows which broke over me like floods of water?

Now I was tortured by the fear that I would have to take the office of mistress of novices, for which I did not at all feel qualified! During the ceremonies of the investiture my soul was completely crushed, but God again had mercy on me and came to my assistance. I knelt in the doorway for it was impossible for me to enter the Chapel.

"O Lord, I am not worthy; O Lord, I am not worthy." My lips could whisper nothing else. I knelt there, completely overwhelmed by sorrow, repentance, and unworthiness. I had always felt unworthy of the grace to be a member of holy Mother Church. Now I was as a child of the desert!

I wished to be a domestic Sister, to do the lowliest work. I wanted to spend my life united with God in profound solitude. That was the desire of my heart which I had entertained for years. Now what would happen?

It is impossible for me to express in words the fear and anxiety of my heart caused by the feeling of my crushing unworthiness. It was again one of those hours during which the storm raging in my soul made the waves rise mountain high, until our Diving Savior raised His hand and both storm and waves obeyed and calmed down.

Sr. Maria Theresia of St. Peter assisted Father Damasus at the investiture. There they knelt before me, shrouded in their white mantles, near the Tabernacle. They were souls entrusted to me by God. Souls to whom I should be mother and mistress. Trusting solely in God and His assistance, I said, "O Lord, I am not worthy," and added to this cry of my heart, "O Lord, Your will be done."

The work, exterior as well as interior, is God's work alone. It is my one consolation to know that my lack of ability redounds to the greater glory of God. I was devoid of everything required for the office. I had but one desire: always to do the will of God and to strive to know His holy will in all things, even to the most minute detail.

Thanks be to God for having given me, at that time in Sittard, the old venerable Fr. Ruetgen as a guide. He understood my soul. With a firm and skilled hand he healed the wounds of my soul. He did not use words as balm only, as Fr. Ruetgen was a man of few words. In few

145

and fitting words he said what he thought and always he was unerring. As he had wide experience in the direction of souls, many sought him as their confessor.

In those years I was often tortured by the fear of being damned. On the one side I saw the many graces that God had given me from the days of my childhood. On the other, I saw a life full of sin and faults, despite efforts and struggles on my part. I wanted to practice every kind of virtue for God, but I never got far. I always remained "black," as I used to call myself. This is why I often suffered from great fear. One time when I suffered extraordinary anguish of this kind, and fear was at its height, I turned to our Divine Savior. A fervent love of Him streamed into my soul. I felt united with Him in so intimate a union that I said, "O Lord, if I am to be damned, You too will be damned with me; for if You are in me and I in You, who can separate us?"

Thanks be to God that from that hour I was never tortured by this fear of damnation. Since that time my soul has been filled with unwavering confidence in the mercy of God, who will be a merciful judge to all those who are of good will. This good will, to give God joy, has never left me.

GOD'S WAYS

A few months of happiness had thus passed when a new misfortune knocked at the convent door. Dear venerable Dean Linders died, and a few weeks later the Lord called the Most Reverend Boermans, Bishop of Roermond. How the death of these two men was to affect us was made clear on the first Friday of June 1899. The new Dean came to inform me, by order of the newly elected Bishop, that the Cathedral Chapter at Roermond insisted on the permission to stay for two years only. In addition he mentioned that the newly elected Bishop Drehmanns wished to see me.

The next day I was received in audience. Bishop Drehmanns told me, in a most amiable manner, that he, having only recently been raised to the episcopacy, could not rescind the decree of the Chapter. Although he was very sorry, he was bound to respect the written permission which extended to March 1900. "However," he added, "I will add six months, and I will give you my assistance for obtaining admission in another diocese."

"The voice of the Bishop is the voice of God," I remarked as I thanked him. God had revealed to me that the Carmel would spread over the entire world, and therefore, I looked upon this expulsion as coming from God.

"Do not disturb your novices. Let them finish their novitiate. Later on you will find a bishop who will permit all of them to make their profession, for at the end of the novitiate they are allowed to make private vows only."

I asked his Excellency, "What will become of me? I never made any novitiate."

"I think," the Bishop replied, "your life up to now was a most thorough novitiate."

I returned to my Sisters and lived happily with them. None of them noticed the suffering that filled my soul. Suffering remains suffering even though we bear it for the love of God. I felt acute distress to which was added my fear and anxiety to know the will of God. My first concern would be to find a place for fourteen Sisters and more than twenty-five children whom we had brought from Berlin. I was even more worried about the house which the good Dean had advised me to buy.

It was the month of the Sacred Heart of Jesus, when the expulsion from Sittard was pronounced over us. This was followed by the expulsion from the Pappelallee, as may be seen from the following letter of Sr. Maria Theresia of St. Peter. Although she was very young, I had appointed her superior and sent her to the main home in Berlin, since she, being a true child of Tyrol, would not yield, come what may. Yes, like the mountains of her native country, she remained loyal and firm. The following is her letter.

Berlin, Pappelallee
June 26, 1899

Dearest Mother:

Today, at 11:30, the Reverend Delegate came, very serious and severe, just to see how things were going, having received instructions from His Eminence to finally settle the affair. "Who is the head of this house?" he asked. "Our Mother in Sittard." "No," he replied, "that is no management from a foreign country. Did we not know we were not religious women?" I replied, "Here we are not, but we intend to become, if not here, then in Sittard. Under no conditions will we separate from Mother."

Then the delegate said, "Either all of you separate from Mother, in which case everything will be turned over to an existing Community, or you must all leave, including the mission stations," and the house must be surrendered to him. "Mother is to write to the Delegate what she intends to do. The Reverend Delegate gives you two weeks to think it over."

We are allowed to take along as many of the the children as we want, the more the better. He thought that there were sufficient accommodations in Sittard. Therefore we ought to be able to find something suitable for us. The Reverend Delegate would like it best if we would let him have the house completely empty. It was not his intention to separate us from Mother. We were at liberty to do as we please in this matter. All that Mother would have to do would be to write to him that she renounced all claims to the house and everything else. I replied, "Mother will never write that of her own free will. She will never part with this place and relinquish all that belongs to her."

The Reverend Delegate answered, "Mother admitted that she was disobedient. She was bound to remove the veil immediately without waiting until the next morning and going on a trip in the veil."

I said that this must be a mistake. Mother could never have admitted it, and that it was impossible for Mother to start out any sooner.

All of us are wholeheartedly children of our saintly Prioress and our Heavenly Mother of Mt. Carmel. Firmly and entirely we are united with our dear Mother and the dear Sisters at Sittard.

> In sincerest love always and entirely
> Your child,
> Sr. Maria Theresia of St. Peter

The news contained in this letter was another draught from the cup of suffering of Divine Love. I called all the Sisters to the Chapel to sing the *Te Deum*, as I used to on the occasions of great trials, but I caused no anxiety to the Sisters or anyone else because I did not tell them this news.

"To suffer in silence, that is what I love. I am not attached to Berlin, nor do I cling to the house. It was built for You, O Lord. Do with it as You please; only let me know Your most holy will." Such were the thoughts in my mind that guided me. Again they made use of the old slander of my having been disobedient, in the effort to rob the Sisters of their confidence in me. Yet the harder they worked to bring about the separation, the closer and stronger we became united.

The Sisters looked for a house in Berlin, but naturally none could be found to accommodate 150 persons. Now we were in two places without a house, and the following month brought another eviction. In Marschen, Bohemia, we had been invited by Fr. Kovac to establish a small Home for children in the homestead of his parents. This we had done. However, the complicated political conditions, it seemed to me, made Father think that the best thing for us would be to unite with the Third Order of the Carmel since they already had the approbation of the government in Austria. The decree was either unite with the Third Order of Carmel or leave the house. Since none of us wished to join the Third Order, we decided to leave the house.

In the town of Bruex, not far away, since the so-called Reformation there were no religious communities of Sisters, and the Dean was very willing to take the Sisters and children. Soon they found a house that was to become vacant in the fall. On November 24, the Feast of Saint John of the Cross, I went to Breux in order to help the Sisters (actually only postulants) to furnish the house. The house was opposite the Capuchin church, and this pleased the Sisters very much. Now, instead of walking almost one half hour to visit the Blessed Sacrament, as in Marschen, it took no more than two minutes. Before I left Bruex, I visited the pilgrimage shrine of "Maria-Raschuetz," to recommend my troubles to the heart of my Heavenly Mother.

The various evictions did not cause me much worry because I clearly saw in them God's will and providence. The situation in Sittard was different because I had bought the house. This did not give me any peace, for I always made myself believe that by purchasing the house I had done wrong, because now we had to move out. Besides I had made considerable changes. Who would buy it now?

With Sister Sr. M. Elizabeth I went to the church, a place of pilgrimage, to visit the altar of our dear Lady. Because of my great grief, I soon forgot the Sister's presence and prayed and wept bitterly. I implored the help of our Lady for our house in Sittard. Then I heard clearly and distinctly an interior voice, "Until later." In that moment my anxiety disappeared and my heart was filled with new trust and confidence.

On my return journey to Sittard I visited our Home in Graupen and then the Bishop of Leitmeritz. I expressed my thanks for the permission to establish a house in Bruex and bewailed my misfortune about the written and illegal oral approbation. I also submitted the recommendation of the Bishop of Roermond and asked whether he would allow some of those novices to come to Graupen and Bruex in the religious garb of Sisters. To my great joy His Excellency granted the permission.

On the way to Sittard I passed through Roermond and called on Bishop Drehmanns. After I had reported about Bruex, I told him how happy I was that the Sisters, after the novitiate, were permitted to come to Graupen and Bruex in their habit.

As a substitute for Sittard, His Excellency proposed that I approach the Archbishop of Utrecht for permission, and in case he would not grant it, to try in Tilburg. Since I did not want the novices to find out about the suppression of Sittard, I thought it best to go on to Utrecht. I arrived there in a few hours and obtained an audience with His Excellency. To my sorrow, however, Archbishop W. flatly refused my petition.

That same evening I continued on to Tilburg. There I retired, as I was completely exhausted. The soul may rejoice over suffering, which it bears for love of the Sacred Heart, but nevertheless the body suffers more or less under the strain.

The next morning after Holy Mass I called on the Congregation of the Fratres. The old Director was still alive at that time. He, as well as Father V. Z., received me with great kindness and compassion. The former promised to obtain the permission of the Bishop of Hertogenbosch; the latter said he would look for a house for us. After that I returned to Sittard.

Christmas passed with its joys and blessings. Toward the end of January, we began the retreat, but the novices were not aware of the fact that they would not make profession. On February 2, I informed them that we would have to leave Sittard because the Cathedral Chapter would not recognize the approbation that Dean Linders had obtained for us. For this reason we could not make profession, that is, such as the Church would accept as valid. Bishop Drehmanns, however, had advised us to make "private" vows and in this manner terminate the novitiate. Later on we would find a Bishop who would let us make profession.

In the spirit of truly admirable sacrifice, all accepted this trial which was great indeed. Then I told them that we would make the private vows in the evening, and on that occasion they were to receive the brown veil. The kind Bishop of Leitmeritz had given permission to wear the religious garb in the two St. Joseph's Homes in Bohemia. In conclusion I also told them that we would move from Sittard to Tilburg where some of them would be stationed. This soon robbed the sorrow of its bitterness, and all were happy and content.

Feast-day and feast-day meal and recreation were not

wanting. I had set the late evening aside for our private celebration. In this manner we would not be disturbed by the postulants or children.

The Chapel was beautifully decorated and illumined. Each individual novice knelt down before the Infant Jesus, placed the written profession into the hands of the Divine Child, and made her profession. Then I clothed them with the brown veil. No word was spoken; yet it was a profoundly impressive celebration!

Great was the amazement and joy of the postulants and children next morning when all the Sisters appeared in their brown veils. All were beaming with happiness and joy because as yet they were ignorant of the heavy cross that weighed upon us, namely, that we had to leave the Home in Berlin.

Toward the end of March, Sr. M. Bernadine, two other Sisters, and myself went to Graupen. It was impossible for me to stay overnight in the small St. Joseph's Home, since it was a tiny house crowded with children, many of whom slept in a house about seven minutes distant with two of the Sisters. However, after many difficulties we found a large room for the four of us in a mill. There we stayed while we looked for a suitable house with a garden.

We had not been in the hermitage for long when Fr. Rector, S.J., sent word that the Annenhof was for sale, and that it was a suitable place. The Sisters whom he had directed to tell me added, "We pass the Annenhof every day. It is a large piece of property with a barn, but there is no house to live in. Fr. Rector thinks that you intend to build right away."

I believed the Sisters, and so I looked for a house myself. I asked others to do the same but without results.

Weeks passed by and still we were restricted to that one miserable room in the mill. Early in the morning we would go to Graupen to attend Holy Mass.

One morning the pastor of Graupen sent word through the sexton that he wanted to speak to me after Mass. Shortly after Mass I went with a Sister to the sacristy while the others returned home. As soon as the pastor saw me he spoke in a loud and angry voice; "Where are your papers? What are you doing here? Who gave you permission to wear the habit? The entire town is talking about it. Don't you dare to come to our church again. You will not be allowed to go to confession here."

All during this painful scene the sexton stood in the open doorway. The conversation lasted at least a half hour. My companion was so deeply affected by the angry speech of the pastor that she suddenly turned pale and leaned against the window.

I remained calm and undisturbed. When there was a pause I promised to show him our papers. This pacified him and he dismissed us. Sister T. felt so bad that only with difficulty could she go down the hill. When at last we had reached our mill home, Sr. M. Bernardine could read from our faces, hers distressed and mine joyous, that something very unpleasant must have happened to us. We told them of our experience and then began to think how we might have caused the ill humor of the pastor but were unable to do so.

I took refuge with our good Bishop of Leitmeritz and told him what had happened, and at the same time I asked him to help us. A few days later I received a letter directing us to continue to go to church at Graupen, that the assistant Pastor had been appointed as our ordinary confessor, and that the pastor had been notified to that effect.

After these disagreeable experiences, we endeavored more anxiously than before to find a house. As I have a special devotion to the Blessed Trinity, I prayed most fervently before Trinity Sunday to God for help. On Saturday I sent two Sisters to our landlord, the miller, to ask him once more if he knew of a house with a garden. Within a short time they returned with the message that the Annenhof would be the proper place. The large property had not only a barn, but also a new villa facing the street and some other solid buildings that could be enlarged.

On the Feast of the Blessed Trinity, we went to the Annenhof. The large garden, which was in full bloom, delighted us as well as the villa within it, and the old buildings could easily be enlarged. We were overjoyed in seeing this feast-day gift from our Heavenly Father. Without delay we discussed the business side, and we closed the deal to the satisfaction of both parties. On July 1 we could move in and take possession of the property and all that belonged to it.

I was sorry that I had allowed myself to be dissuaded by the Sisters and did not inspect the Annenhof right away as Fr. Rector had advised, although we could not have moved in any sooner. In the early morning of July 1, we left our mill hermitage and moved into the new St. Joseph's Home. A few hours later there appeared a wonderful rainbow in the sky that gave me great joy. Every rainbow symbolizes for me God's love and peace. It is a sign of the merciful love of the Father for His poor, weak, and sinful children who are of good will but are not always able to translate it into deeds.

A few days later we transferred the postulants and children from our first small Home. The joy of the children was indescribable, for up to now they did not have a garden or playground. Soon a contractor came, and I discussed with him the changes to be made on the building. The first thing to be done was to erect a small wall around the garden.

But how could we erect a Chapel? An old building that was standing by itself, with walls twenty inches thick, lent itself to that purpose. The interior was plastered, vaulted windows were installed (but not without great difficulties), and thus the building became a devotional oratory.

When almost everything was arranged and the building had progressed satisfactorily, a telegram called me to Tilburg. I started out in company with one of the Sisters who had come to Graupen in March. When we arrived there we learned that a house, though a rather small one, had been found. The Pastor of St. Anne's, in whose parish it was located, would be glad to take us. In the absence of all hope of finding something better at the time, I rented the poor little house. By this time it was August, and on September 15 all the Sisters had to leave Sittard. I was grateful to have found a place in which to live.

Now we were busy packing, and the many things for which we would not have room in the new home were put together. On August 25 I took some of the Sisters and the Netherland children to Tilburg. The equipment had already arrived, and many goodhearted Netherland men helped, so that when I returned to Sittard in the evening, the small house with a little Chapel was ready.

A few days later we finally left Sittard. I went once more to Roermond to visit Bishop Drehmanns. As in the past, he again received me. This time most kindly. Concluding the audience His Excellency remarked that since it would be very difficult to exist without the German mail station, he would permit two of the postulants, in civilian clothes, to remain in Sittard to take care of the mail. I was very grateful for that. I would not have dared to ask for this favor, although I did not know what to do without the German mail, for I still endorsed everything. My dear St. Father Joseph had obtained that favor for us!

September 15 dawned. The last Mass had been celebrated. Our Divine Savior had left the convent! Deep sorrow rested upon all of us as long as we remained, but my grief was softened by the words of our dear Lady, "Until later." These were words which I could never forget. I was convinced that our dear Lady would later on bring us back. The two postulants stayed in Sittard under the protection of Fr. Ruetgen.

The wagon came, the children wept bitterly as they climbed into the wagon, and our eyes likewise were filled with tears. After a few hours on the train we were in our new St. Joseph's Home at St. Anne's Place. This small house reminded me of our first Home in Graupen, which also was without a garden. St. Joseph and our dear Lady had transformed the little Nazareth house of Graupen into a charming Carmel of the Divine Heart. Later on St. Joseph and St. Anne transferred the little Nazareth house of St. Anne's Place to the beautiful Wilhelmina Park, and changed it, by and by, into a stately Carmel of the Divine Heart.

God's blessing works miracles every day. Sad to say, most men are blind to the wonderful works of God!

Time flies. One month had passed and we celebrated the Feast of our St. Mother Teresa on October 15, 1900. Despite extreme poverty, we were happy. As we gathered in our small community room in the attic, the pastor of the Church of St. Anne was announced.

His Reverence expressed his regret for coming on the Feast of St. Teresa, but he was acting under instruction from the Bishop of Hertogenbosch. The introduction of his message left little doubt that my St. Mother Teresa was to offer me a draught from the chalice of suffering which I loved so much, and so it was.

His Excellency gave me notice that he had indeed granted permission for a foundation in Tilburg, but this did not mean a Motherhouse and a novitiate, and for that reason I was not permitted to stay in Tilburg. For wherever I lived, there the Motherhouse would be. His Excellency granted me six more weeks to stay in Tilburg.

Where should I go now? To go back was impossible; neither in north Germany nor in the southern part was it possible to obtain approbation. Neither was it possible in the Netherlands. Once more I had to venture out on the world's sea in my little bark. Trust in God was my rudder and the steering I left to God. At such hours I often pity "poor heaven." Everything is there except sufferings, the cross, pain, and sorrow. Passion flowers bloom only in this world. Isn't suffering, borne joyfully, "balm for the Savior's wounds?"

CHAPTER SEVEN

ENGLAND

In this time of need I once more had recourse to God, my Father, who always had been my refuge, and until now had shown me the way and guided me. After all, the Carmel of the Divine Heart of Jesus was the work of God, not mine. In our little oratory I entreated God, "Lord what would You have me do?"

The Lord heard my prayer and directed my thoughts to England. I recalled a story that I had heard in Rome. It was about the son of a Calvinist preacher from Zurich. He was quite young; I believe he was only about seventeen years of age. With some friends from the best families in Zurich, he turned Catholic, joined the Discalced Carmelites, then went to England and now lives in the Carmel of London, Kensington. This is the Carmel which Fr. Herman Cohen, the famous Jewish convert, had founded.

I wrote to him directly, describing my situation, and asked him to petition Cardinal Vaughan for admission into the diocese. The good Father Benedict complied with my request and sent an immediate answer.

"His Eminence did not grant the permission," Fr. Benedict Zimmermann wrote, "but if you come personally, you certainly will obtain it." What else could I do but follow his advice? I asked Father Benedict to make arrangements for us, and we would arrive in London on November 13 or 14.

Sr. Maria Theresia of St. Peter accompanied me again. From Vlissingen we went to London and then through that endless sea of houses to East End, the section of the

159

poorest people. Fr. Benedict had obtained a place for us with the French Sisters living there.

The next day we looked up Fr. Benedict who advised us about the best way of obtaining the permission. Following his advice, we were soon admitted to an audience. His Eminence was very kind. He concluded the audience with these words, "I am going to Rome. There I will make inquiries concerning you. In the meantime you may remain in my diocese."

Since Kensington was very far from East End and it cost money to get there and we had but little, we endeavored to locate a German-speaking priest to whom we could go to confession.

I asked the French Sisters the location of the nearest church. It was the Church of St. Michael. Trusting in the help of the Archangel, we made our way to that church, but we were sorry to be told that none of the priests spoke German. "But the pastor of the Guardian Angels Church, Fr. Green, speaks German," the sexton remarked. The next morning we went to Fr. Green and inquired if he knew of a good woman or family from whom we could rent a room, for it would probably take weeks before we would hear from His Eminence. The good priest showed great interest in us and gave us his assistance. After thinking a while, he gave us the name of Mrs. Buttler, a very good old lady who, although Protestant, had at various times boarded Catholic ladies. She lived not very far from the Guardian Angels Church. We looked her up without delay and found her to be an amiable old English woman who occupied a cozy home with her family. She had one spare room, and since it was vacant, we could rent it for the time being.

We were very happy, since the next day we could kneel

before a little house altar that we had hastily arranged and could pray, thanking God for this place of rest on our pilgrimage. At once I notified all my Sisters about our new address, and that there was hope that after the return of His Eminence from Rome we would get permission to establish a new home.

In Berlin conditions remained the same as when I had left in the year 1898. The eviction from the St. Joseph's Home had not taken place. Those in charge could not find a house suitable for the many Sisters and children, and the Reverend Delegate of St. Hedwig's did shrink, after all, from putting them out on the street without a roof over their heads. Nor could he find a Congregation that was willing to take the children free of charge.

Every morning we went to the poor little Guardian Angels Church. I think it had formerly been a Methodist Chapel. Due to necessity it now served as a dwelling place for our Divine Savior. The poor rectory harmonized with the poverty of the church, but as the miserable Chapel became a throne of grace through the King of Heaven, so did the rectory conceal a jewel in the person of the pastor, Fr. E. Green. As were many English priests, he was a convert who combined the spirit of self-sacrifice with a holy zeal for winning souls for the Divine Heart. For us, at that time, he was a gift of grace from God. Along with us he confidently hoped for the approbation of the Cardinal.

Not very far away was a German church, and repeatedly I was advised to call upon the German priest. An undefinable feeling prevented me from following the well-meant advice. Years later I learned that at that time Father S. of Bohemia was stationed there. He was the same Father who had caused me so much trouble and who intended to make use of the Homes at Marschen and my Sisters for his foundation.

How grateful I was to my guardian angel when I learned this, for certainly it was he who kept me from paying the German pastor a visit. How painful it would have been for me if suddenly I should have stood face to face with the priest who even in Berlin had left nothing undone to wrest from me or to destroy God's work.

This again was a lesson for me. How faithfully and attentively we must heed the voice of our interior! Above all else, we must preserve our soul in constant peace and the most profound tranquility. Come what may, nothing must penetrate that secret chamber, for it is God's dwelling place within us. Here abides the Divine Savior who dispenses His graces insofar as He finds us so disposed.

At times God reveals His will to us directly through the holy angels. This happened to me in Altstaetten where I clearly and distinctly heard the words, "Go to Schlieren." It is a wordless feeling that we must heed or else run the risk of straying from the way of God.

Toward the end of November, we moved into the little room of Mrs. Buttler. There we celebrated Christmas in seclusion. My companion shed many tears. She was homesick for St. Joseph's Home, for the forsaken Sisters, and for the children. Dense fog covered everything outside. At times we could barely see our hand before our eyes. Thus also my future was shrouded in thick, heavy fog. Furthermore, we suffered from physical ailments. Sr. Maria Theresia was troubled very much with pain in her stomach. It was a severe test, but likewise a great grace that the great God never allowed my confidence to weaken or wane, not even for a second.

His Eminence had returned from Rome in February, perhaps even in January, and daily we waited, but in vain, for the promised message. About this time we visited the Benedictine Abbey at Ramsgate and came in contact with the Order of St. Benedict, a very well-known Order in England. In the beginning of March, we received an invitation to come to the Abbey for the Feast of St. Benedict. There we would meet the Bishop, himself a Benedictine, and there was hope of obtaining his permission for a foundation.

I informed Fr. E. Green of this dim ray of hope. Without my knowledge he went directly to Cardinal Vaughan and told him about it. Now we immediately received an invitation to come to His Eminence. He received us very kindly and, after our conversation of some length, he took a piece of paper and wrote. He gave the paper to me, and with tears in my eyes I read it. It was not only permission to establish a house but also to open a novitiate.

"Now go to Maldon where you will meet a German Priest, Fr. Verres. He will help you find a house." With these words His Eminence closed the audience. Filled with gratitude, we knelt down, and His Eminence blessed us in the same manner as on the former occasion. As earlier I felt the hand of God in benediction upon my head. When the hands of His Eminence touched my head, I immediately recalled the blessing in the Chapel and in the refectory of the Pappelallee.

After a few days we went to Maldon. Fr. Verres had been informed of our coming, not only by us but also by His Eminence. He had been very busy trying to find a suitable, large house for us. He conducted us first to an old abbey, about one mile distant. A villa had been built adjoining this abbey. It was a beautiful property but not suitable for our purpose. However, just opposite the extremely poor Catholic Chapel, four small houses were being built. We selected those; two of them were almost finished. We fixed March 18 as our day of occupancy. We agreed to get the key at Fr. Verres' rectory. The owner lived somewhere else, and for this reason the agent had to obtain permission to connect the four houses with one another. All we had to do was to cut openings with doors and the four houses would form one unit.

I was overjoyed when M. Gabriela and some Sisters arrived in London on the morning of March 19. We went together at once to the station to take the train to Maldon. Our amiable landlady, Mrs. Buttler, and her youngest daughter accompanied us to the station. They insisted on doing so. I made use of this occasion once more to speak to Mrs. Buttler, that poor soul, regarding God.

She replied with these words, unforgettable for me, "I never needed God."

I asked in surprise, "But how is this possible?

She said, "I have a good husband and good children. We always enjoyed good health, not counting little ailments, and we have had all that we desired. I never needed God." These words spoken by the kind old lady of seventy-five sounded horrible to me.

I replied, "Dear Mrs. Buttler, since you had such a pleasant life, you ought at least thank God for it." This she promised to do.

How many millions of people there are with whom "all is well" and so "they do not need God!" Oh, those unfortunate people; how will they fare in their last hour? God, whom they never needed, for whom they have no regard, and whom they never worshiped, will stand before them as their judge. Some forsake God because, "all goes well with them," others because of their misfortune!

I would be willing to do anything in order to lead souls to our faith and to God. Nevertheless one is powerless before the will of the individual. Our Divine Savior Himself was not able to convert Israel to the faith. Thoughtlessness and overactivity lull the powers of the soul to sleep and frequently are the cause of infidelity. How is it possible that men endowed with reason and aware of the fact that one day they must die - and no one knows when death shall knock at the door - no one knows if he shall die young or old, after a long illness, or suddenly, how is it possible that they do not think of the beyond? What unhappy souls!

MALDON

After a two hour ride we reached Maldon and immediately went to Fr. Verres to obtain the house key. A surprise awaited us there. The owner of the houses had not given permission to the agent to make any changes, and for that reason the agent could not give us the keys. What were we to do now?

Without hesitation I went to the other two houses which were not completed and tried to open them. Sure enough, they were not locked. They were ready to be occupied except for the wallpaper and the plumbing. "Here we are," I said, "and here we stay." We began in great haste to unpack, looked for straw to fill the sacks, and arrange the rooms so that we could live in them. For seats we used the suitcases, and large boxes served as tables. Kind neighbors allowed us to draw water, after which all of us left for Mass. The house simply remained unlocked. Since no one disturbed us in the house of which we had taken possession, we procured the necessary furniture and used our time studying the English language. M.M. Francis and Sr. M. Rosa arrived on March 21.

From week to week we hoped that the owner would yield to our wishes, but he would not do so. The weeks had already become months when one day a neighbor of ours, a contractor, informed me that all the houses, two of which we occupied were up for auction sale. Now we might obtain the permission to make the changes that we had planned.

"No," I said, "we start immediately, but you must do it secretly."

"That will work fine," he said, "since my property borders on yours, I can bring my tools through the garden, and no one can see anything from the street."

The next day Mr. Baxter started to work. We were all very glad, for without the connection we were unable to arrange for a Chapel. Good Mr. Spurgeon, the agent, now handed us the keys, not only for the two houses of which we had taken possession, but also of the other two which we had rented. In consequence of this we had water. In the meantime, Bishop Brindle, auxiliary bishop of the diocese of Westminster, approached us concerning another foundation. He wanted us to purchase a house located in the center of the nearby city of Dumnow in order to gather the Catholics of the surrounding country.

I had little or no inclination to accept the offer. However, the least I could do was to inspect the place. Therefore we went to Dumnow. When we visited the little Chapel, we found our Divine Savior lonely and forsaken in the city, which was almost entirely Protestant. No priest resided there. On Sundays and feast days a Priest came from a monastery quite a distance away. We were moved by compassion and decided to accept the second foundation.

The work on the two houses in Maldon progressed very well without any disturbance, and we hoped soon to have the Blessed Sacrament with us.

I had left Sittard on September 15,1900, and thereby separated myself from the Blessed Sacrament for an indefinite time. Since November 14 we had lived in London like hermits and the days seemed endless indeed because of the uncertainty! We had been in Maldon since March. The end of June was near, and still we were waiting for our Divine Savior! Hopefully and joyfully we hastened to Maldon knowing not what lay ahead.

God had listened to my prayer to suffer for the return of England to the Church. For over twenty years (all the time we were in possession of the house in Maldon until we sold it), it was a source of trouble and trial. I am thankful to God, and confidently hope that in His mercy He has graciously accepted our "sufferings of atonement." On my part it was a sacrifice of love and gratitude. This was in view of the fact that St. Boniface and the other great missionaries who had won pagan Germany to Christ were Englishmen.

From day to day my yearning for the Blessed Sacrament grew stronger. I could no longer hide my tears. Even in the presence of the Sisters I wept bitterly, so great was my desire for our Divine Savior in the Tabernacle.

When the Chapel was almost finished, that is, when the mason work was finished, I asked Fr. Verres to obtain permission from the Dean to bless our Chapel and reserve the Blessed Sacrament. He went that same day to the Dean and returned on July 1 in the evening with the news that the petition had been granted. Our joy was indescribable until he added, "Tomorrow morning I will celebrate Mass here, and notify the Catholics living nearby as they will be glad to come."

We were frightened at first and I said, "That is impossible." Although we raised objections because of the debris lying in heaps in the Chapel, we could not make Father give up his intention of blessing the Chapel on July 2 in honor of our dear Lady.

Now we all went to work. Night was turned into day and by the next morning we had a sanctuary, poor indeed, but very devotional and ready for our Divine Savior. The Tabernacle was made of wood as was the manger in Bethlehem. Nevertheless it was ready to welcome Him as were the hearts, full of loving desire, of His brides who awaited Him.

July 2 is deeply significant for the entire Carmel of the Divine Heart of Jesus and for me. By this new grace it also became a special day for Maldon.

In the meantime we had also bought the house on Dumnow. On August 25, I went there with some Sisters for the purpose of making a foundation. The Blessed Sacrament was reserved on the Feast of St. Michael. Here we immediately opened a Home for poor children, that is, for little girls. In Maldon we made preparations for a Home for little boys.

November 21 was another day of great joy when twenty-two postulants, whom we had called from various St. Joseph's Homes, were invested. That is, it was a day of joy for the Sisters and novices, but for me it could hardly be called a day of joy. For me it was painful beyond words to see the oldest postulants here, while far away I knew that many children were in the hands of young candidates, most of whom I scarcely knew or did not know at all. The postulants who had just been invested had withstood every kind of opposition, persecution, and distress caused especially by some of the clergy.

My anxiety grew from week to week. I had been away from home for almost four years. Neither any of the oldest Sisters who had made their novitiate in Sittard nor I had ever visited the five houses in Berlin. It was indeed the work of God, or else it would have been impossible for them to exist under those conditions. True, all superiors were in constant correspondence with me, but they themselves were wanting in the necessary training, both as religious and as educators of children.

In my great concern about the Carmel of the Divine Heart in Berlin, I dared to ask Cardinal Kopp of Breslau for permission to visit Berlin in my religious garb. I enclosed a letter of Bishop Brindle, permitting the investiture, and stating that he himself would perform the ceremony. This, however, did not take place, since he was prevented from doing so. In reply to this letter I received the desired permission for a visitation of the Homes in Berlin.

In the first years, moved by compassion, I had admitted Mrs. Hiltl into the St. Joseph's Home. She was a good old lady who had become impoverished by the bank crash of 1874. The Sisters and children called her "Grandmother," and she was also loved and honored as such.

I think it was in the Fall of 1900 that I was instructed by the ministry in Berlin either to come to Berlin, since I was the superior of the St. Joseph's Homes, or else the institutions would be closed.

What was I to do? Cardinal Kopp remained firm in his resolution not to help me obtain either the approbation of the government in Berlin or the ecclesiastical approbation in Rome. The ill will of his Eminence toward the St. Joseph's Homes was no secret either to the ministry or to the government at Potsdam. In order to return as superior in my habit, I needed permission both of Breslau and of the ministry. Under the existing conditions, a permanent return was out of the question. I therefore proposed to the ministry that they recognize Mrs. Hiltl as my representative and superior of St. Joseph's Home and to grant her the concession. The ministry agreed to my proposal, and thus I had a rest for the time being from that side. It was a makeshift as it could not work for a long time. I could see no escape from these painful relations with Cardinal Kopp. It was a crushing cross and remained so until His Eminence departed this life in March 1914.

In January 1902 I went from England to Berlin. I found that Mrs. Hiltl had worked with great circumspection and that the candidates also were interested in the work. I was sorry, however, to observe among them quite a number who manifested little vocation for Carmel, and the future proved it so. I did what I could to inspire them with renewed enthusiasm and encouraged them to persevere. It was not possible for me to stay with them any longer, since a letter from Fr. Benedict Herzog, in Rome, informed me that if I wished to see the Father General I should come to Milan, as he was there on visitation.

I chose Sr. M. Bernardine and Sr. M. Mechtildis as my companions. The former was superior in Graupen, the latter was a very faithful postulant who suffered from ear trouble which the doctors in Berlin had declared serious. She had joined us in Zurich where she received treatments from a very good doctor. I took her with me so she could receive treatment once more from him.

How it happened I do not know, but I had a foreboding that during this trip we were to have a new foundation. Therefore I took along the necessary equipment for a Chapel and for the use of the Sisters.

After I had seen Father General, we returned by way of Lugano so that Sr. M. Mechtildis could go to Zurich. The other Sister and I planned to continue our journey.

The moment we left the train I saw a Visitation Sister at the station. It was Saturday, and since we wished to attend Mass the following day, we were compelled to stay there overnight. Thus I was anxious to find a suitable place to sleep. Quickly I walked up to this sister and was pleased to hear that her companion spoke very good German. With Italian cordiality and vivacity she took care of us. First she conducted us to an academy and remained for a while with us. During this time we made her acquainted with the Carmel of the Divine Heart of Jesus. She was very enthusiastic about this work of God and exclaimed, "I must call Madam Friedmann. She comes from Vienna every year and lives here for a few months. She is very interested in what is being done for the poor. She practices a great deal of charity herself, and they call her the 'Mother of the Poor.'"

It did not take long and both ladies knocked at the door. Madam Friedmann immediately recognized the value of our work, both for the children and the poor. Then she told us of Dr. Pestalozzi, a doctor from Zurich. "He is a saintly gentleman, full of zeal. I will write to him today, and you must found a convent here in Zurich. That will be a field of labor for you!"

Sunday morning after Mass the two ladies called again and Madam Friedmann informed us that she had already announced our coming to the Sisters of the Holy Cross in the hospital of Zurich, and that she had written to Dr. Pestalozzi.

The meeting of these two zealous ladies, their enthusiasm for the Carmel of the Divine Heart, and now this mission to Zurich appeared to me to be the work of the guiding hand of God. Consequently I anxiously waited as to where Divine Providence would direct us. After all, it had been my intention to let Sr. M. Mechtildis go alone to Zurich for her medical treatments while we other two had planned to travel through Switzerland without stopping. Again I anxiously waited to see where Divine Providence would lead us.

CHAPTER EIGHT

CARMEL OF THE DIVINE HEART OF JESUS
IN SWITZERLAND AND ITALY

In the dark of night we passed through the magnificent mountains of Switzerland. At daybreak we were in the valley, and soon Zurich lay before us.

While my eyes rested upon Zurich, of whose infidelity I had heard so much since the days of my youth, indescribable compassion gripped my heart and tears filled my eyes. Instantly I recalled the Divine Savior's grief and sorrow over Jerusalem, and the great desire seized my heart to be allowed to suffer, to pray, and to work for Switzerland.

The shrill scream of the whistle startled me out of my reverie. The train came to a stop; we were in Zurich. Dear Sr. M. Mechtildis was very well acquainted here, and we were soon in the beautiful new hospital of the Sisters of the Holy Cross, who welcomed us most cordially.

Since all the mail was still forwarded to me, it was again my first duty to inform my Sisters of my new address in Zurich. While my companions rested from the trip I mailed my letters. In the hall I noticed a priest and the Sister Superior standing together. In order to remain unobserved, I endeavored to gain the side entrance, but I did not succeed in my ruse, as I was to discover later.

Toward noon a Sister approached me and said that the pastor of Altstetten wished to see me. I thought it was a mistake, since I did not know anybody here. "No," the Sister replied, "the pastor wants to know whether he could speak with the Sister Superior after dinner."

We met the pastor of Altstetten in the parlor after din-

ner. He told us that he was out collecting money to pay
the debt on the church. He had seen me in the hallway,
and all morning he was pursued by the thought to speak
to me and ask me to come to Altstetten. Thirteen hamlets
belonged to his parish, which made it a great field of
labor. This labor was even more difficult as not only were
the villages far away, some were located in the mountains. For two years he had made a momento in Holy
Mass to obtain Sisters.

We had followed his words with great interest and
promised to come to Altstetten to look at the place. In the
meantime we had learned that Dr. Pestalozzi was not in
Zurich at the time. Hence the invitation looked to me as
coming from God.

Our visit to Altstetten stimulated me more than ever to
do all in my power to establish a convent there. First of
all we had to obtain the approbation of the Bishop of
Chur. If we could obtain that, I would make certain that
this foundation would be in accordance with the will of
God. The pastor promised to take care of the approbation
himself. The next day we inquired if one or two rooms
could be found in Altstetten where we could stay until we
got word from Chur. The pastor declared that after having given the matter more thought, he was of the opinion
that it would be best for us to go to Chur ourselves. Two
rooms were found near the church, and while I went to
Chur, the other two Sisters moved to Altstetten.

In Chur I met the ailing Bishop B. His Excellency listened with great interest, but no matter how expedient
our work might be for the Swiss conditions, a foundation
could not be considered, since all foundations of religious
were prohibited by law.

"But," I replied, "we are still without ecclesiastical

approbation. Perhaps this might make it possible to obtain permission." Even then His Excellency did not think there was a possibility.

Once more I asked for his permission to let me try to obtain permission for the opening of a Home for children in Altstetten. "In case I obtain it, may I hope for your permission?"

He replied, "Yes, go and try, but I believe it will be in vain. However, I give you my blessing." Full of joy, I returned home. It did not appear to me that there were anymore difficulties or obstacles to overcome.

My Sisters shared my happiness. So did the pastor, although, like the Bishop, he did worry concerning the civil approbation.

First of all we had to find a large house or estate. The pastor made various propositions, but after a close inspection we found them unsuitable for our purpose. One morning, while engaged in writing letters in my spare time, as was my custom, I clearly and distinctly heard, though inaudible to my companions, these words, "Go to Schlieren!"

In a moment I was convinced that it was a command from God. After dinner I proposed to my companions that we take a walk to Schlieren. None of us knew the place. When we came to the main street Sr. M. Bernadine suggested that we take the road to the right. On the contrary, I thought that Schlieren was to the left. Both Sr. M. Bernadine and Sr. M. Mechtildis followed me although they were in doubt. Soon we met a young woman who positively assured us that we were on the right road to Schlieren. All we had to do was to follow the streetcar tracks.

After about fifty minutes we reached the first houses of

Schlieren. A few paces away in the middle of the road two men were standing and talking with one another. I approached them and asked if they perhaps knew of a house that was for rent here in Schlieren. I had barely spoken the last words when one of them, instead of answering my question, said, "A Catholic woman lives in this house." At the same time he called, "Mrs. Mathis!" Immediately a woman appeared in the window, and when she saw us, she quickly came down and greeted us very cordially, for in Switzerland, Sisters are seldom seen. I told her of the purpose of our coming, namely, that we were looking for a large house suitable for a Home for children and a Chapel. I further stated that we would either rent or buy the property. "There," she said pointing to the house across the street, "this house is for sale. It has no garden but you can buy the meadow which belongs to the neighbor."

"Is this not Divine Providence?" I thought to myself. We find the town, the name of which we had never heard and stop in front of the house that is for sale. Since it was without a garden, we continued our search for another house, but our efforts were in vain. A larger house could not be found. We obtained the address of the owner, returned home, and asked the pastor what he thought of Schlieren. He reported that he found the town to be an excellent one. He said that it was the best of all the villages, and that a Chapel was most necessary there. Four-hundred Catholics, mostly laborers, lived in Schlieren. Some of them were Italians. Because of the great distance, only a few, perhaps ten or twenty persons came to church in Altstetten. The pastor was very surprised, and his joy was great when we told him that we had already found a house. I asked him for the name of a man who knew how to handle the transaction and could be of help to us. He promised to introduce us to a gentleman worthy of our confidence. Soon the transaction of the sale began; yet before I closed the deal, I had to get the permission of the President of the Canton of Zurich (I think that was the government official) or his representative. Confidently I called the gentleman. In reality the Sisters and I were private persons who had founded a private society since we lacked everything required for an ecclesiastical congregation. We were without a Motherhouse and had no ecclesiastical approbation. We did indeed have episcopal approbation for establishing Homes for children, but each one was valid only in the diocese for which it was given. Hence, by right and by law, we did not fall under the law of restrictions which applied to "ecclesiastical congregations."

The official received me politely. I calmly answered all the questions he asked me, and obtained permission to open a Home for children in Schlieren but for Catholic children exclusively.

Immediately I brought the good news to the pastor, and there were no further obstacles to the opening of a home. I informed the Bishop of Chur and asked him at the same time for the promised approbation and for permission to establish a public Chapel.

After a few days I received from the Bishop all that I had asked for and his blessing for the new foundation. Full of gratitude and joy that we could offer a St. Joseph's Home to the Swiss children, we soon moved to Schlieren.

The house had thirty-eight rooms and was arranged for many small families. One suite, consisting of three rooms and all the necessary furnishings was vacant. Therefore on Wednesday of Holy Week, March 25, 1902, we moved in.

I was compelled by a severe cold to remain in bed. It was no small sacrifice for me to be unable to attend Holy Mass during the Easter days, but another cross was added to this misery.

For about two years, despite trying circumstances, peace and harmony had reigned in St. Joseph's Home in the Pappelallee. This home was under the provisional management of good Mrs. Hiltl. In the Spring of 1902, however, our opponents succeeded at last in convincing most of the postulants that they could never become Sisters as long as they remained with me. The discontented ones at last upset the peace of the house completely.

Silence was no longer kept from morning until night, but standing here and there the postulants discussed when they should follow the recommendation of the Pastor or the Chaplain and leave St. Joseph's Home. The postulants who paid no attention to the disturbers of the peace were stopped any number of times and asked to leave with them. The reason, they were told, was that St. Joseph's Home would never be a success, and that within a short time it would be closed, and the postulants would have to join another community. The few who remained faithful and loyal declared firmly and emphatically, "We stay as long as the Blessed Sacrament remains in the Tabernacle." Such were the contents of the letter that reached me during the Easter days of 1902 in Schlieren!

From my bed I wrote Cardinal Kopp that for the first time in all these years a great dissatisfaction had been caused among the postulants of St. Joseph's Home, and that we could no longer continue under the direction of the laywoman Mrs. Hiltl. I besought him most earnestly that he permit me to send two Sisters in their religious garb. These Sisters were suitable for this mission as they had finished their novitiate at Sittard. This time His Eminence did me the great favor and sent the desired permission without delay. Immediately I sent a telegram to M. Paula Maria, who was in Tilburg, to go to Berlin with Sister C. I had already informed them concerning the entire situation and of my petition to His Eminence, and they were instructed to hurry to the Pappelallee in order to restore peace and harmony. M. Paula Maria departed without delay and wrote a letter to me from Berlin. She had been received with joy and great cheer, and after she had dismissed the worst troublemakers, peace and quiet returned.

As soon as I was well again, I did all I could to clear the house in Schlieren of the many renters. Most of them left within a short time, but we had considerable trouble with the family that occupied the best rooms on the first floor. We were most interested in these rooms because we planned to remodel them for a Chapel. I think it was not until May that these rooms became vacant. At that time a few walls were hurriedly removed, an arch was built over the sanctuary, and we found an Italian painter who decorated the sanctuary and Chapel. All was simple but tasteful. By the middle of June, all was in readiness for the reception of our Divine Savior. To the great joy of all Monsignor Schmid von Grueneck, Vicar General at that time (later on Bishop of Chur), came himself to bless the Chapel and reserve the Blessed Sacrament.

After the blessing, about one hundred persons hurried up the steps and filled the Chapel to the hallway. During Mass Monsignor preached a touching sermon, and when the Mass was ended he went to the organ and not only intoned the *Te Deum* but also accompanied the singing. That day, June 16, 1902, was a day of great joy not only for all of us who had been led almost miraculously to Switzerland by Divine Providence but also for the Catholics of Schlieren.

I had appointed Mother M. Bernardine as superior. Some Sisters and postulants had already arrived, and thus we could open a Home for children within a short time.

Two of the Sisters coming from England had traveled by way of Tilburg. I was surprised and shocked to hear that in that place Sisters and postulants were about to leave the Carmel due to the persuasion of the pastor of St. Anne Church. The Netherland postulants had already left and the other Sisters had their belongings packed. The pastor had declared that we would never get the approbation of Rome. Can anyone blame the young Sisters from weakening when a priest robs them of their confidence in such a manner?

On June 18 I left Schlieren. First I went to the two Homes in Bohemia for a brief visit. There the Sisters lived in peace and charity while making every effort to please God by making the poor children happy. Their contentment in the face of great poverty was most touching.

Next I went to Berlin to the little hospice in Anhalt Street. As fast as possible I sought to remove the obstacles and difficulties that had again developed in the four Homes for children. I worked in haste in order to get to Tilburg as quickly as I could.

On the eve of the day I had set for my departure for Tilburg, I received a post card from Monsignor (later Archbishop) Pisani telling me to hurry to the Pappelallee because the following morning Bishop Bonamelli of Cremona wished to celebrate Holy Mass with us. Bishop

Bonamelli happened to be in Berlin at that time on a visit to the Italian emigrants.

I immediately rode to the Pappelallee in a closed carriage, because I was not permitted to be seen on the streets in my habit. This also applied to the two Sisters who lived in St. Joseph's Home. They were permitted to wear the habit only in the house.

The next morning after Mass we had over 200 children assembled in the hall. His Excellency was visibly touched at the sight of the great number of little children dressed in white who, like little angels, crowded about him without fear.

When I expressed my regret at not having a house in Italy, the Bishop manifested his satisfaction by saying, "Come to Cremona; I hereby give you my approbation for establishing a Home for boys." Joyfully I accepted the offer, and we agreed that toward the New Year I would come to Cremona with some of the Sisters.

In the evening I took the train to Tilburg and arrived just in time to save one of the Sisters who had made her novitiate in Sittard in 1899. This Sister has persevered. I remained until some Sisters came to help them, and after inspiring them with renewed confidence, I returned to Maldon.

We stopped in London to call on Monsignor S., a Belgian, since all religious of the diocese of Westminster were subject to him. I asked for permission to have the profession of the novices made in Maldon. The permission was granted. However, when half of the retreat exercises preparatory to the profession were over, Father Benedict, O.C.D., received a telegram from Monsignor S. stating, "Stop retreat—letter follows." I cannot recall whether the letter arrived or whether Father Benedict went to London of his own accord. At any rate, we received the order not to allow the novices to make profession for the reason that our Constitutions had not been approved.

Thanks be to God! The novices bore the sad news in the same spirit of sacrifice shown by the novices in Sittard a few years previous. To serve God and save souls was their heart's desire. We left the decision to God as to whether or not we would have a profession. With renewed zeal we offered ourselves to God as victims; then I clothed the novices with the brown veil.

Shortly thereafter I sent some of the Sisters to Switzerland. Others I set aside for the new foundation in Cremona, while I believe some of them went to Tilburg. The foundation in Italy meant much to me, but I did not want to leave the Sisters in Maldon before Christmas. Therefore, if a ferry would depart on that day, I decided to leave with M. M. Johanna on December 26.

I was in a hurry, for I seemed to be haunted with a foreboding of an obstacle that would detain me. In my excitement it never occurred to me that on December 25 and 26 there is no mail delivery in England. As a precaution I had ordered the Sister who had the key to the mailbox not to go to the mailbox on December 26, but to keep it locked until we had departed. In addition I instructed her to forward the mail on December 27. This was done.

Cardinal Vaughan, who was always well-disposed toward us, was seriously ill and died in 1903. For that reason in Maldon and Dumnow we were entirely under the jurisdiction of Monsignor S., who showed us little good will. On the occasion of my very first visit, when he learned that I had altered the Rule and Constitutions of

St. Teresa to fit modern conditions, he tried his very best to draw me away from Carmel. When he realized that I was willing to die for Carmel, he was compelled to desist from any further attempts. Because of my devotion to Carmel, we had to suffer very much at his hands during all those years. Whenever an opportunity offered itself, he let us feel his ill will.

We landed safely in the Netherlands and continued our journey through Bavaria to Italy. In Nuernberg we stopped to call on Fr. Hauck (later Archbishop of Bamberg) who welcomed us most cordially. In the meantime the mail from England had been delivered here, and I received a letter from Monsignor S. "forbidding" me to leave England in the course "of the coming year."

Thanks be to God, we said, that we had left England when we did, as it would be impossible to comprehend how many commands and prohibitions would have been directed to the ten St. Joseph Homes during my absence.

CREMONA

While crossing the Brenner, we were held up by an avalanche, and we were forced to return to Innsbruck. In consequence we did not arrive in Cremona until January 2, 1903. Monsignor Lombardi, who was at that time the secretary of the bishop, received us most cordially. He was dismayed, however, when he noticed that I did not understand him and could not speak Italian! I did understand a little Italian, but the preceding sleepless nights had deprived me of all my ability in the language; still less could I speak it. However, after a few days I fared better.

Until we could find a home, a lady had offered us free of charge some vacant rooms in her "palazzo". M. Johanna and myself were busy in procuring the most necessary furniture for a number of Sisters. To our great joy the Sisters arrived from Maldon, and now we studied Italian with great diligence. We had a teacher, a most amiable lady, who lived in the same "palazzo" and who instructed us without pay. She had been educated by the Sisters of the Visitation in the convent of Zangberg and spoke German fluently.

All the Sisters learned the beautiful language with great enthusiasm and soon became accustomed to the new surroundings. Every nation and country has its own customs and practices. Consequently, whoever wishes to educate children must first of all adapt himself to the chacteristics of the people and learn to love the nation. Indeed every nation has its own way of living, its own character, and every nation has something worth loving.

As in all other places, here also we started in greatest poverty, since we were practically without income. Bishop Bonamelli paid us a visit, and he was touched when he saw our poverty within the enclosure. At the same time, however, he was edified by the spirit of the Sisters, all of whom were cheerful and content.

In Cremona the bark of my life was anchored for the present in calm and security. I was busily engaged with the Sisters in the study of the Italian language. Yet this time of peace was of short duration! As a dream or a sunny day in April vanishes, so did our peace. A fresh storm arose which to all appearances threatened not only to tear my bark from its moorings but also to drown me within the depths of the sea!

Monsignor Lombardi, at that time Don Emilio, called on us one day. He made the introductory remark that today he was a harbinger of bad news. Bishop Bonamelli had sent him to deliver the following confidential information. His Excellency had received a letter from London from Canon S. concerning me, in regards to my disobedience to Cardinal Kopp and the Bishop of Roermond. It stated that contrary to his prohibition, I had permitted the Sisters in Sittard to make profession at the end of the retreat. His further wrote that contrary to the orders of Cardinal Vaughan of Westminster in London, who had forbidden me to leave England "within a year," I had left Maldon. It was a long letter full of "misdeeds" on my part.

After Bishop Bonamelli had read this letter he remarked, "Whoever writes a letter of this kind about another person, without any provocation, must be a bad character." Monsignor Lombardi added, "Now, His Excellency wants me to tell you to go to Rome and do all in your power to obtain the approbation. His Excellency will give you a recommendation to Cardinal Ferrata who is a good friend of his."

This was the conclusion of the confidential message. Although externally calm, internally I was completely crushed for the moment. Again it was injustice that wounded me so deeply. The letter containing the order "not to leave England" had reached me in Bavaria on my way to Cremona, and now my departure, which had taken place on December 26, was looked upon as disobedience on my part.

Cardinal Vaughan was ill, near death, and certainly knew nothing of this letter, nor did he ever learn of the order to close both convents of the Carmel of the Divine Heart. When the priest of Maldon hastened to the sickbed of the Cardinal to obtain the revocation of the two communities of Maldon and Dumnow, the Cardinal remarked, "I have never heard anything evil of the Carmelite Sisters, and therefore they remain in both places."

Full of gratitude, I went to the Chapel next to the parlor and sank on my knees. I was filled with gratitude and joy, although my nature recoiled from sufferings. Many, many times I sent this ejaculation to God, "O Lord, refresh my soul with trials!" This was my source of grace.

CHAPTER NINE

THE SECOND JOURNEY TO ROME

On May 9, 1903, I went to Rome with Sister C. with the idea of looking for help. This time our misfortune started soon after we had begun, for our traveling money lasted only as far as Florence. There was nothing else to do but to look for some generous soul who would help us in our need and then take the next train. Through the kind help of a Sister of the Holy Cross we obtained sufficient money to reach Rome. However, the funds were not sufficient enough to take us from the station to St. Martha, the Vatican Hospice in which the Vincentian Sisters have charge of visitors who come to Rome.

Sister Theresia Bong, the superior of the house, had been born in Cologne, and was the sister of Monsignor Bong in Cologne. M. Johanna and I had paid Monsignor Bong a visit on our way from England. We wanted to stop at Sittard, and thus we had to pass through Cologne. At the time when I was in Lindenburg, he was rector of the house of the "Good Shepherd" at Melaten, a suburb of Cologne. As we had known each other since 1886, our conversation consisted of renewing old memories. I owe very much to the prayers of this saintly priest and the Sisters of his convent. At the end of my visit I made use of the opportunity to ask Monsignor on which feast day I had made the decision to join the Church. In his inimitable composure he took his little notebook from his inner pocket, paged for a while, then said, "It was June 17, 1887, Feast of the Sacred Heart." It was a great joy for me to learn at last (in December 1902) on which feast I had received the inexpressible grace which prompted me to join the Church, or rather, to ask for admission into it. I was filled with honor, praise, and thanks to the Divine Heart of Jesus for all eternity!

Now let us return to Rome and to St. Martha. Monsignor Bong had announced our coming to his sister. She received us kindly but told us that even though she was superior, we could have a room only for a short time in the hospice. Therefore we were instructed that we should look for another place as soon as possible. She explained that the small number of Sisters were overburdened with work. I told her that in order not to add to the work of the Sisters, we would gladly prepare our own meals as we had done on previous occasions. I did mention, however, that we would appreciate it if we could take our breakfast at the hospice. She agreed to my proposal. Naturally it had never occurred to me that we would have nothing to eat or drink until the next morning, but that is what happened, due, no doubt, to a misunderstanding. Luckily, our Sisters had provided us well with bread and fruit. They were also willing to send us money from different convents. With this in mind I sent my companion every day to the Superior to call for my mail. Nevertheless her visits were always in vain. She was always told that no letters had arrived for me.

Now we had no money to buy anything. Coffee and bread and a few fruits from Cremona had to suffice not only for the day but for six days! At last, on the sixth day, we received the expected letter. The letter had come the first day after our arrival, as Sister Theresia remarked, but she had believed that we were Franciscan Sisters and therefore had forwarded it to a convent of Carmelite Nuns, and only today the letter had been returned, but it had been opened.

Holy Father St. Joseph had watched over the contents, for it still contained the eighty marks. Without delay we bought the necessary provisions to recover from our strict fast.

In the meantime I was constantly pursued by the thought of continuing this mode of living to the end of my life. This I would do (if my confessor would permit it) in reparation and for the salvation of souls, in union with the intention of the Divine Heart of Jesus. The thought was very painful for me, but I overcame myself. The Father immediately gave the permission. I now vowed to God, "Never to eat cooked food to the end of my life." This mortification, like all other sufferings and hardships, I endured in reparation.

After two weeks, Monsignor Jacquemin was kind enough to permit us to stay for a few weeks with his Sisters until we could find a place where we could board. We had lived there only a few weeks when my companion developed a fever and became very sick. At last I found a large room with the Gray Sisters in the Via Olmata, and there we stayed until September. Since Sister C. was too weak to accompany me on the many trips I had to make, I was compelled to call for another Sister.

During the first days of my stay in Rome, I had called on Cardinal Ferrata with the recommendation from Bishop Bonamelli. His Eminence received me very graciously. He then asked me, "Where is your Motherhouse?" I replied that we had no Motherhouse because Cardinal Kopp would not give us his permission to consider the first house in Berlin to be the Motherhouse. His Eminence responded, "That makes your case very difficult." After thinking a while, he sent me to a monsignor to submit the affair to him. This I did, and this monsignor, in turn, referred me to another. Thus I went from one to another and in the meantime also to some cardinals. All of them were kind and sympathetic, but no one could do anything for me until we had a Motherhouse outside of Rome.

Formerly the situation had been different, but when Leo XIII was Pope, a decree had been published not to give approbation to any Congregation which did not have a "Motherhouse outside of Rome approved by the bishop." The Motherhouse forms the natural foundation of an Order or Congregation. It is the root out of which the trunk and crown grow and where its life originates. We were wanting in a foundation although we had houses or St. Joseph's Homes in seven dioceses and numbered about one hundred Sisters, including the postulants. Because Cardinal Kopp refused permission to consider the first house in Berlin as the Motherhouse, none of the other bishops would grant the approbation for me. This was an act of Divine Providence.

From this difficulty with Cardinal Kopp arose a chain of difficulties that appeared to be endless, even insurmountable. However, though I could get neither advice nor find help, my confidence remained firm, and my hope of success never wavered. God had showered many graces upon me; they too formed a chain that was deeply engraved upon my memory. A glance at this chain of graces sufficed to spur me on and enkindle in me renewed courage, confidence, and energy to continue my efforts to break, with a strong hand, this chain of difficulties and thus arrive at the goal: the Motherhouse and ecclesiastical approbation.

Prayer was the anvil on which I hoped to break that chain. I prayed every spare moment. By myself I made three novenas, climbing the Scala Santa (Holy Stairs) on my knees. How easy it is in this quiet spot to meditate on the sufferings of the Divine Savior! When one sinks down at the "Confessio" in St. Peter's, then the soul is immersed in God and in the heart of God which is full of infinite mercy! My great devotion to St. Lawrence led me to his holy relics. Before his feast I made a novena there early in the morning accompanied by a Sister. I prayed for help and asked for light to get out of this labyrinth of difficulties. Yet (and I admit this in a whisper), I personally had a nervous anxiety. This anxiety was that after our affairs would be well ordered and we had our Motherhouse, our dear Lord might have no more trials for me!

To live without suffering appeared unbearable to me. At the present I seemed to float on storm-whipped waves, carried along by confidence in God and love. How would it be possible to practice confidence and love if I were no longer on the stormy sea and on the ocean of suffering?

One of the oldest Sisters, M. Gabriela, made me promise not to pray for further "sufferings" for fear we would never reach our goal. For love of my Sisters, I did violence to myself and did whatever the highest and wisest counselors told me to try. Therefore, with one exception, I likewise kept my promise to pray no longer for sufferings.

On one of the feast days in July, I asked Sister C. to accompany me to "Quo Vadis," a little Chapel outside Rome. According to a legend, St. Peter was fleeing from Rome, and here on the Via Appia, where the Chapel stands, the Divine Savior, with a cross in His arms and walking hurriedly, appeared to the Apostle. St. Peter was frightened and exclaimed: *Quo vadis?* "Where are You going?" The Savior looked at Peter sadly and said, "To Rome, to let Myself be crucified." St. Peter lowered his eyes in repentance, but before he could say anything, his Master had vanished. Peter, however, had understood the look and words of his Lord. He hastened back to Rome to let himself be crucified. Peter had yielded to the urgent entreaties of his friends who wished to preserve his life, and so he fled. However he was now strengthened again by grace, and he returned to become the "Rock" upon which the Savior could build His Church.

It was a very hot day. At last we reached the Chapel. I knelt down on the floor, at the feet of the Savior carrying the cross, and began to pray. Yes, my passion for suffering immediately overcame my resolutions and promises, and I prayed for sufferings. As a traveler dying of thirst begs for a drink, so did I pray to God to let me drink further from the chalice of suffering.

"My dearest Savior, heaven has all things, but it has no sufferings; therefore, let me suffer and suffer, only suffer on this earth."

To save souls was the one desire of my heart. Souls, which pride and every kind of passion have violently torn, and will tear, out of the arms of the Divine Savior. The will of God and the purpose of my life was to gain those souls again for the Divine Heart.

A religious preacher can hasten out into the world and with fiery sermons stir up souls and lead them back to the faith and to the Church. What is a poor Sister to do in order to attain the same purpose and gain the same end, that is, to win unnumbered souls for the Divine Heart? The solution is nothing else, but to suffer, atone, and pray!

I had prayed quite a while when, becoming conscious of my companion, I arose and left the Chapel. Before the door she told me that she had prayed for my intention. I was frightened and asked, "Now what did we do? Forgetful of my promise, I prayed for sufferings."

On Sunday, during the novena to St. Lawrence, the three of us were walking in the Via St. Giovanni, south of the Lateran, in order to see if we could find a suitable house for us. Cardinal S. has advised me to look for a house so that in the event that we obtained the approbation we could immediately furnish it.

Toward the end of the street Sister C. asked me, "Mother, have you seen the cross above the door of the house we just passed?"

"No," I replied, "but let us turn back and inquire what it means."

The house, above the door of which there was a small cross, was open. We met a woman in the hallway and asked the meaning of the cross over the door. She replied, "Here is the Chapel which our Cardinal prepared because the church is too far away."

Then I asked, "Who celebrates Holy Mass here?"

"Don Adolfo, don't you know Don Adolfo, the chaplain?"

"No, I do not know Don Adolfo. Where does he live?"

"Opposite the Lateran," she replied.

The good woman was still more surprised when I continued to ask, "Who is your cardinal?"

She replied, "Cardinal Satolli."

I thanked her for the information and returned with my Sisters to the city. Yet while quietly walking along I was interiorily agitated. I could not rid myself of the thought that this insignificant incident was the finger of God and the answer to my novena to St. Lawrence.

We reached the church of the Lateran at the time when Vespers were ended and a number of priests in surplice were leaving the Chapel. I went to one of the servers and asked for Don Adolfo.

After a little while Don Adolfo appeared. In a few words I explained to him that we were looking for a parish in which we could take care of little children.

"Wait a minute; the Cardinal is still here." With these words he hurried away. A few minutes later he returned with the message, "Come tomorrow forenoon at 10 o'clock for an audience with Cardinal Satolli."

At the audience the next morning I submitted my case to His Eminence. I did not forget to tell him that we had no Motherhouse. Our work in behalf of the people and the poor children won the interest of His Eminence. More than once he remarked, "That is a holy work." Then he expressed the wish that we open a home for children in the Lateran parish, but first of all he would have to speak to the Cardinal Vicar of Rome. In great expectation I waited for the answer. But in place of the desired permission, I was told the permission for the foundation in Rome could not be granted until we had a Motherhouse outside of Rome.

Once again we received the same response. . . the same answer!

In the meantime August had passed, and in September most of the Cardinals leave the Eternal City and the Congregations are closed. Hence, there was nothing further to do or accomplish.

Five months passed. They were months full of trials, efforts, and sacrifices of every kind and to all appearances without results. Yet this was not the case, as the future will show. Now I was advised by Monsignor Jacquemin to go back to Cremona and return to him in January in order to resume the work anew.

We were in Rome at the time of the death of Pope Leo XIII, the time of the conclave, and the coronation of Pope Pius X. Despite all this, our life was a penitential life rather than anything else. To be restricted to one room in the hottest days of summer in Rome calls for self-denial and is far from being a pleasure.

In Cremona I still found the Sisters in the "palazzo" as I had left them. The Sisters at least had advanced one little step. They finally had found two houses which were for sale. I inspected them but neither was suitable. However it would not seem advisable to wait any longer. Hence we bought the house owned by Signor Sacchi, who was a minister. Though anti-religious, he was always kind and benevolent toward us.

On the Feast of All Saints in 1903, we took possession of our own convent. We prepared a Chapel with great energy and joy, and soon the Blessed Sacrament was reserved. In a like manner we got everything ready for the admission of the boys. After a few weeks the large rooms were filled with lovely little brown-eyed boys. This was a great joy for me.

CHAPTER TEN

THE THIRD JOURNEY TO ROME

In the beginning of January 1904, I again went to Rome with M. Bernardine. This time we stayed with the good Sisters of the Holy Cross in Via St. Basilio. On February 12 we moved to the Sisters of St. Charles Borromeo behind St. Peter's. We stayed there until June 17. A very kind French Superior was generous enough to let us have a large room.

One of our first visits was to Father Antonio, O.C.D., provincial at the time and consultor of the Sacred Congregation of Religious. He later would become Archbishop in Sicily until his death in 1924. After a friendly greeting he informed us that we were now permitted to use the little breviary of the Sacred Heart in Latin, since it had been approved. I was very glad. I had anxiously awaited the approbation because before that I could not arrange our office. While most Congregations have the Little Office of the Blessed Mother, our office is composed of the same psalms, but the hymns, antiphons, and prayers are taken from the office of the Sacred Heart. After the arrangement was finished, it was approved in writing by the Vatican and then immediately printed in Rome. Since 1904 the Carmel of the Divine Heart has its own proper office of the Sacred Heart.

Again all our efforts to obtain a Motherhouse seemed to be in vain. Easter was approaching, and there was no sign of help. As we had done on our first visit, we again had recourse to St. Mother Teresa of Jesus and began a novena to Maria della Scala. On the third day of the novena, I went to Monsignor Jacquemin and asked whether a bishop in the neighborhood of Rome would be willing to give us permission for a Motherhouse, for I had learned that there were a number of dioceses in the neighborhood of Rome. Monsignor Jacquemin replied, "Stay by all means with Cardinal Satolli; he is interested in your work. He is Bishop of Frascati. I will speak to him myself."

At last there was a ray of hope! Monsignor Jacquemin spoke to us on Tuesday morning, and on Wednesday we were to hear from him. You may easily imagine how anxiously we awaited that message, for, notwithstanding our numerous failures, I was firmly convinced that we would have success.

Monsignor Jacquemin, with his usual kindness and charity, had called as early as Tuesday evening on Cardinal Satolli, and His Eminence awaited us on Thursday to grant us the desired permission. Monsignor Jacquemin, our saintly counselor, shared our happiness. He left it to His Eminence to give us the details.

At the appointed hour His Eminence received us graciously and with great kindness. He gave us the permission to found a Motherhouse and novitiate in his diocese. In Rocca di Papa some Sisters moved out of a convent which we were to buy.

"Come to Frascati Tuesday after Easter. I will meet you there. Don Lorenzo will accompany you to Rocca di Papa," he added as he closed the audience.

Was it true? Was it reality? It had seemed impossible to procure a Motherhouse, and now, within a few minutes we had obtained the necessary permission. It seemed like a dream, yet it was the truth. It was a fact. Everything had been given us, assurance was given that we would become a religious Community with ecclesiastical approbation. Full of gratitude we hastened to the Tabernacle in the nearby Lateran church.

Early Tuesday morning we rode for about an hour's distance to Frascati where His Eminence received us very kindly and graciously. Then His Eminence introduced us to Don Lorenzo, who formerly had been procurator of the major seminary and now was chaplain in Rocca di Papa. After a brief discussion, we were on our way to Rocca di Papa accompanied by Don Lorenzo.

The convent which we were to take over was the former Plazzo Overbeck, named after the well-known German painter who lived there. Achtermann, the famous German sculptor, had lived a little higher up on the hill. He had built a little Chapel and had ended his saintly life in Rome.

There was also a private Chapel in the Palazzo Overbeck. Don Carlo, the oldest priest in Rocca di Papa, told us many things about Achtermann, whom the people venerated as a saint. His kindness and benevolence had won the hearts of all. He was like a pioneer to us German Sisters who were told to settle here.

The magnificent view and the woods that belonged to the convent gradually made us forget our first terrible impression caused by the dilapidated condition of the building. First of all it was necessary to settle the very complicated transactions of the sale of the property. Fortunately, Signor Passarelli, who had built the Carmelite Church of St. Teresa, assisted me a great deal. After we had agreed on the price, we decided to move in on June 17. A number of the older Sisters from the novitiate of Sittard and Maldon had already arrived in Rome. After we had obtained the blessing of the Holy Father, Pius X, we rode up to the "Rock of Peter," Rocca di Papa.

We got the old Chapel of Overbeck ready for the time

being and already on July 2 the Blessed Sacrament was reserved. To my great joy Don Carlo, the venerable old priest, celebrated Holy Mass here for the first time in a long while. In fact, it was he who celebrated the last Mass offered there.

Praise, glory, and gratitude filled our hearts as well as awe and wonder. We certainly had experienced that the ways of the Holy Spirit are wonderful indeed. Wonderful are the ways of Divine Providence.

From Berlin, the fortress of Protestantism, as it was justly called until the overthrow of the imperial power, Divine Providence had guided the Carmel of the Divine Heart of Jesus from south to north, from north to west, again south, and farther to the south to the Rock of the Holy Father. The Carmel of the Divine Heart of Jesus was to be founded on this rock.

After a struggle and battle for thirteen years, the impossible became a reality. If the Carmel of the Divine Heart had been the work of man, its enemies and adversaries would have lived to see their prophecy fulfilled: that the St. Joseph's Home will never become a Congregation. But it was the work of God, and God permitted these uninterrupted trials and obstacles for His own glory.

Thanks be to God, a new trial welcomed me immediately on the "Rock of Peter." The house was not free from occupants, as we had expected. A lady, a Sister, and a housekeeper still lived in it. The lady had paid the Sisters for the right to stay there for life and would not vacate the room until her money was refunded.

Furthermore, an old lady, the former superior of the convent, now refused to move. On the record, the deed was in her name. These painful negotiations were protracted for eight weeks, but the deal was finally closed on

August 25 after some very exciting negotiations that lasted for hours.

With the exception of these three persons and two other ladies, the Community had left the convent a few years previously. Hence the entire estate, woods and garden included, looked like a wilderness.

As soon as the strangers had departed on August 25, we started our project with renewed energy and labored like bees. The main building was arranged as a Home for the children. Beginning in September we accepted children, and soon all rooms were filled. They were the poorest children, who until now lived in shacks and caverns and whose main food consisted of fruit that, not infrequently, they had to steal from various gardens. You may easily imagine that they thought that they had been transferred to paradise.

The wing and front of the building toward the street were remodeled and enlarged to make a Chapel with an oratory. At a later date a large refectory, parlor, and halls for the novitiate were added.

On October 15 the Chapel was completed and Cardinal Satolli sent a monsignor to solemnly bless it. The day became a real "fiesta" for Rocca di Papa.

The best feature of the convent for me was the large door on the steps that led through the convent to the upper garden. The view of the heights of Rocca di Papa from this point gave me joy such as I had never imagined. Often when I mounted these steps and looked upward I beheld the vision of July 2, 1891. I saw the Divine Majesty, God the Father. I saw the cross, myself, and the Sisters grouped about me, and the Divine Savior in the clouds as His face expressed indescribable love and benevolence.

THE LARGE SHIP

Cardinal Satolli insisted that I do everything possible to obtain the first decree of approbation. Immediately a second obstacle arose which hemmed me in like an insurmountable wall. That was the suggestion to become a Third Order of the Carmel. After many unsuccessful negotiations I was told that if I didn't want this, then we would have to become a Congregation of the Divine Heart.

I should leave Carmel and our holy Mother Teresa? No, a thousand times no. Yet what else was there to do? Third Order? Never! I rather would not become a Sister at all.

In these days of anguish and doubt God assisted me with a new grace. In my sleep I dreamed I was on the shore of the ocean where the calm, boundless sea, bathed in a bright light, stretched out before me. The seashore was flat and a number of little boats rocked gently back and forth in the bright sunlight. All boats were shining white, and a blue strip ran around the upper rim. It was a delightful sight, and I felt invited to enter one of the boats.

I approached one of the little boats near the shore. I was about to step into it as there was no need of assistance of any kind. They were so very small and the gunwales so low that a person could conveniently step in. At that moment a heavenly figure stood at my right side and stopped me. Not only did it stop me; it did more. It pointed to the left, and there I beheld a ship, a large, dark brown ship. It was so high that a person could only board it with the help of a ladder. Still further to the left I saw another ship, gigantic and dark brown, and to this giant ship the large, brown ship was moored.

I understood the vision immediately, and God arranged

everything as he had decreed from all eternity. Attached to the Carmel, forming a ship of its own and upon which no number III was to be found, was "Carmel of the Divine Heart of Jesus."

God is and remains Master and Lord. He carries out His will and His designs no matter who opposes it or works against it.

St. Teresa of Jesus had paved the way. Why should I not be allowed to walk the same way without strict enclosure? Why not be permitted to follow her? I could not understand that. Times had changed, but the spirit, the love, and zeal to work for the salvation of souls ever remained the same. It is rejuvenated with every generation without weakening. Zeal does not grow weak, love does not grow cold. God is almighty, and as long as the world exists, His creative power will never come to an end!

The spirit of God moves souls in all the hundreds and thousands of years, and where the spirit of God works and is active and moves the souls, all opposition will break down. The Holy Spirit knows how to overthrow all difficulties and obstacles towering mountain high. He, the Holy Spirit Himself, makes the soul courageous and willing to fight joyfully.

How often in the course of those years did I look upon myself as a race horse which gracefully and easily takes one obstacle after another, one more difficult than the other. It leaps over them as though they were nothing. One gallant leap and it had won another victory for its master.

This is what had happened to me until now. I had overcome one obstacle after another because one difficulty was followed by another. I had heard that before a race the jockey gives the horse some bread soaked in cognac or wine in order to incite its highest spirit and courage and thus give it extraordinary powers and strength. God acts in a like manner as I experienced innumerable times. Before great difficulties, when human help, which I might call the daily fare, is not sufficient, God sends help from heaven. This help bestows special graces which give life and understanding and the ability to achieve anything. Man is but a tool in the hands of God. God has proved this to me again on this occasion.

I asked Professor Pisani (who would later become Archbishop), whom I knew from Berlin and Cremona, to come to my assistance, and he was kind enough to grant my request. Through his counsel everything was accomplished as I desired.

We had to be aggregated to the Carmelite Order, otherwise we could not participate in the indulgences and privileges of the Order of our dear Lady of Mount Carmel. According to God's will, we were to form an independent branch which would be subject to the Sacred Congregation of Regulars and not be subject to the superiors of the Carmelites as the Third Order.

Thanks be to God who accomplishes all according to His Will. Beginning in 1904 the Carmel of the Divine Heart of Jesus became a ship by itself but chained to the giant ship, the old venerable Order of Carmel whose great founder is St. Elijah the prophet.

So far everything was finished, but the name came up again. It did not please them. What now? Even Cardinal Satolli thought over the matter, along with Fr. Pisani and myself. Once they struck out the "Carmel" and another time the "Heart of Jesus," but I would relinquish neither the "Carmel" nor the "Heart of Jesus."

During those days we paid a visit to Father Antonio, the provincial of the Carmelites, in the monastery Maria della Scala. Immediately after we greeted one another, he joyfully exclaimed, "I have the name! 'Carmelitane del Divin Cuore di Gesu' ('Carmelites of the Divine Heart of Jesus')."

I was delighted. "Magnificent!" I exclaimed. "All that I love is united in this."

Father Provincial continued, "This name came to my mind last night."

Without delay we went to the Generalate to announce our great joy. Father Procurator met us with these words, "I have the name: Carmelitane del Divin Cuore di Gesu." When I told them that we came from Father Provincial to whom the name had also occurred last night, all of us (Father Procurator, my companion M. Maria Theresia of St. Peter, and I) were greatly amazed over this double inspiration. Thus our name was changed for the third time. This time it found universal approval.

CHAPTER ELEVEN

GERMANY AND THE NETHERLANDS

Now that the work had been firmly established in Italy, duty called me to the cold North where my Sisters were working under constantly difficult conditions.

In the beginning of 1904, therefore, I journeyed to Vechta with Sr. Martha Maria. Our journey took us to Freiburg in Baden. There we stopped off to make a personal acquaintance of Monsignor Wehrtmann who had shown great interest in us and to thank him for his kindness.

He strongly urged us to go to Osnabrück and to do everything possible to get into the northern Diaspora territory, as, "that was the real field of activity" for us. He gave us the names of those at the chancery whom I was to see, and I was instructed to call upon the Bishop. Although I expected little success, I followed this well-meant advice, but as I had anticipated, our efforts were fruitless.

Therefore, we went on to Vechta. I was there only a short time when I was called to Berlin by a special delivery letter. The priest-members of the Center party who were living in our hospice in Anhalt Street thought that Cardinal Kopp was better disposed now toward me and that I should travel in secular clothes to Breslau and seek an audience.

I received this letter on Saturday, and on Monday morning I was in Berlin and went straight to Breslau, where I spent the night. His Eminence could not be seen until the next morning. When I arrived at the Cardinal's Palace, I had to wait a long time. Finally the servant who had announced me returned and said in a contemptuous manner, "For you, His Eminence is not to be seen."

The Priests at the hospice were very disappointed at this news. Yet I consoled them by explaining that after my previous experiences and my vain efforts to get an audience, I had not expected anything else.

From the hospice in Anhalt Street, I visited the other houses. I was horrified when I saw the house in Schoeneberg. During my absence the Sisters had moved into the house in Sedan Street. It was wholly unsuited for us and very far from a church. I immediately gave an agent the order to look for a house suitable for a children's home. He took me to several of them, but none suited our purpose.

One day, after returning from long, fruitless wanderings, I told the Sisters that no house with a garden and a playground could be found.

"Oh," said Sr. Maria Magdalena Nueschen, "I forgot that Mrs. Gross was here a few weeks ago with a newspaper clipping. I was to send it to you. She thought the offer would be acceptable to us." She found the clipping which was an advertisement about a convent in Charlottenburg vacated by the Sisters of the Good Shepherd. These Sisters had built a much larger convent in another suburb and had already moved there. Consequently, the Sacred Heart parish had bought the old property and presently was offering it for rent.

The next day I went to Charlottenburg with another Sister to inspect the buildings. The archpriest, Fr. Faber, was not at home, so the caretaker took us around. Everything made a terrible impression on me.

When Fr. Faber heard of our visit and its purpose, he wrote me a letter in which he urged me to come again. He wrote about the large field of labor open to us. He further mentioned that there was no parish mission work being done and that no home for poor children existed in this parish of 36,000 souls. As far as the building was concerned, we were advised not to let ourselves be discouraged by its run-down condition. We could remodel as we pleased, and we could get as much as we liked from the property for a playground and a garden.

Following his urging, I once more looked at the place and promised Fr. Faber to consider the matter. Nevertheless, 6,800 marks for rent seemed very high.

I had sent Fr. Faber's letter immediately to my wise counselor in Rome, Monsignor Jacquemin. His advice had so far always brought me blessing. Hardly a week had passed when I received his advice which was to accept Fr. Faber's offer. I trustingly rented the house.

The lease of the house in Sedan Street, Schoeneberg, expired on March 16. Therefore, hasty preparations had to be made to get the place ready for the Sisters and the children. Alterations were made on the building, and everything went well. To the joy of all concerned, the Chapel and the Home were blessed, and the Blessed Sacrament was reserved on August 2.

While the little Nazareth Home of Schoeneberg had become a large, imposing St. Joseph's Home, Weissensee did not lag behind. First, an adjacent piece of property was bought. In place of the Home on Delbrueck Street in Neukoeln, which my Sisters had opened in my absence at the request of the pastor, I bought a house with a garden. This I had done with the approval of Cardinal Kopp. We moved in on April 1, and the Blessed Sacrament was reserved in the Chapel. Later the neighboring house was also bought.

I had come to Berlin without money, and my enemies

triumphantly boasted that I would come to financial ruin because of these many projects. My holy Father St. Joseph did not let me down but obtained for me the grace that I could make all necessary payments. God visibly blessed the unending labors and hardships, which, after all, had but one purpose: to glorify God, serve the church, and save souls. As soon as the existence of the St. Joseph's Homes in Charlottenburg and Neukoeln became known, they were filled with children.

I have merely mentioned the changes in the Home in Berlin, since I described each one in the fourth letter from St. Joseph's Home. I must mention something about the trouble we had at our hospice in Anhalt Street, which belonged to St. Hedwig's parish. The Chapel there was on the ground floor in a wing with no rooms above it which extended into the garden. The rooms of the hospice itself, however, occupied the second and third stories. The pastor of St. Hedwig's considered the dwelling unsafe for the Blessed Sacrament. Nevertheless, I very much wanted to have the Blessed Sacrament there for the Sisters who were overworked and lived far from a church. I therefore fixed up a cozy little sanctuary for our Savior in the top story. The priest-members of the Center Party, as well as the bishop, lodging there at the time, declared that the pastor would no longer have a reason to refuse to reserve the Blessed Sacrament. Yet, the Sisters never received this permission! At times, however, in both Chapels there were as many as ten to twelve Masses said every day by priests who belonged to the Center Party.

The time of my stay was up. The clothing ceremony of the postulants called me to Rocca di Papa. Cardinal Satolli had permitted the opening of the novitiate for January 1906, and he also allowed all the Sisters of the Sittard and Maldon novitiates to make their profession.

To my great sorrow the superiors and the Sisters of Rocca di Papa had neglected the precautions which the climate demanded and which I had urgently recommended. Some of the Sisters had contracted the fever and were still very sick. The others were almost sick from the hardship of caring for the other ill Sisters.

I knew not what to do. I was told that a change of climate was the best. I immediately went to Rome, rented a few rooms, and alternately brought all the Sisters there for a few weeks. I did all I could to restore the health of the Sisters, and, thanks be to God, I succeeded. All recovered with the exception of one postulant who died suddenly and found her last resting place in Rome. The postulant's name was Sr. Beatrice. She had brought the germ of the disease with her into the convent. All loved her and grieved over her death which occurred a short time before her investiture.

We then went ahead with the preparations for the investiture of more than fifty postulants and the calling together of the novices for profession. My festive joy was extremely heightened by the presence of Father Antonio (later Archbishop), a Carmelite whom I highly esteemed. He had always been well disposed toward me since 1897, and now he received the postulants and also the first vows of the Sisters. This faithful friend visibly shared our joy, just as he had previously shared our sorrows in those hard times. Now I confidently hope he is our mighty intercessor before God's throne.

While I was busy at Rocca di Papa and often marveled at God's wise dispositions, dark thunderclouds were massing in the North in Charlottenburg.

With a great deal of trouble Father Faber had obtained

the permission of the Potsdam government (under which Charlottenburg was before it belonged to Berlin) to open a Home for children but on condition "that only Catholic children would be received."

Shortly after I had left Charlottenburg, a Lutheran workman had asked M. M. Catherina of the Divine Heart to admit his small child for a short time. The workman's wife was sick and had to be taken to the hospital. He did not know of another place to put his child, but as soon as his wife was well, he said he would return for the child. M. M. Catherina told him that she could not take in a Lutheran child. He pleaded insistently and said that he would not report to the police where he had placed the child, and that the Sisters would not have to report the placement either. Besides, he urged, it was only a matter of a few weeks.

Mother M. Catherina let herself be persuaded and took the child, who was about a year old. Several weeks passed and then the man returned in deep grief over the death of his young wife. He pleaded even more strongly that the child be kept a little longer until he found a place for him. M. M. Catherina yielded once more.

Not long after this, a policeman arrived and asked whether the child was staying at St. Joseph's Home. The child had not been registered, and furthermore he was a Lutheran, and the government had allowed only Catholic children to be admitted. Mother M. Catherina explained the whole story. The policeman replied, "At least it should have been registered," made a few notes, and left.

The father of the child was immediately summoned, and he took his child away, but it was too late! Not even a month had passed when Fr. Faber received the following order from the Potsdam government: "On account of the violation of the directive, all those children of school age as well as small children, are to be placed elsewhere within two weeks. Hereby the Home is closed, and its permit revoked."

How much hardship and sacrifice it had cost to establish our home, and now, after being a home for over one hundred children for almost a year, it was to be closed! The most bitter part of this incident was that it had taken place through our own fault!

I was immediately informed of the calamity. I advised M. M. Catherina and the other superiors to transfer as many children as possible into the other Homes. I left some of the Sisters in the Home to keep affairs in order and to acquire the rent money. M. M. Catherina and the rest of the Sisters were transferred.

It was a great storm, but God also controls the storms or allows them to happen when and where he wills! I had this thought right away: this is a disposition of God. God, in His Infinite mercy had mercy on me again and in a dream showed me the future of this convent.

In the small garden of the Sisters, I saw a very large tree and right next to it was a sawed-off branch as thick as the tree. The place where it had been sawed off is still before my eyes today. It had been the lowest branch, over which the mighty crown of the tree had risen. I awoke and was filled with consolation and confidence.

This great tree always remained in my memory, just as God's first blessing remained when the Home in Goltz Street was founded in 1894. The large tree could only signify the great future of this house. The years that have since gone by have proved this sufficiently.

Again and again it was reported to me that Fr. Faber had

found a buyer for the whole property including our house and the garden. These reports left me cool, for I was convinced that it is nothing for God to nullify the plans of men.

The Sacred Heart parish kept the ownership of the former convent and grounds until I returned from the United States in 1920 and visited Charlottenburg. The opportunity then offered itself to buy a large part of the property and the villa on Luetzow Place for the Provincial House of the Carmel of the Divine Heart. Only a few decades more and a convent of the Most Holy Trinity would rise. Then the golden cross will shine from the little tower on Luetzow Place, and hundreds of children will come to know and love the Divine Cross bearer and be made good members of the worldwide Christian family.

The story must be told of how permission was obtained to reopen the Home. Despite the efforts of Fr. Faber, who himself was a member of the school board, four years went by before the permission was granted. Yet this permission was granted "only for children not of school age." It was only after repeated petitions that permission was granted for the Home to admit children of school age as well.

The inspections and the harassment, however, to which the Sisters were subjected up to the fall of the empire, defy all description. I will relate a few of these incidents.

One morning at about eight o'clock five men appeared before the greatly surprised Superior and demanded to inspect the house. They not only entered the parlor but went all through the house. They were amazed to see such neatness and order in a place which housed over one hundred children, more than half of whom were under five years of age.

Even the cells of the Sisters were not spared. Not only were the cells inspected, they were searched. During one of these "inspections" one of the men found a discipline under a Sister's straw mattress. The Sister was subjected to insufferable questioning. These were the kinds of humiliations the religious had to endure.

How wonderful the saints protected their devotees is proved by the following example. The Sister who was to awaken the others on that morning when the five men came to inspect, told me herself that through an oversight she woke the others at four-thirty, instead of five-thirty. Nobody noticed this error until after the meditation. The Sisters then used the extra hour to tidy up all the rooms before Mass. It was only after the inspectors had left the surprised and frightened Sisters that they thought of the wonderful foresight of holy Father St. Joseph who, for the honor of his St. Joseph's Home, had the Sisters awakened an hour earlier without them noticing it.

The hardest burden, however, which the Sisters had to endure were the reproaches heaped on them during the four years in which the house was empty. "To collect alms year after year for an empty house just to pay the rent of 6,800 marks is more than wrong, it is sinful." One priest commanded the Superior, "Write to your superior that I think it is a mortal sin to pay the rent for an empty house from the alms that are given."

All these charges did not disturb me, even the one which stated that paying rent on an empty house was a mortal sin. My conscience did not accuse me of any sin. On the contrary, I saw with thanks and joy how God visibly blessed the efforts to get the money, for mostly always the Sisters managed to have the large sum of money ready.

Almost thirty years earlier, I had regarded it as a blessing of God that I was able to raise money for the salary of a Lutheran city missionary, as I had written before. At that time I started a society of forty young ladies for this purpose. Throughout the year we made fancy articles, and then held a bazaar, and thus obtained the salary for the missionary. The thought that hundreds of children, innocent little ones, would thereby receive the grace of baptism filled me with joy.

This missionary often found over one hundred unbaptized children in one tenement building. After the introduction of the registrar's office, the Evangelicals thought that baptism and church marriages had been abolished. Hence, thousands of children remained unbaptized in Berlin where religion had been thrown overboard by countless people. Who can count or know how many children have died without Baptism?

The house in Charlottenburg belonged to the Sacred Heart parish. When I wanted to rent it in 1905, I was frightened by the high rent, but thinking of the Sacred Heart, I lost my anxiety, for by paying the rent, we directly helped the Sacred Heart parish. Every bit of the alms we collected for this purpose went into the church treasury. Therefore I was determined to do all I could to gather the money. To stand fast, not to lose confidence, and to persevere with great patience was our task.

During these years, I urged and encouraged my lonely Sisters in this big house to persevere in firm confidence. Thirty years earlier I regarded it as a "grace of God" to support a Lutheran missionary. How much greater then was the grace of being able to put 6,800 marks into the treasury of the parish church? Was not this an alms box, just as the one in the temple of Jerusalem? Did our Divine

Savior think less of our portion placed in it than of the alms of those days long past?

We gathered the alms and placed them "with joy and gratitude" into this "alms box of God." May we not believe that the Sacred Heart has blessed all benefactors as well as the Carmel of the Divine Heart of Jesus for these alms?

SITTARD

"Until later. . . . " These were the words of the Queen of Heaven with which she consoled me in Maria-Raschuetz, Bohemia. They were also the same words which led me in April 1906 to write once more from Rocca di Papa for admission into the Roermond Diocese. This time my request was granted.

The diocesan decree, which did not allow further foundations of religious communities had been lifted on behalf of the religious who had been expelled from France. Consequently, we too received permission to return to our abandoned convent in Sittard.

In the beginning of July 1906, I left Rome and went directly to Roermond in order to thank Bishop Drehmanns. My heart was filled with joy and gratitude because I was able to reopen our convent and restore the cradle of the Carmel of the Divine Heart of Jesus in the "City of Mary," as Sittard had been known in ancient times.

Those of us who had lived there for two years (from1898 to1900) and who had been invested and spent the sunny Spring of the Order there, clung to Sittard with tender love. Did this little town not deserve to be loved? Did not Sittard, the "City of Mary," stand fast as a rock among raging waves when the storms of the so-called

Reformation shook other cities like Limburg and other countries too? Yes, this "Fortress of Mary" belongs to the few places in the Netherlands which have always remained faithful to Holy Mother Church.

One could call Sittard "the Rock of Faith," just as Rocca di Papa means "Rock of the Pope," if the Kollenberg were only higher and made of rock. However, it is only a small, humble hill of sand. Even the "City of Mary" is small and modest as was Nazareth and, in a like manner, our convent. Yet, as it had been proven from year to year, the blessing of our dear Lady rests visibly on the place of her beloved Carmel and will remain so in the future.

I traveled from Roermond to Sittard where I had expected to be met by my Sisters of Tilburg. We had abolished the position of "Guardians" since in almost all the Homes the Sisters were superiors (although in Germany the Sisters could not appear in their habit). I had given full power to the Sisters so they could completely manage the financial matters.

In Sittard an elderly couple lived in a wing of the building and were responsible for maintaining the house and garden.

I was shocked that no Sister met me in Sittard, for everything was locked except the corridor, and the keys were in Tilburg! I therefore sat down in the corridor and waited hour after hour. The elderly couple were kind enough to give me some milk and bread.

Finally about nine o'clock or later two Sisters arrived, and now we could begin to air the rooms and get them ready. This was an unforgettable reception for me! It had been five years and nine months before the words of our dear Lady, "Until later," had become a reality!

We worked very diligently to prepare the Chapel as the

first step in reestablishing the convent. In honor of our dear Lady, we wanted to have the Blessed Sacrament reserved in the Chapel on August 15. Our labors were finished in time, and this day became a day of great joy and thanksgiving for the Carmel in Sittard.

Would that I had been able at that time to look into the future and see the new, big Motherhouse, the postulate, and the juniorate with more than fifty Sisters preparing for perpetual vows, and the many Sisters with perpetual vows. Had I been able to see them walking into the Chapel praying the *Miserere*: more than one hundred professed Sisters with lighted candles returning from making their perpetual vows and singing a hymn of praise and thanks to the Sacred Heart in the hall, that would have been too much happiness. Divine Providence, however, had hidden all this under the veil of the future.

As soon as the convent had been prepared, I longed to show the good God our thankfulness. Sittard itself offered little opportunity for mission work, and at first there were few children to be cared for. To gain souls, many souls, for the Divine Heart always has been and still is my one desire. I therefore suggested to the Sisters that we should conquer another country, namely France, for Carmel where many souls could be gained. I asked Fr. Ruetgen for his advice. He thought it would be a good idea to try to get into France in secular clothes. The Church was being persecuted there, and many Tabernacles were empty. Convents were closed and thousands of children were growing up without religious training. All the Sisters were enthusiastic for the project. We prayed fervently to know God's will, hoping that it would be to go to France.

Our prayer was heard. Instead of France, however, God

gave me a country of which we never dreamed. Yes, "my thoughts are not your thoughts," was true here also. God had looked with pleasure on our longing for souls and our readiness for sacrifice in our hearts. He gave us what we desired: a new country and many souls. Instead of France the "new" country was Hungary.

CHAPTER TWELVE

HUNGARY

In the year of 1907, the Carmelite Fathers held their General Chapter in Rome. Fr. Soos, the founder of the Carmelite monastery and church in Budapest, had also been in Rome. Father Benedict happened to tell him of our new branch of the Carmel and took him to Rocca di Papa for a visit.

After returning to Budapest, Fr. Soos wrote to me that he had been to Rocca di Papa and about what he had seen. He further stated that he had learned of our mission work and that it was just what Budapest needed. He begged me to come to Budapest with some of my Sisters as soon as possible.

This letter and this challenge brought us inexpressible joy! God had heard our prayers and instead of sending us to France He was sending us to Hungary. Such was the opinion of all.

Father Soos' letter contained another suggestion that had to be considered before I could give an affirmative answer to him. For about a year fourteen women had been living in community and trying to establish a new branch of the Carmel, really a missionary congregation. Yet, despite all of our efforts and sacrifices nothing had developed. Father Soos, therefore, proposed that I take over this community and receive these fourteen women into our Carmel as postulants. I remembered a similar offer which was made to our St. Mother Teresa of Jesus, and although she was reluctant at first, she finally accepted.

First of all I sought the advice of Fr. Ruetgen. Indeed, he

considered it a difficult task, but since I was never deterred by difficulties, he advised me to accept the offer. Filled with courage and confidence I decided to follow his advice. While we prepared the foundation, I exchanged several letters with Fr. Soos, asking him urgently not to rent a house for us and not to make any purchases.

Before traveling to Hungary, I first had to go to Schlieren in Switzerland. After a short stay, I went on to Bohemia by myself, since the Father General of the Carmelites had given me permission in 1897 to travel alone. There my three traveling companions awaited me in Graupen.

When I arrived in Bruex, Divine Providence saved me the second time from the hands of a possible murderer. This is what transpired. While waiting for my baggage in the station a policeman came up to me and asked quietly whether I had traveled alone. When I said yes he continued, "A very sinister looking man left the train with you and is still waiting over there keeping you in sight. Stay here quietly, we two policemen will accompany you, and then we will see if we can arrest the man."

With one policeman at my side and another behind me, we started on our way to the city, while the suspected individual quietly followed me, as the policemen observed. Finally, he must have realized that the police were watching him, for suddenly as we passed a little woods and a side path, he hastily darted off. Had the police not been so observant, how easily he could have robbed and killed me!

The policemen accompanied me to our convent and told me not to worry, as they would keep an eye on the house during the night.

The next day I went to Graupen where I met Sr. Mary, Sr. Maria Magdalena, and Sr. M. Irene, who had arrived in the meantime from Sittard. We started our journey on July 31 and arrived in Budapest on August 1, 1907.

Initially I had written that we would arrive on August 2, so I sent Father Soos a telegram from Graupen, telling him of our early arrival. However, he was gone on a journey and on his return he found the unopened telegram on his desk.

There we stood in the station. Not knowing the Hungarian language we felt unspeakably lost. Just at that time there was a strong anti-German movement in Budapest, and even those who knew German perfectly would not let this be known. We waited in vain for the postulants who were to call for us. Finally, tired of waiting, I sent two Sisters with a porter to show the way to the Carmelite monastery, for that was the only address we had. The monastery was quite distant so it took a long time before the Sisters returned with the joyful news that the nuns teaching school at the Carmelite parish would take us in for the night. Fr. Soos was not at home, yet he had wanted to take us to the community of the fourteen women himself. We were sincerely grateful to the superior of the Salvatorian Sisters for her great act of charity.

In the afternoon of August 2, 1907, Fr. Soos took us to our new companions, but the superior was not home. They received us joyfully for they hoped that we would make it possible for them to lead a real religious life.

It is remarkable what sacrifices these women had made and what ridicule, and what hunger these young girls had to endure solely in order to serve God! They occupied themselves with making fancy articles that they hoped to sell for their support, but this was not the case. Several of these young women went a few days each week to a hospital to be trained as nurses. This was a blessing for them as there they were given enough to eat.

The extreme need that these young creatures had endured for a year could be seen not only in their pale, sunken cheeks, but was experienced by us when we came to the dining room for supper. There was nothing on the table but bread and water and some brown flour. Of this fare each one received a little with a small piece of bread. That was the whole supper. In the morning when we returned from Mass, there was dark soup. At noon there was nothing on hand but a case of canned soup. The treasury was as empty as the cellar.

Every minute showed us more and more into what a precarious position we had come. Nevertheless to this position we had been led by God. We had not only ourselves to support now but also these fourteen people, and we, too, were also without means.

Fr. Soos gave us the addresses of some women who would help us, but the Sisters' visits were in vain. The summer heat was terrible and the wealthier families always left Budapest in the summer.

In this predicament I asked M. M. Catherina of the Divine Heart to send us some money. At the time she was the Superior in Graupen. In the course of the years I had sent so much help to the convents there for the support of poor children that it seemed no more than right that help should be sent from Bohemia to Hungary. Dear M. M. Catherina, always ready to give, quickly came to our rescue.

For our mere livelihood a thousand kronen was a large sum, but also we had to acquire all the furnishings for the convent. It was obvious that we could not stay where we were. Though our companions were good and willing, it was nevertheless clear that we could not receive the whole group into our Order. The superior was a sick, young widow and her assistant a sixty year old who had been discharged from another Order. Among the others was one who was fifty-six years old, another a poor, little cripple, and a number of young girls who had no vocation to the religious life. Yet we knew not how to get away and to separate from this devout group and this house.

Fr. Soos had asked us to come to Budapest; he would have to give us advice. I went to him, explained our situation, and urged him to help us. He promised to do everything possible, and especially to consult the pastor, who was the director of the community, regarding the best way to bring about a separation.

Every day seemed endless in this hot prison. August in Budapest is unbearably hot, and the sun burned down all day on the one room into which we had withdrawn. Here we slept, prayed, and lived, except for the short time when we went out. In this time of hardship and distress, God in His fatherly love strengthened my courage and my trust, as I will relate shortly.

Finally Fr. Soos and the director appeared, but they did not know how they could help us out of our distressing situation. Bereft of all human help in a strange land, I again had recourse to my dear saints, St. Father Joseph and St. Lawrence, who had so often helped me. With one of the Sisters I made a novena in St. Joseph's Church, and my beloved saints did not let us plead in vain. The thought came to me and turned into a firm resolve. This resolve was to look for a house ourselves and simply move away.

Despite our decision we were unsure how we could

locate a house in the city where we seldom found anyone who understood us.

I set out courageously with Sr. Maria Magdalena. After fruitless questioning we went to a bank in Calvin Place. There we met a man who could speak German. With great friendliness he gave us advice and provided useful information. "It is not advisable to look for a house through an agent in this city," he said, in reference to my question about employing an agent, "it is better to use a newspaper. There you will find something suitable." He pointed to a bookstore across the street where a newspaper listing houses for rent could be obtained. We immediately purchased a paper and hastened home.

It was Saturday evening. We said our prayers as usual, and then the Sisters went to bed. For me sleep was impossible as I had to look for a suitable house. We had been here only four weeks, and the newspaper was in Hungarian, and I knew only a few words of this language. Trusting firmly in God, I opened the paper and began to search. Suddenly I located what I wanted. I saw an advertisement which I translated to mean, "A house with garden and twelve rooms, etc." I was electrified with joy, made a large "X" on the advertisement, and hastily awakened the Sisters from their peaceful sleep. My joy was so great that I had to share it. I showed them the advertisement and explained by signs that this was the house we wanted. They rejoiced with me, and then went back to sleep. After Compline we observe strict silence even here, and that was why the whole explanation was done in sign language.

The night seemed endless. When morning came we went to Holy Mass and then, after our return, I broke the good news to the Sisters with the words, "I have found a house, and I am going there right now with Sr. Mary to look at it."

We set out and soon reached the streetcar line which would take us to Dr. Bonta. This was the name of the one who was to give us further information. We found him in one of the large rental houses in the newer part of the city. After I told him that I wished to see the house that was advertised, he answered in fine German that this could not be done that day. It belonged to his mother-in-law, an elderly lady who had to be prepared for the visit. He asked us to return the next day at nine o'clock. He then would take us to the house.

Another day to practice patience! Monday came, and we found ourselves punctually at Dr. Bonta's residence, and then we set off. We changed from one streetcar to another. It seemed to me that we were coming to a different town. After a one hour ride and passing hundreds of small cottages and workers' homes, we arrived at a country home.

The ladies of the house, mother and daughter, received us very affably and showed us the house. It was situated in a beautiful garden surrounded by shady trees. The dwelling was very suitable for the Sisters. There were small buildings suited for the children and also a space for a playground. Everything was perfect for a beginning.

The ladies left the arrangements concerning the rent to Dr. Bonta. When we started discussing details, it soon became apparent that the owner wanted to rent only two or four "furnished rooms!" "That's what the paper said," replied Dr. Bonta.

"Oh," I exclaimed, "I read it to mean twelve rooms and a garden."

"There is nothing like that in the paper, but perhaps we can arrange matters so you can get the whole property, for my mother-in-law has wished to leave this city of Ujpest for a long time. I will talk to her about it, but let us look at the little summer house now." He was already leading the way to the little house that was at the far end of the garden. There we walked up a flight of small stairs. We kept following him and found ourselves on a balcony. I looked up, and what did I see? Where was I? There, in the bright sunshine was indeed the great river, the green riverbanks, and in the distance the elevation. Everything was exactly as I had seen it, wondrously beautiful. Only the glorious rainbow was missing. The entire scene was indeed spanned by an arch of bright, green leaves, and blossoms of unearthly beauty. It was a garland of heavenly charm. I thought of this arch as a symbol of the blessing which God's goodness was to pour out on the "Carmel of the Divine Heart of Jesus" here in Hungary.

There were no words to express my amazement! Trembling with inner excitement, I turned to Dr. Bonta with words of admiration for the beautiful view, and added that we would like to have Fr. Soos come here and view the property, since it was through him that we had come to Hungary. This was agreeable to Dr. Bonta, and in the meantime he intended to speak to the ladies and suggest that they rent all of the houses and the garden to us.

We decided to return and see Fr. Soos. On the one hour streetcar ride I was in spirit before the throne of God while my heart was aflame with love and gratitude. I was completely overwhelmed by this new proof of God's favor. Fr. Soos was pleasantly surprised that we had found a place so soon and was ready to go with us without delay.

On our return to the house, we were happy to learn that the ladies had agreed to rent the whole property to us. Our joy was increased when we were told that we could move into four of the rooms on September 7.

Fr. Soos could hardly find words in his amazement over our find, the beauty of the location, and its suitability for our purposes. On the way back I asked him to do me the favor of telling Madam Margaret of our intentions to leave her. We wished to part peaceably. He promised to do this.

We had begun slowly to get our furnishings together, and we continued our preparation during the week. To my greatest astonishment it was during those days that the whole Community came to our room and asked for admission into the Carmel of the Divine Heart of Jesus! I quickly gathered my wits and told them that we could not admit all of them in a group, but they were to come singly on the following days.

We then consulted among ourselves as to which ones we were to admit. When they came one by one and asked to be received, Divine Providence disposed that the eight whom we had chosen were the first ones to come one after the other. These eight were admitted as postulants. The others were told that they could not be taken at the present time.

On September 7 all went to Holy Mass except for the four of us Sisters and the eight postulants. These I sent to Ujpest with two of the Sisters. At the proper time the furniture van appeared, and our belongings were loaded upon it. Before it could start, however, Madam Margaret and her companions appeared on the scene.

As we soon discovered, neither Fr. Soos nor the director had told them of our plans. One can easily imaging her shock and amazement when she saw the items which she thought were intended for her convent being taken away. As soon as Madam Margaret had recovered, I asked her to step into the parlor. First of all I expressed my regret that Fr. Soos had not prepared her for our leaving and moving to Ujpest. Then I explained to her that the merging of her community with ours was impossible. This was so because she, the foundress and superior, was a widow and her assistant was an ex-religious. In conclusion I wished her God's blessing for her institution and then we, Sr. Maria Magdalena and I, left this house in which we had spent such a miserable time.

The feast of our dear Lady's Nativity in 1907 was indeed a day of festive joy for us. Fervent prayers of thanksgiving were sent to heaven, to God, who indeed tries His own but never abandons them if they firmly trust in Him, and to our dear saints who had protected and guided us to the place chosen by God. We recommended this foundation in particular to our dear Lady, our Father St. Joseph, and our Mother St. Teresa of Jesus.

Joy does not seem to feel at home with me. For here, as elsewhere, it soon changed to suffering and grief. We had spent only a few days in sunny happiness when Fr. Soos came with the sad news that we would never have Mass there. He said that he had spoken to the priests of Ujpest, and they had declared that no priest could go to Vac Street in Megyer (the part of the city in which we had settled) without risking his life. Only a short time before the people had threatened to kill a Franciscan Father on the street in broad daylight. This occurred without any reason or provocation but merely out of hatred for priests and religious. The Father owed his life to a woman who had quickly opened her garden gate and let him in.

At that time there was in Budapest, and especially in the suburb Ujpest, a very bitter feeling against priests and religious. Meetings were held in which the people were incited against God, the Church, priests, and religious. Evidently these were preparations for the revolution which followed later. Naturally I was greatly disturbed for the moment, but my courage soon rose again, and I was able to reassure good Fr. Soos.

We did not, in the least, let ourselves be hampered either in our work or by these fears. While some of us were busy with getting the house ready, Sr. Mary, a German professed Sister who had a great talent for languages (after six weeks the children called her the German-Hungarian Sister), together with Sr. M. Theresia, one of our Hungarian postulants, went from house to house asking the people to send their children to our nursery and kindergarten. On these visits they also inquired about going to church and found that in this whole section of the city hardly anyone went to Mass. When the Sisters urged them to go, they often got the answer, "What will the neighbors say if I go to church since nobody else does?"

The children had the same spirit, for as soon as they saw the Sisters from afar they fled into their homes. However, love and sincere friendliness overcomes all. This was proved to be true here also. It did not take long before our rooms were overcrowded. Not only did those under six years come, but more than forty children of school age appeared. This took place in the forenoon! The surprised Sisters asked the children why they did not go to school, and they answered, "Her ladyship (that is the title they gave the teacher) sent us away because our clothes were too shabby."

We were more than surprised at this condition. All these children were not to learn to read and write and be instructed in religion because their parents refused to dress them in anything but rags? Thanks be to God that conditions since have been much improved in Budapest for the poor and their children. Would we, however, find the same condition in the country far from the capital?

From day to day we recognized more and more into what a large mission field God had led us. Trusting in His help, we hoped for a rich harvest of souls. After a few weeks Fr. Soos came to us with the happy report that the attitude of the people of Megyer had changed completely. In place of the ridicule and slander one heard the people speak of the "dear Sisters" of whom they could not say enough good things.

"What have you done to win their hearts in such a short time?" asked Fr. Soos.

I replied, "We have done nothing special. We practice charity for which there was always an occasion. We know from experience that one can accomplish everything by heartfelt, sincere love, and we love these people and their children, and they feel that."

"Since the attitude of the people has changed," said Fr. Soos, "a priest will no doubt venture to say Mass for you now. I will go to the pastor right away and ask if one of the assistants would be willing to do so."

How happy we were that we did not let ourselves be kept from our work in the house and in the Chapel. On the Feast of Saint Francis Xavier on December 3, the Chapel was blessed and the Blessed Sacrament reserved with a large number of people in attendance. Many were there who had not been to Mass since their first Holy Communion or their wedding! Tears of emotion or, perhaps, contrition were seen in the eyes of some.

The ice was beginning to melt and spring soon would be here, we said trustfully. God did not let us put our trust in Him in vain. I must not forget to mention our benefactors. Our first ones were the merchants (all of whom were Jews) of the neighborhood. We were without income and forced to rely on the alms of generous people. The furnishings of the rooms, of the Chapel, and our own poor furniture all cost money. Great was our joy when the mail brought us twenty kronen! One time we were in extreme need and Sr. M. Rafaela heard of Bishop Kohl who was the almoner of the Cardinal. She went to him and told him about our institution in Ujpest. She received not only eighty kronen which we needed badly just then, but from that day on the Bishop became the helper in need of the Carmel of the Divine Heart of Jesus.

Time swiftly passed since we had plenty of work, and Christmas was fast approaching. We had one great wish and that was to make all of our children happy. The Sisters went to Budapest and wandered from store to store asking for gifts for the poor children. They did manage to get one gift for each child. A young Jewish boy, of whom they could not rid themselves, joined Sr. M. Rafaela and Sr. M. Alfonsa on this trip. He led them from one store to another, where he said good people lived. Before Sr. M. Rafaela could say a word, he would ask for a gift for the poor children. Again the Sisters tried to get him to go away but did not succeed. He also helped to carry the packages. Their worry about the gifts that he was carrying increased greatly when one of the women in the store said to them, "But Sisters, who is that with you? That boy is a thief!" At the same moment the boy and the packages disappeared! However, when the Sisters turned the next corner they saw the youngster with all the packages. He waited for them and swore that he was honest. He said that he just wanted to help them because they were strangers and knew so little Hungarian. He would not think of stealing their gifts.

Just as they were unable to get the boy to leave, so it was also impossible for them to carry all the packages. Therefore they took him with them hour after hour until, finally, loaded down with their treasures, they reached home in the evening. The boy had spoken the truth. He had been honest that day. May God reward him one hundredfold! After he had been given a good supper, he left. The poor boy, like so many others, wandered about homeless.

Since I have a great love for the people of Israel, this good deed of the Jewish boy on Christmas Eve gave me a special joy and pleasure. Without his help we would not have been able to make our children so happy.

Christmas was over and the New Year began. We looked back on 1907 with deep joy and thanksgiving. To the great joy of all it had brought us to Hungary, where the Carmel of the Divine Heart of Jesus had found a new home. In the meantime several professed Sisters came to help us. All were filled with admirable zeal and were ready to regain the many straying souls for the Divine Heart by their labors and sacrifices.

ST. JOSEPH'S HOME OF OUR DEAR LADY—BUDAPEST X

In the beginning of our stay in Budapest, when we were still living with Madam Margaret, God made known to me that we first would have a small house in Budapest and later a larger one. We now had the small one in Ujpest, but how were we to acquire the large one?

It was January 19, 1908, when I inwardly felt moved to start looking for a house. I rode to Calvin Place in company with Sr. Maria Magdalena. We went to the same bookstore and bought the latest edition of the newspaper that had helped us to settle in Ujpest.

This time we boarded the streetcar right away and searched the advertisements. We found one of a villa in Maglodi Street. Sr. Maria Magdalena asked the conductor how to get there. He assured us that we were on the right car, but later we would have to transfer to another car.

We had ridden for about one hour when we began to doubt whether a large villa could be found here outside the city, where only isolated workers' homes stood along the country road. A gentleman sitting across from us, and who had been riding with us for the past few minutes, noticed our impatience and uncertainty and asked us where we wanted to go. "125 Maglodi Street," was our answer.

"I am going there myself," he said, "so you ladies may feel safe."

Finally the car stopped. The gentleman led us to the villa for which we were looking and in which he himself lived. It was a large, beautiful villa located in a garden. Behind it there was a small park and a large vegetable garden. I did not like the property. The house seemed too luxurious for a convent. After we had looked at everything, I thanked the man for his kindness in showing us around and added that we would have to consider the matter.

A short time later we again went to Budapest to look for another house since I did not regard the one on Maglodi

Street suitable for us. Wrapped in silent prayer I was riding along with Sr. Maria Magdalena, when suddenly we left the streetcar in a section entirely strange to us and we walked along the road. The road led to the church in Koebanja, as the people of whom we had inquired the way had told us. We first went to see the pastor, but since he was not at home one of the assistants received us. When we told him the purpose of our visit, he was very willing to help us. He thought for a while and then advised us to see Mr. N. who was a tax official and was very familiar with the territory that belonged to District X of Budapest.

Thanking the good Father for his advice, we went to see Mr. N. We were received very kindly by his wife and mother-in-law (they were an Austrian family). As soon as they learned that we had come on business and not for alms, they called the master of the house, who also received us affably. All three listened to our story of the Home for poor children in Ujpest and of our plans to open a similar Home in this section provided we could find a suitable dwelling. After some thought the gentleman said, "In this section there is only the villa. A baron lives there with his sister. This villa has a nice garden, is located near the workhouse, and is well-built. It is outside the city but belongs to District X. An open road leads there, and you can reach it in twenty minutes. I will show you the way. You will not find a more suitable property," he assured us.

I turned to Sr. Maria Magdalena and said, "Isn't that the villa which we have already seen?" She thought so too, but Mr. N. declared that this was impossible as its location was so hidden that we could not possibly have found it.

He showed us the way and in about twenty-five minutes we stood before the villa which we had seen at 125 Maglodi Street. I was taken by surprise and said to myself, "Perhaps the good God has chosen this place for us or rather for His abode." We would have to open a Chapel first of all because there was no church close by. No doubt the people here were as neglectful, as irreligious, or as lax as those living in Ujpest.

The Baron was very friendly again, and this time we asked for the name of the owner who happened to be a widow. When we met her the next day we quickly agreed upon the financial terms. We could not settle them definitely since we had to get the episcopal approbation in Graan. There we were received by Auxiliary Bishop Rajner who was not only agreeable but seemed glad to see us again. "You received the approbation for your establishment last year, but then you went into another diocese," he said in answer to my request for permission to settle in District X of Budapest. This was the same District in which we had lived while we stayed with Madam Margaret.

I excused myself for settling in the diocese of Vac, but I had done so without any intentions on my part. It was only after I had rented the house in Ujpest that Fr. Soos told me that it belonged to another diocese. His Excellency smiled and said, after granting the approbation, "But now remain faithful!"

The villa did not become vacant until July. The Sisters made all the arrangements in the house and have labored there with great blessing to this day. Unfortunately, the great poverty with which we always had to struggle did not permit the building of a much needed Home for children and a Chapel. It was only in 1924 that this project could be undertaken. It was done so with the approval of Cardinal Csernoch, primate of Hungary, of the ministry, the mayor, and with the help of generous benefactors. For sixteen years the children occupied the beautiful, high, and airy rooms of the villa, while the Sisters had to be content with miserable sleeping quarters under the roof. These accommodations were hot enough to suffocate the Sisters in the summer and cold enough to freeze them in the winter.

Nevertheless, these were small sacrifices. In 1919 the storm of revolution raged throughout the country and especially in Budapest. It did, indeed, cause our Sisters and superiors to tremble with fear, but they stood firm as rocks in the defense of their faith and of the children. They were determined to hold out with great confidence in God, come what may. As they had been informed, their names were on the list of those condemned to death, but a few days before the orders could be undertaken the revolution came to an end.

ST. LAWRENCE

Just as our St. Mother Teresa of Jesus had built a hermitage in the garden where she could pray for the salvation of souls in quiet and solitude, so we too had arranged the summerhouse in Ujpest for a hermitage of prayer and penance and had placed the Stations on the wall. It was a tiny little Chapel which we loved and to which all of us, despite snow and cold, made a daily pilgrimage, as the footmarks in the snow would show. We went there not only for our own spiritual benefit but also to obtain graces. These great graces came from God for Hungary, which we had come to love, and above all for the souls around us in Ujpest and Budapest.

One morning I was saying the Stations there, as I did

almost every day, when I heard the loud and clear words, "Go to St. Lawrence!" I had begun to pray devoutly, and so I was exasperated by the distraction. Collecting my thoughts again I continued my devotions and again I heard the words loud and clear, "Go to St. Lawrence!"

"My God, if this be Your holy will, I will go immediately, as long as it is not the devil who wants to distract me," I replied.

I finished the Stations. From one Station to the other I became more and more convinced that God had given the command. The order perhaps may have come through an angel, just as had happened at Alstetten where I was told, "Go to Schlieren!" I did not know Schlieren at that time, and I did not know St. Lawrence now. Just as I had found the former and was given the grace to found a convent there for the good of many souls, so I now was sure that this foundation at "St Lawrence" would also become a place of blessing.

Returning to the Sisters, I asked Sr. Maria Magdalena to accompany me on an errand. With my thoughts raised to God, I rode to Calvin Place with my companion who had no inkling of the purpose of my errand. Here I inquired about the way to St. Lawrence. We were told what train to take and where to transfer. After a ride of about two hours, we arrived at our destination.

Near the station I saw a small inn. I went there with the purpose of asking the owner whether he knew of a place for sale. The owner was very reticent, and after pondering for a while, he said he did not know of such a house. We were about to leave the inn when an elderly man arose from somewhere in the back of the room, walked up to us, and said, "I am a Catholic also. I will take you to a man whom they call the 'Pope of St. Lawrence.' This name was given him because he looks out for the Catholics who have no church or priest in this section, although we number about 5,000. He has also been to the Bishop. Mr. N. has recently fixed up a schoolroom as a Chapel, and occasionally Holy Mass is said there on a Sunday or a Holyday."

We soon met Mr. N. who was a German-Bohemian and owned a factory. As soon as he heard of our plans to establish a home for children and a Chapel, he was full of enthusiasm. He said that he knew of a suitable property which he would immediately show to us. It was sure to please us and, as it was vacant, we could move in without delay.

On the way to the place, he entertained us in a lively manner by telling us about the history of the suburb of Budapest and how neglected the Catholics were in the area. In the meantime we had reached the villa. It was situated in a small park with very beautiful trees. A nobleman of Galicia had built the house and sold it recently. The villa was, unfortunately, not very large. Since Mr. N. assured us that no other place was to be had in St. Lawrence, we asked to be taken to the owner, in order to make arrangements about the amount of rent. I told him that he could have a definite answer within a few days. I first had to get the approbation of the Bishop of Vac.

Deeply grateful to Divine Providence we returned to the convent where the Sisters were greatly surprised to hear that a third St. Joseph's Home was planned in or near Budapest.

We received the necessary approbation for a Home and a Chapel so that work could be started at once. It was early in March or somewhat later during the carnival days of 1908 when we moved to St. Lawrence. Our greatest joy in making a new foundation is always this: to erect another dwelling for the Divine Savior. We have the greatest confidence that in this way faith and love of God will be awakened and increased in many souls.

I had the wish to have the Chapel blessed on March 21, which was the feast of St. Benedict. Everybody worked with zeal and great joy. We could not hire any laborers except masons and carpenters because we were so unspeakably poor. As the feast day came nearer we had to work through two nights in order to be finished on time. On the feast of St. Benedict, the Chapel was ready for dedication, but, alas, no priest appeared on that day (Saturday, March 21) to bless the Chapel.

The dedication took place on Sunday morning before Holy Mass. The Catholics of the neighborhood had gathered for the occasion and were overjoyed to have the Blessed Sacrament in their midst. Some came daily to Mass after that.

At the same time we opened a Home for girls in the large room downstairs. Later on, another property was acquired and a Home with a larger Chapel was established for boys.

ERZSEBETFALVA

When the Bishop of Vac gave us his approbation to establish a Home in St. Lawrence, he also urged us to open a Home in Erzsbetfalva, where the need was even greater.

With another Sister I set out without delay and found a section with more than 30,000 Catholics without a church! This large parish had nothing but a tiny little Chapel which was anything but properly furnished. I could not believe that the Blessed Sacrament was reserved there. The sanctuary light, however, indicated the presence of the great God in this wretched place. I cannot express what I felt! I cannot put my indignation into words. My blood boiled!

I hurried to the pastor and asked him the reason for such conditions. I clearly expressed my horror at such a state of affairs. He replied that the plans for a new church were ready, but that he could not get the bishops approbation to build until he had the necessary funds. This would take about two years.

Those of you who know me (if only through my words) will understand how indignant and excited I was. God is "my God" and His souls are "my souls" and here I saw the great and almighty God treated so shabbily. This Chapel certainly was not "a dwelling of God." Now the souls, these precious treasures of the Divine Heart for whom the Savior had given His life on the cross in such unspeakable torments, were allowed to go to ruin.

Filled with the deepest compassion for these poor abandoned souls in Erzsebetfalva, I, on the same night, wrote a letter in which I described the existing conditions to the Bishop of Vac. I still remember that I added that one church after another was being built in Berlin at the cost of great effort and sacrifice and pleaded for sympathy and help. In conclusion I asked that the pastor be given permission to build and that the building not be postponed for two years until the funds were on hand, but to trust in God's help for obtaining the necessary means.

God be praised for having my plea be heard in Vac. When I saw the pastor again he had obtained permission, and the preparatory work was already underway.

To our great joy we soon found a small villa with a large

hall which was suitable for a Chapel. More and more Sisters came to Hungary to help us, and they prepared a very devotional Chapel for the Divine Savior. In addition some good people donated the statues for the Chapel. It did not take long until we had Holy Mass every day. Even on weekdays some devout people were present.

An addition was built, giving another room for the girls, and later an adjacent one-story building was bought as a Home for boys. The quarters for the Sisters were indescribably poor, and they lived in them from 1908 to 1924. In this year the Apostolic Nuncio, Bishop Schioppa, dedicated the children's Home. A generous benefactress, Baroness Napos, had built it. This truly noble woman took the poor Carmel of Erzsebetfalva to her heart and collected, with great personal sacrifice, the funds for this splendid Home. A temporary Chapel was furnished and also a section reserved for the Sisters. May the Divine Heart of Jesus reward in time and in eternity this devoted benefactress and all the others for their labors and sacrifices!

There is something I must add about St. Lawrence. During those busy weeks of preparation in March, my sweet Jesus came to me in a dream.

In the first villa at St. Lawrence, where I was at the time, an outside stairway led to the upper story. In front of the entrance there was a small balcony. Here in the wide open door, I saw the lovely Child Jesus who appeared to be four years of age. He was standing with both arms outstretched and beckoning me to come. The right arm was held in a peculiarly stiff position, which seemed very remarkable.

Filled with wonder and rapture I gazed at the Divine Child, and then He pointed into the distance, and I saw a river that wound around a hill covered with woods. On this hill I saw several large buildings which were quite close together. It was an exceedingly charming picture: the sweet Child, the bright river glittering in the sun, the rich, deep green of the riverbanks, and above all the delightful woods.

I awoke with the firm conviction that this was another command from God. Soon my thoughts wandered to Schlieren where the Sisters were just then looking for a house. They were searching again because the factory from which they had rented the garden and playground now needed more space, and without this space the Sisters could not stay in the Home with the Children.

At the end of March, Sr. M. Irene and I left our beloved Hungary. First, however, I visited all my dear ones in Ujpest. Then for the last time I walked up the little stairway to the little balcony of the summer house and looked down upon the beautiful Danube and across it to the heights. There in spirit I left this world and sank down adoringly and gratefully before the throne of God.

It had been granted me to live eight months in Hungary and establish four convents and children's Homes for the Carmel of the Divine Heart. Grace upon grace had been granted. Picturing to myself once more the rainbow of divine blessing, I quietly left the work that had been begun, trusting in God's help and protection, and in the faithful cooperation of the zealous Sisters.

I esteem myself fortunate in having found the noblest and most loyal people among the Hungarians.

CHAPTER THIRTEEN

HERMETSCHWIL

Upon our arrival we were most heartily welcomed by M. M. Mechtildis and all the Sisters of the Carmel in Schlieren. After the greetings were over, M. Mechtildis asked me whether we had met a priest on the way. Just a few minutes earlier, the pastor, Fr. Keusch had left the Home. He had come to offer us his institution in Hermetschwil. I replied that I had met a priest who had given me a friendly greeting. Somewhat later I inquired about this offer and asked, "Does Hermetschwil lie on a river?"

"No," M. Mechtildis answered, "it lies on a hill. There is no river."

My interest was gone now, and I declined the offer by saying, "We will not take over this institution under any conditions, so we will not even look at it."

The next morning after Holy Mass, my good Guardian Angel persuaded me to change my mind and go to Hermetschwil without delay. I therefore went to M. M. Mechtildis and asked her whether it would be better if we were to go to Hermetschwil. She stated that as it was nearby and easily reached, that the pastor might feel offended if, indeed, we did not visit. Following this advice, we were soon on our way to the electric railway that runs to Hermetschwil. For the last stretch of the trip we were alone in the car with an elderly couple. The husband told us all about his son who was a missionary priest. He then called our attention to the monastery, Muri, which could be seen in the distance. Since he seemed to know the country so well, I asked him about Hermetschwil and especially whether it was situated on a river. "Certainly," he replied, "it lies on the Reuss."

We finally reached Bremgarten, the end of the line, crossed a bridge, and then followed a road through the woods upward to Hermetschwil. Since it is almost impossible for me to walk slowly, the elderly gentleman and I went on ahead, while M. M. Mechtildis and the lady followed us at a slower pace. My companion kept up a running conversation and acquainted me with the conditions in the Aargau.

We had walked for some time, and I had been listening to him without giving further thought to the surrounding country. Suddenly I stood still and looked around and was unspeakably amazed. To my left the silvery river wound its way through the valley, bordered by deep green banks which rose to the tree covered heights, and above were the buildings. Everything existed in the most minute detail just as the Divine Child had let me see it.

We kept on climbing. The kind gentleman kept on talking, but I could hear no more, for my soul had flown to God who again had shown plainly that I was an instrument in His Hands.

We met Fr. Keusch near the buildings, and soon M. M. Mechtildis and her companion caught up to us. We bade farewell to the fine elderly couple who continued on their way to the convent of the Benedictine Sisters, while Fr. Keusch led us to his institution. First of all I viewed the front, and to my great joy St. Benedict greeted us from very far on high. A statue of St. Benedict, in whose honor we had worked so hard to get the Chapel ready in St. Lawrence, was occupying a place of honor here!

The pastor now opened the Chapel. Mother M. Mechtildis and I knelt down in one of the front pews. I greeted our Divine Savior in the Tabernacle. Next, I looked on the altar on the right side on which stood a statue our Lady of Lourdes. Then, as I turned my eyes to the left, I saw the lovely Infant Jesus with the stiff arm, just as I had seen Him in St. Lawrence! Forgetting everything and being carried away completely, I jumped up and ran to the altar and sank to my knees.

Mother M. Mechtildis, frightened by my abrupt rising and running to the altar, followed me and asked what had happened. In my extreme excitement I forgot myself and told her something of my dream. Except for a later time in Detroit, Michigan, when I was also very excited, I very seldom have spoken of this.

Naturally I now agreed to accept the offer of the pastor and take over the institution, but only on condition that it would become our property and that we could change it into a St. Joseph's Home of the Carmel.

God knows why He led us there. We had been in the Home of St. Benedict for twenty-three years, and it was always difficult, and had become even more difficult. St. Benedict had been for us, in truth, "a carver of crosses," for Hermetschwil had brought us nothing but crosses and suffering until now. Perhaps my great love for suffering is to blame. Perhaps the future would bring sunny days for the Home up there. That was my heartfelt wish for my Sisters.

After many years I returned to Hermetschwil, but my beloved little Infant Jesus was no longer there. Mother M. Alexianna, who was superior there at one time, was so displeased with the crippled little arm that she had the statue renovated. The artist, who knew as little about the story of this Infant Jesus as Mother M. Alexianna did, renovated it to such an extent that it lost all resemblance to the "miraculous Image," as I called it. Fortunately, however, during the first weeks of my stay in Hermetschwil I had a photograph made of the little statue, and the Divine Child still stands before me in the way it appeared when directing me from St. Lawrence to Hermetschwil.

ROCCA DI PAPA 1908—1912

I left beautiful Switzerland in the summer and returned to our Motherhouse in Rocca di Papa. This time I had the pleasure of finding all the Sisters and children in good health, although the convent as well as the Home was overcrowded. Of course, the dear Italian people live almost entirely in the open. In Rocca di Papa there are bitterly cold days, besides the rainy season. I looked over the whole property carefully, hoping to find further accommodations. I looked thoughtfully at the large barn or shed of broken stone which we had left facing the road. I then asked our builder, Mr. Santangeli, to come and see whether he could build a refectory on the ground floor and a Chapel above it from the old stable. After examining the masonry carefully he said he was willing to undertake the work. To everyone's great joy the rebuilding began on November 2, 1908. But more stones were needed and these, of course, cost money. Our treasury in Rocca di Papa, like all the treasuries of the St. Joseph's Homes, was quite empty.

Two of the Sisters thereupon went to the owner of the quarry, told him of our need for more stones, and the kind gentleman gave us permission to take as many stones as we needed from those "lying around."

The quarry was not far from the foot of our wooded hill. As soon as this generous offer became known, the young

Sisters and the children besieged me with their pleas to be allowed to carry the stones. I granted them this favor, but I also hired a few donkeys besides.

Every day the procession started off jubilantly for the quarry. It was really something to see the caravan returning from the quarry, a sight that could be seen from the upper garden. The older children carried a stone on their heads, as the women and children carry everything here. They climbed the hill with that grace so peculiar to the Italians. In between the children, Sisters appeared now and then leading a donkey laden with stones. It was an amusing, yet picturesque scene.

Now that we had a place to get stones without cost, a number of the Sisters volunteered to repair our convent wall. This very ancient wall was completely in ruins in certain places, and we were too poor to have it rebuilt. About twenty of these "master masons" went to work with spirit and zest. They succeeded in rebuilding the wall in several places. Two portals, named St. Peter and St. Paul, were made in the wall, and so it did not take long before our whole beautiful property was closed off all around.

Unfortunately, the new Chapel was not yet ready when one of the greatest feastdays of our Carmel approached on January 3, 1909. On this day, fifty Sisters came from all our convents and assembled here on the "Rock of St. Peter" to make their perpetual vows with the approbation of Cardinal Satolli.

Besides these there were fifty-six novices on the Rock. It was a day of joy for all. This was so especially for the older Sisters who had suffered so much and made so many sacrifices in the years of persecution, not only in Berlin, but also in other places where we were treated with the same ridicule. They had finally reached their goal, and the Divine Heart had lifted the burden of scorn from them. Happy beyond all measure, they returned to their convents and to the countries from which they had come.

VIENNA

It was the same year, I believe in the fall, that I received a letter from a Sacred Heart Father in Vienna in which he proposed that I take over the Boys' Home of Fr. Krassa. This offer was very unappealing to me. We wrote to Fr. Krassa for further information, sought the council of others, and considered the matter for a long time. We finally came to the conclusion to accept the proposal, but only for a time, for we hoped to establish our own Home in Vienna. It was with this intention that we sent several Sisters in 1910 to the institution of Fr. Krassa in Vienna.

If we in Rocca di Papa would have had an idea of what kind of existence our dear Sisters, forced by the circumstances, were to lead in Vienna, we never would have sent them there. Unfortunately, I was unable to visit Vienna until the summer of 1911. The institution, filled with older schoolboys, was located in the middle of the city. There was no playground, garden, or balcony, and there were no arrangements whatever for the Sisters' convent.

What a life of sacrifice the members of a congregation have to assume when they take over schools or other institutions and then have to depend on the pastor or the director. The circumstances in Vienna made this fact very clear to us.

God be thanked for leading me to the Carmel and thereby to the wisest teacher, our holy Mother Teresa of Jesus.

She is called the "seraphic" or also the "mystic saint" and that with good reason. In a miraculous way she not only soared to the highest heights of the mystical life of the soul, like a seraph, she was at the same time a superior according to the heart of God. Yes, St. Mother Teresa was a true, loving, always solicitous Mother toward her daughters and proved herself in all her undertakings to be an excellent businesswoman, as she herself had stated.

God gave me this great saint as a lawgiver, and I always tried to follow her directions scrupulously as far as this was possible in our times and under our totally changed conditions. Thus our holy Mother ordained that we have separate convents with a garden enclosed by a wall. In consequence, the Carmel of the Divine Heart of Jesus also has its own convent with a garden, enclosed by a wall or a high fence. Connected to every convent is a children's Home or a Home for the aged with a playground and a garden, also enclosed by a wall.

I am firmly convinced that if our holy Mother Teresa had founded her Carmel in the nineteenth or twentieth century, instead of in the sixteenth, she would not have restricted herself to prayer and penance for the salvation of souls. Like us, she would have joined to this life, the work for souls.

I must now return to my story of the Home in Vienna where God visibly blessed the sacrifice we made in taking this Boys Home. If I remember correctly, Father X. of Ebersdorf District XI, called our attention to the Children's Home of Miss A., whose home was located in his parish. This lady was looking for Sisters who would buy her property and take over the Home including its sixty children.

After looking at the house and garden, we stated our readiness to buy. On August 2, 1911, we obtained the long-awaited approbation of the Church authorities for the founding of the Carmel of the Divine Heart of Jesus in Vienna.

On August 15 we moved into this place, which is in District XI, and in the course of time, we purchased several more pieces of property. Unfortunately, the first addition, which was badly needed, could be started only in 1921, and in 1925 it was still not finished because of the lack of funds.

I had been at the Carmel in Ebersdorf only a few weeks when I discovered another wonderful field of labor for our mission in another suburb in District XXI. At the same time I found a new and vacant house. Though not suitable for a convent, it had enough room for the beginning, as well as a garden.

To my great joy I received the approbation of the Church authorities for this second foundation. This St. Joseph's Home of St. Bernard was opened in September 1911. During the Great War a generous benefactor, having pity on the poor children of Vienna, took a great interest in the Home and bought a newly constructed house which was added to the Home. However, this was soon overcrowded and a certain Count agreed to have a Chapel built at his expense. The building was begun and had reached the height of three or four feet when the terrible inflation made it impossible for the noble benefactor to complete the work. In 1925 the Chapel was still unfinished and awaited some generous benefactor who would bring it to completion.

The building of this Chapel is a truly social work. It will not only serve the public as a place of worship, but the rooms now used as a Chapel will be put to use as a kindergarten, a nursery, and a sewing school for the children of the working class of the neighborhood.

Many will be trained there to become good Christians and loyal members of society who are now being inoculated with the poison of Communism. Unfortunately, many people of that section are Communists.

IN THE NEW WORLD

A few months before we left Sittard, in September 1900, I went once more to Roermond to see Monsignor Drehmanns and told him that, despite all efforts. I could not receive approval for a Motherhouse and novitiate, and that I was determined to go to America.

"Don't do that," Monsignor replied with determination. "You have always followed my advice; follow it now and do not go to America. I am telling you, your Congregation is too young, and you cannot leave it now even for a short time. I will help you get approbation."

How right he was! Our Carmel family was too young at that time (1900), much too young to be left by itself. I knew this well, but what else could I do since I could not find shelter anywhere for my Sisters?

In August we received the approbation of Bishop van Veen of Hertogenbosch for our convent in Tilburg. The events that occurred there on the feast of our St. Mother Teresa on October 15, 1900, have already been chronicled. I also reported how we found refuge after that in Maldon, Essex, England.

Years of labor and hardship had passed since then, but despite all of that, the Carmel of the Divine Heart of Jesus was growing steadily. Apparently it feels at home in the waters of tribulation and thrives best when watered with suffering. Just as some fruit trees demand much sun and water, the Carmel of the Divine Heart was not only watered copiously by God's providence, but it also enjoyed the sun of blessing and grace at all times.

The following review of the status of this young religious family up to the year 1912 is the best proof of God's blessing. He not only kept this work alive but also made it grow and thrive despite the storms of many trials.

1891 – Beginning in Berlin with five hundred marks and three poor children.

1899 – First novitiate at Sittard opened with fourteen novices and the approbation of theBishop.

1900 – Closed without profession.

1901 – Second novitiate opened in Maldon, England with twenty-one novices, with the approval of Cardinal Vaughan; closed in 1902 without profession because the constitutions first had to be approved.

1904 – Motherhouse and novitiate opened in Rocca di Pappa with the approbation of Cardinal Satolli.

1906 – Third novitiate opened in Rocca di Papa with fifty novices. At the same time all the Sisters of the first and second novitiates were allowed to make their profession, with the approval of Cardinal Satolli.

1910 – The *Decretum laudis* was received.

1912 – The total number of Sisters is 205, of whom sixty-two have perpetual vows and 143 have temporary vows, fifty novices and eighty-two postulants. The Sisters labor in thirteen dioceses and twenty St. Joseph's Homes. Of the latter there are established five in Germany, two in Bohemia, two in the Netherlands, one in England, two in Switzerland, two in Italy, four in Budapest, and two in Vienna.

1912 – The total number of children in the Homes is 1,000 boys and girls, from one to fourteen years of age. The number of day charges is 900, from three to fourteen years of age.

Besides working in the Homes, a part of the Sisters devote themselves to parish mission work. That is, they visit the families who have fallen away from the faith and endeavor to bring them back to the practice of the faith and the reception of the sacraments.

The result of these labors are as follows: 950 children up to the age of ten years, and some older, have been baptized; 1,200 people, mostly men, have been brought back to the church after five, ten, and even twenty to forty years. In many cases instruction had to be given. Some had merely been baptized and had to make their first Holy Communion after twenty and even forty years.

Three hundred marriages were validated. A priest was obtained for 120 dying persons, who received the last sacraments.

All the baptisms of children took place in Berlin and Switzerland.

Most of the returns to the faith occurred in Budapest, some of them in Berlin and Switzerland.

Since the beginning of the 1890's, I had been sending appeals for alms to the United States, and through this I began a correspondence with a number of priests. One of these appeals must have reached the Pastor of St. Peter's Church, Cleveland, Ohio. In 1912 this priest wrote to me that he thought our work would be very well suited to the conditions there, and he urged me to come to Cleveland.

Filled with great joy and emotion I read this letter again and again. In spirit I saw this large field of labor, ripe for

General Motherhouse
Sittard, Netherlands

Motherhouse Chapel

Provincial Motherhouse of the Northern Province
Wauwatosa, Wisconsin

Provincial Motherhouse of the So. Western Province
La Mesa, California

Provincial Motherhouse of the Canadian Province
Mississauga, Ontario

Provincial Motherhouse of the Central Province
Kirkwood, Missouri

In every child we love the Divine Child, and this sincere love affects the heart of the child as the sun affects the tender growing plants.

--*Mother Mary Teresa*

Aging has something wonderfully attractive, when from the eyes of elderly people shines forth kindness and peace, and a gentle smile plays on their lips.

--*Mother Mary Teresa*

Adoration before the Blessed Sacrament –
the source and center of our personal, communal and apostolic life

An informal gathering of Sisters with Mother M. Katharina and
Sister M. Philiberta during their visit to Wauwatosa in 1990

I conceived such a great, tender devotion to dear Father St. Joseph, as I called him, that I thought I ought to make reparation for the coldness of all unbelievers toward him.

Mother Mary Teresa of St. Joseph

His Holiness Pope John Paul II greeting Mother M. Katharina,
Superior General, and Mother M. Siegfrieda, former Superior General

Wauwatosa's Celebration of The Centennial of Carmel D.C.J.

A MASS OF THANKSGIVING was held at St. Anthony Church in Milwaukee
on May 12, 1991. The Ministers of Celebration (left to right) were:

Rev. M. Patrick Cremer, SCJ
Spiritual Advisor of Carmel DCJ

Rev. Edward S. Tobijanski, SAC
*Chaplain of Provincial
Motherhouse*

The Most Rev. Leo J. Brust
Auxiliary Bishop of Milwaukee

Rev. Msgr. Fabian W. Bruskewitz
*Pastor of St. Bernard Church,
Wauwatosa, (recently consecrated
Bishop of Lincoln, Nebraska)*

Rev. John L. Gigl, Ph.D.
*Former resident of Carmelite
Home for Boys*

Rev. Msgr. Joseph P. Springob
*Former Director of Catholic Social
Services*

the harvest which we would find in the United States. I also remembered vividly the words that I had uttered in that dream vision on July 2, 1891, "I shall not die before the Servants of the Divine Heart are spread all over the world."

Were these words to be fulfilled? Was it God's will that I was to lead His servants, my Sisters, to the New World, now after twenty years? I was ready to do so joyfully. As I had been doing up to this time in Europe, I was willing to sacrifice myself for the salvation of souls in America. However, before I accepted this proposal, I had to be sure that it was God's will. I hurried to Rome to consult Monsignor Jacquemin. After thoughtfully reading the letter of the Pastor, he advised me to follow the suggestion immediately. His own Congregation was laboring in the United States with God's manifest blessing, and he was unable to send enough Sisters there. There was so much work to be done, he added. I told another Priest in Rome of my plans, and he also was of the same opinion.

I then wrote to the Priest in Cleveland that I, along with another Sister, would come to that city in a couple of months. In answer to this letter, Father stated that he would first ask the Bishop's approval, but that the latter was absent just then. Thereupon I wrote to him not to do this but to wait until our arrival. We would leave Naples in the beginning of September. It seemed to me that it would be a very risky endeavor to ask for approval before I knew the conditions and the demands which would be made upon us.

If Father did not obtain episcopal approval, which seemed quite likely, then perhaps we never would have gone to America.

At the moment all was going well in the convents and

the St. Joseph's Homes. Superiors and Sisters were content and endeavoring zealously to sanctify themselves and to work for the salvation of souls by prayer, penance, and works of charity according to the purpose of our Order. We therefore set about preparing for our journey to America.

About the middle of August, a plan for the building of a Chapel in Ujpest was sent to me for my approval. The estimated cost was 25,000 kronen. The Sisters were wholly without funds and had no prospect of generous benefactors. As much as I favored the building of a Chapel, I was still entirely against the expenditure of 25,000 kronen.

I hurriedly set out for Budapest, traveling via Ancona and Fiume. Mother Maria Magdalena accompanied me. After our arrival I called in several masons but no general contractor or architects. I led them to a large, imposing stable which belonged to our property and formerly housed fourteen pedigreed horses. After I had explained to them where the arch for the sanctuary and the oratory and the walls of the sacristy were to be placed, and that all walls were to be newly plastered, I asked them to have an estimate ready for me the next morning. I had 3,000 kronen, and the estimate of one of the masons was 3,000 kronen. I gave this mason the contract for the work. I was overjoyed that now the neighbors would have a Chapel and the Sisters an oratory, and this without incurring a heavy debt.

I hurried back to Rome and Rocca di Pappa the same way as I had come. A few days later, on September 5, M. M. Canisia and M. M. Rita accompanied us to Rome and from there M. M. Johanna and M. M. Alexandra went along with us to Naples. At 2 o'clock in the morning, the

Grosse Kurfürst of the German Lloyd Line steamed away from Naples. Now Naples, the beautiful city, like our future, lay covered with darkness.

Indeed, our future was again veiled in darkness, but God's hand was guiding us through the shadows. This firm confidence enabled me to board the ship trustfully and to enjoy the ocean trip without trepidation. From my youth I had a real passion for traveling on the water. Until now I had only made the short trip from the Netherlands to England and from Ancona to Fiume, but this time I was to have the great pleasure of crossing the ocean.

On September 7 and 8 there were no Holy Masses, although there were two priests aboard. There were about one hundred passengers more than the regular accommodations, and therefore absolutely no place was available where the priests could celebrate Mass. They therefore suggested that they say Mass in our cabin at six o'clock in the morning if we agreed. Naturally we gladly agreed to this suggestion. Very early in the morning we got everything ready for Holy Mass in our small, cozy cabin. There was a portable altar on the ship with every-thing necessary, and we found a few items to beautify the little Chapel. An elderly Italian lady, our neighbor, came to Mass every morning, as did two Franciscan Sisters, when they were well enough. Unfortunately the poor Sis-ters were very seldom well enough, and the same was true of the ship's chaplain. In my travel notes I wrote:

> *September 10:* Glorious weather—sighted Spain; on the heights one could see Arimeda and Trafico, made famous by the battle against the Moslems. We drew near Gibraltar and to the south we could see the coast of Africa.
> *September 11:* Weather bad, only one holy Mass.
> *September 12:* Weather more quiet, two holy Masses.

September 13: Only one holy Mass. Glorious weather, so that the ship could pass between the Azores (island group). This happens only when the weather is unusually clear and quiet, otherwise it would be too dangerous. The islands are covered with luscious vegetation with villages and houses between. Everything is shimmering in bright sunlight, and all around the sparkling waves are flashing like diamonds. Words cannot describe it! What can be compared to the ocean? It is a book that speaks to those who understand its language. Like no other book it tells of God, of His might and splendor, and of His love and mercy.

September 14: Exaltation of the Holy Cross. Two holy Masses. Windy.

September 15 and 16: Cloudy and windy. Daily two holy Masses.

September 17: Thunderstorms. Because of the storm there was no Holy Mass.

September 18: Clear. Storm subsiding. Two holy Masses.

September 19: The last day. Beautiful weather. One holy Mass in our cabin and one on deck for all Catholics. Landed in Hoboken at 6:00 p.m. An agent of the St. Raphael Society met us and took us to St. Mary's Hospital for the night.

September 20: Had an audience with Cardinal Farley of New York. He received us very kindly, read the "Review of 1912" with visible interest and expressed his admiration over the success of the work among the men. He thought our mission was very suitable for American conditions. In conclusion he advised us, as we already had intended, to seek the approval of the Bishop of Cleveland, and then gave us his blessing.

When we returned to the hospital, we were told that in the meantime Father P., a brother of the pastor in Cleveland, had been there and had left word that we were to go to Cleveland without delay and see his brother. This made it impossible for me to visit my sister Lisa and other relatives. We took the night train and reached Cleveland about 4:00 p.m. on September 21. The Pastor seemed to be highly astonished at seeing us and told us that the Bishop had not yet returned, and that he was still in Rome.

It was evidently a disposition of God that Father had not informed me of this while I was in Rocca di Papa, so near to Rome. If the Bishop had refused us admission into his diocese while he was in Rome, we would have been deprived of the opportunity of going to America. And who knows whether another invitation would have been extended to us in the short time before the outbreak of the war of 1914. Now after this war it is almost impossible, under the new immigration laws, to get across and establish a new foundation.

God guides and directs everything wonderfully! After a little while Father took us to his school Sisters who gave us shelter until September 27. We waited for the return of the Bishop from day to day, but in vain. Since I had always regarded time as more precious than gold, I gave up waiting.

The Superior, Mother Leonarda of the Alexius Hospital, was kind enough to give us a small attic room where we could lodge and also store our baggage. It was here that we heard from the Sisters, who were German, that the Bishop had little liking for Germans, and that it was extremely doubtful that he would admit us into his diocese.

These conditions in Cleveland led me to resolve to go to Canada. The Pastor had kindly translated my petition for admission into the diocese. I copied it and left it at the chancery so that His Excellency would find it waiting for him when he returned.

On the ship there had been another priest besides the ship's chaplain, Fr. Aloysius Scafuro, an Italian. Weather permitting, he said Mass daily and gave us Holy Communion. When we parted, I asked him for his address. His Monastery was in Berlin (now Kitchener), Ontario, Canada.

On September 30 we left for New York where we stayed with the Sisters of the Sacred Heart Academy. Then after two days we moved to the very kind Sisters on Pine Street because the Sisters at the Academy had no room. I began to look for a counselor, and Divine Providence led me to Fr. Maeckler, S. J. (a native of Oldenburg) a pious and wise counselor. As soon as he heard of our work, he wanted to keep us in Buffalo, but his plans failed. He had thought it best that we go to Canada and advised me to send my request for admission to a number of bishops whose addresses he had given me. To this request he added a few words of his own. In my request I was to state that I would reply in person for the answer. Fr. Maeckler then gave me his blessing and promised us great success in the New World. Filled with gratitude, we left the good Father and the dear Sisters in Pine Street.

No longer did we feel alone and abandoned in a foreign country and in good spirits we set out for Canada. It is about a one hour ride from Buffalo to the bridge that connects Canada and the United States. This bridge crossed the river below Niagara Falls. The falls are most beautiful and are formed by the drop of the water from Lake Erie into Lake Ontario, which has a much lower sea level. We did not have time to tarry at this place for the duty to establish a home of the Carmel of the Divine Heart in the New World had complete possession of me. Every minute that could be spared I spent communing with God in prayer that I might know His holy will and carry it out.

After crossing the bridge, we had to use several trolleys

and also a railroad. Finally at one of the stations we were directed to a wagon covered with gray canvas. This vehicle, supposedly an omnibus, was completely filled with country people, who, however, moved even closer together to make room for us. I do not know how long we rode in this conveyance. We arrived in Berlin, Ontario, in the darkness of late evening. A friendly woman, who had made the journey in the wagon with us, came up to us as we got off and said that if we wanted to go to the Sisters she would be glad to take us there. Although she was a Protestant, she knew where they lived. We thankfully accepted her kind offer and after a ten minute walk we arrived at the convent of the Notre Dame Sisters. We were received very warmly and were told by the superior, who just happened to be leaving, that we could stay until Monday.

This was Saturday evening and Fr. Maeckler had ordered me to rest at least a week. This rest was now narrowed to one day, Sunday, and on this day I had to write to four or five bishops as I was seeking admission into their dioceses.

The next morning as soon as we had returned from Mass, I began to write. In the course of the day, we were told to see the superior of Father Aloysius. He advised us to see the Bishop of Hamilton and the Archbishop of Toronto, for in both cities we could find a rich field of labor among the foreign born. I thanked him and asked him to give us the addresses of both prelates.

Monday morning we went on to Toronto. We arrived toward evening and had just enough time to look for lodging with some Sisters. In the morning we went to the residence of Archbishop Neil McNeil, who had been appointed only recently. However, he was in Rome. We then submitted our request to his delegate. The city pleased me very much. I felt completely at home in it.

Without further delay we then traveled on to Hamilton. Unfortunately the Bishop was very advanced in age and did not receive any visitors. The Vicar General would gladly have admitted us on account of the many Italians, but the Bishop would not admit any new Congregations.

We took the next train to London, which is a small city in the Province of Ontario, where we would spend the night. We were very warmly received there by the daughters of M. Barat. The following day we continued our journey to Detroit. The Bishop of Detroit was very old. He received us very amiably and was friendly, but he would not take any more Sisters into his diocese. That was the end of this audience.

We stopped over in Toledo where the Bishop promised to send his answer to our petition to Cleveland, but it never reached us.

We had now traveled around the whole of Lake Erie and returned to Cleveland after vainly asking for admission into five dioceses. To us poor, shortsighted mortals it looked as if our journey had been to no avail. This, however, was not the case, for Fr. Maeckler's advice and blessing finally brought us the success prophesied by him. Though it did not seem so at present, it was certainly true of the future. He was undoubtedly the leader given to me by God who directed me on the right path and then Divine Providence taught me to keep pursuing it farther and farther.

The next day, October 14, the Bishop of Cleveland received us in audience. In the presence of several priests, he replied bluntly to my request for admission into his diocese, "I have no place for you in my diocese."

He left the room abruptly without giving us his blessing. Although I had entertained little hope of obtaining his approval, the manner of his refusal wounded me deeply. Nevertheless, immediately a *"Deo gratias"* rose from my heart to God. What else did I seek in America but souls? What else had I been able to do in Europe but to suffer for souls? Until that moment the same was true in America, and no doubt it will always remain so. Has not suffering accompanied me for many years like a shadow?

M. Leonarda allowed us to leave our belongings with her until we could find a home of our own. In the evening of the feast of our St. Mother Teresa of Jesus, October 15, 1912, we arrived in Chicago. We had no address except that of the Archbishop, so we went to his residence. A very friendly, elderly housekeeper took us to Columbus Hospital, which is run by Italian Sisters. There we found welcomed lodging for the night. The housekeeper also told us that the Archbishop was not at home at the time.

The next morning we went to see the Archbishop's secretary who had received and read our petition. He, a German, told us briefly and positively that we, as Germans, would not receive permission to settle in the Chicago Archdiocese, and we should not make any further attempts to obtain it.

Nothing was left but to approach the last Bishop, Archbishop Messmer of Milwaukee, to whom I had sent a petition.

MILWAUKEE

Without losing any time, we traveled to Milwaukee and were very warmly received by the Sisters of St. Joseph's Convent, a young, flourishing Congregation, whose foundress, Mother Alphonsa, had to endure hardships just as we had experienced when she arrived America.

The Archbishop was not at home but returned after a few days, and on October 21, 1912, he graciously granted us permission to establish a Home in Milwaukee.

It was only for about a month that we had been forced to wander about in a strange country, and then the good God took pity on us and let us obtain admission into a diocese. Yet we were unsure how we were going to get a house. Just as it was in Berlin in 1891, I had no money here in America. Our treasury was practically exhausted by our constant traveling. Nevertheless, we did all we could and crossed the city in all directions looking for a house. It seemed very difficult to find property with a garden and a playground suitable for our purposes. In this predicament the Superior of the Sacred Heart Sanitarium advised us to look on South Pierce Street at the Boys' Home which had been vacant for two years and belonged to the archdiocese.

We looked at this Home on October 27. The first impression was horrible, but when I learned the history of this ill-fated Institution, I was convinced that God had intended this house for us. The places for which something had to be atoned were often the places where God led the Carmel of His Divine Heart.

This former Boys' Home now became ours for a rental fee of $400.00, or we could purchase it for $12,000. It was a large structure with a garden and playground. At first the negotiations dragged on. The superintendent with his family had to be given time to move out, and so we could not begin to get the place ready before the feast of the Presentation of our Lady on November 21. Fortunately, our baggage had arrived from Cleveland and the necessary furnishings were still on hand in the poor home. We destitute pioneers had to work very hard cleaning and getting this big house ready to some extent for our Sisters for whom we were ardently waiting. We could not hire any help because we had no money. The few dollars we had were just enough to buy the most necessary food.

Had not Divine Providence guided us? How else could we have found approbation and a home so quickly?

Filled with gratitude and joy I reported our experiences in the United States to all my dear ones in Europe and gave them our address. Some of the Sisters were already on their way to America and arrived in Milwaukee on the night of December 7. Our joy was indescribable on meeting them in our new home, and particularly on the day of the Feast of our dear Lady. That made our joy all the greater.

A temporary Chapel was prepared and the Blessed Sacrament was reserved on December 15, 1912. Fr. Leist was kind enough to say Holy Mass for us every day until he was relieved by Father Fabian, Capuchin.

The Home had hardly been opened when the first children were brought in. It did not take long before the Home was filled. Some of the Sisters devoted their time to mission work and had great success among their respective countrymen. How many had neglected their religious duties and now, urged and encouraged, had begun a new life!

In February 1913, more professed Sisters and postulants arrived. At the same time I received a request from the Archbishop of Toronto to come as soon as possible to establish a Home there.

Heeding this request I left with an Italian Sister for Canada on March 24. We were very hospitably received by the Sisters of St. Joseph, and then had an audience with His Grace, Archbishop Neil McNeil of Toronto. After receiving us most graciously and inquiring about our mission work, he spoke of the many Italians who had settled in Toronto and needed spiritual guidance. But first we would have to look for a home. In order to help us in our search he gave us the addresses of several pastors in whose parishes the largest number of Italians lived. He then dismissed us with his blessing.

What was our amazement the next morning when we were called to the parlor after breakfast and there found the Archbishop who asked us to get ready to go out. In a moment we had put on our mantles. Waiting for what would come next, we returned to the parlor. His Excellency went along with us into the street, led us to his carriage, and urged us to get in. I thanked him and said, "Your Excellency has an Irish heart."

He smiled and replied, "My mother was Irish."

The friendliness and warm-heartedness of the Irish is something unique. I have often thought and said that our Divine Savior must have been friendly and warmhearted like that when He was on earth. How else would He have been able to captivate the people in such a way that they followed Him for days and forgot about eating and drinking!

We now drove from one pastor to another. Those who were at home were very friendly, but none of them knew of a house suitable for us, so we returned to the convent at noon. For a whole week we looked around for a house, but all was in vain. On April 2, we not only found what we wanted but what Divine Providence had destined for us.

After we had gone quite a distance on that day by streetcar, we got off and turned into the next cross street. We had walked for only a few minutes when we saw a "For Rent" sign in a window. We rang the bell, and a young woman appeared and took us through the house, saying she wanted to rent it to somebody as soon as possible. It was a two family house, and since I wanted the whole property including the garden, I inquired about the owner. We were told that the house and garden was the property of the archdiocese. The nearest Catholic Church was that of St. Francis. We went there directly, and the kind and zealous pastor, Fr. McCann, was greatly surprised that we had found this particular property of the archdiocese. Divine Providence must have led us there, he said, and so he was willing to take us into his parish. The Archbishop, too, was surprised when we reported to him that we had been able to find the house, and he gave his consent to our renting the property. He also encouraged us to make every effort to purchase the entire property as well as the garden.

Since the upper flat was vacant, we moved into the house a few days later. The family left the house on April 15, and a number of our Sisters arrived from Milwaukee, for our family had recently grown. Three professed Sisters and one postulant had come from Germany. M. M. Fabiana also came along, and now everybody got busy. We ourselves carpentered and painted and decorated. Yes, we even succeeded in getting the Chapel ready on the last day of May. I named the Home "St. Joseph's Home della Madonna" (dear Lady). That's why, in honor of our dear Lady, the first Holy Mass was celebrated in this small sanctuary on May 30.

Here my dear Italians showed themselves to be generous benefactors. They had not only supplied us with the necessary food, but also collected money and brought it to us after work. They helped us most faithfully through all these years, and we, on our part, have done all we could to get them to observe their religious duties. Since May 1913, their orphan children have always found a home in the Carmel of the Divine Heart.

In Toronto we found benefactors of all nationalities faster than in any other foundation. They vied with one another to make a real Home here for the poorest of all children. Later we obtained the second house and garden, which was then used entirely for the children.

In June the approbation of the Bishop of Fort Wayne reached me, permitting us to settle in Lake County, Indiana, and do mission work among the thousands of immigrants. A number of towns, each with a population of twenty to forty thousand, offered a large field of labor. After a few days, Sr. M. Elizabeth and I left Toronto for Chicago, and from there we went to Lake County, where we were allowed to choose a place.

I went to see one pastor after another. They were of various nationalities, and finally we came to a Hungarian parish with a temporary church. The former church, which had been dedicated to the Most Holy Trinity had burned down. The poor priest was highly nervous. Everything I saw awakened my deepest sympathy, and so I decided to found a Home of Carmel among my beloved Hungarians. This Hungarian parish was located in East Chicago, Indiana.

EAST CHICAGO

For several days our efforts to find a property were in vain until we were directed to the "Land Company" of which Mr. Riley was president. This excellent gentleman, an Irishman and Catholic, took great interest in us. He found two tiny workers' homes, which were being built but were almost finished. We bought these with some land, and were promised that we could occupy them on July 1.

In the meantime, we traveled to Milwaukee in order to greet our newly arrived Sisters and to pack the items necessary for the Chapel and our new home

On July 2, M. M. Aloysia, Sr. M. Elizabeth, and I went from Milwaukee to East Chicago, Indiana, where we were met by M. M. Fabiana and her companion who came from Toronto. Together we went to the little Nazareth houses to prepare a dwelling for our Divine Savior and to establish a Home for His favorites.

These two little houses that we bought were located in a new section of East Chicago called Calumet, where, besides our houses, only two or three other framed houses like ours could be seen at some distance. As far as the eye could see, there was nothing but flat, sandy land. There were no trees, no buildings, nothing, hence, we called our new home "the Desert."

Our poverty had surpassed everything we had experienced so far. I think we did not have one dollar when we arrived at Calumet. We were, therefore, dependent on the charity of kind souls. It gave me special pleasure when a Jewish lady gave me the first loaf of bread. Soon our neighbors, friendly and kind Hungarians, generously came to our aid. More assistance came from some friends in East Chicago, among them Mrs. Fleck and her daughters. All these wonderful people became our faithful and generous benefactors.

The altar of the Chapel was donated by the Extension Society of Chicago, an organization similar to the Bonifatius-Verein of Germany. This Society also gave various other articles, besides altars, to later houses established by us. Mr. Daleiden of Chicago donated a Sacred Heart statue for East Chicago, and a kind, French woman gave us a statue of our Blessed Lady.

A few weeks later, the second little house was made ready for the children, and as soon as its doors opened, it was filled with children whose fathers worked in the mills and whose mothers had died. The fathers paid for the board of their children and gradually the number of benefactors increased. This provided a small, steady income for the Home.

Our main mission work, which was house visits among the people, was begun soon after. Some of the Sisters went out regularly and contacted those who had become estranged from the church. The Sisters sought to awaken new religious life in them, and they were quite successful. They also furnished a small Chapel for the Italians and obtained the services of an Italian priest who later became our chaplain and offered his second Mass on Sunday in the Italian Chapel.

The new Carmel grew amid increasing labors and sacrifices. Even our short recreation period, which we spent in the shade of the house, was not a time of rest. The mosquitoes, which thrived in great numbers in the willow bushes, tormented us so much that often we had to light a small fire and thus drive them away with the smoke.

Our "desert" life was something unique, and yet we came to love it despite everything. Only then did we learn to understand the life of the ancient hermits. The solitude, the beautiful cloud formations, the gorgeous colors of the sunset, and later the sparkling stars, indeed, all these attributes beautified our Indiana desert. Even the howling, or, rather, roaring of the king of the desert was not missing. The seven railroad lines which connect New York with Chicago (the latter is the central point of the United States), passed only a few hundred yards behind our property, and the locomotives gave out their whistles that sounded like the roar of the beasts.

With pleasure I still remember our Sunday walks through the desert. When the sun began to sink, and with our thoughts on the ancient hermits, we strolled to a tiny hill covered with wild roses. At this time the holy prophet Elijah, Spiritual Father of the Carmel, particularly came to mind. To him I dedicated the hill. Happy and peaceful were the hours we spent in this unique place. Ten years later the "desert" had disappeared, and a colony of Croatians had settled in its place. There is a church and a school, now surrounded by several hundred frame houses such as ours.

To make room for a Chapel in our little dwelling was not easy. It took much thinking and planning, but we succeeded in arranging a miniature cathedral in the attic. It included a sanctuary, an arch, and an oratory for the Sisters behind the altar. Even side aisles were not missing. Bishop Alerding of Fort Wayne came in person to bless the Chapel. He was welcomed at the station by over a hundred Hungarians, children, and adults. Later he told me that he kept searching (but in vain) for a house which could be a Chapel. Finally, the whole procession stopped in front of a small workers' cottage. "How can a Chapel be in there?" he thought. He was led from the porch into the parlor and then along a narrow corridor to a very narrow stairway. When he had climbed this and entered the Chapel, he was greatly surprised. Truly he was simply amazed at the sight of this beautiful little sanctuary.

We had not been a month in East Chicago when I received an offer to establish another Home, and of all places, this home was to be founded in Texas. The offer was from Bishop Shaw of San Antonio, the city where we were to administer to more than 40,000 Mexicans. All the Sisters, like myself, were in favor of taking over this mission work. Thus, in the late fall I accepted this offer.

In the beginning of October, I returned to Milwaukee from East Chicago. On the 30th of this month Bishop Koudelka, who had recently been transferred to the diocese of Superior, Wisconsin sent word to me that I was to come to see him. When I did so, he urged me to go to Superior with some of my Sisters. I resolutely declined to accede to his wishes because I had accepted the offer to go to San Antonio. But all my protests were in vain. The Bishop practically forced me to concede.

SUPERIOR

On November 5 Sister Sr. M. Elizabeth and I traveled to Superior, where we were hospitably received by the Poor Handmaids of Christ.

After some futile efforts and difficulties, we finally succeeded in finding a house in a fairly short time. It was located in South Superior and was part of an amusement park situated in the woods. It had been closed recently by the police because a man had been stabbed to death there in a fight.

For years this place had been the source of scandal for the good people of the neighborhood. They were mostly Norwegians, good Lutheran immigrants, who therefore welcomed us with joy. To us, however, this house became a "house of atonement."

There was a Catholic Church in South Superior, but the Blessed Sacrament was not reserved there. To the great joy of the small parish, the Blessed Sacrament was reserved as soon as we began to attend Mass there. The church was about a mile away, and the road led through the woods. Only near the church were there houses.

The cold was very severe there in the North, near Lake Superior. It is a cold such as Germany does not experience. It was horribly cold as early as December 8 on the Feast of our Blessed Lady. The gorgeous colors of the sunrise helped us to forget the biting cold and made this December 8, 1913, unforgettable. Yet these sunrise colors could not compare with the wondrously beautiful coloring of the evening sky. We had never seen anything like it.

Due to the climate and the distant location of the church, we made every effort to get the Chapel ready as soon as possible. The pastor, too, preferred to say Mass with us in the warm Chapel than in the cold, empty church, for beside Sundays and Holydays there was seldom anyone at Mass. On December 25, the great God, hidden in the Blessed Sacrament, made His entrance into our little Bethlehem and brought us true Christmas joy.

When the Home had been made ready, the Bishop came to see it. He was not only satisfied but pleased, not only with the Home but also with the success of the Sisters' mission work among the people.

On December 29 I left Superior with Mother M. Fabiana and Sr. M. Josefa. We stayed one night in East Chicago and then traveled via St. Louis to San Antonio, where we were warmly received by the Ursuline Sisters.

·The Bishop had obtained a house for us, which we later purchased. It was located in the Mexican section of the city and near the Mexican church. As soon as we were ready, we opened a day nursery, and soon over one hundred children were there. The mission work among the Mexicans also flourished. They are good people and are easily led. They had become lax on account of the lack of religious training and instruction. They were all baptized, and that seemed to be enough for them!

Around this time in 1914, thousands of fugitives flocked into San Antonio from Mexico where the revolution had broken out. What misery! The poor Catholic people sought help and refuge. Yet, where did they find it? They found their refuge with the Protestants! However, soon articles of clothing in large quantities were sent to us, and in a short time this new place of refuge became known among the Mexicans. To our great joy, the poor women with their many children were constantly at our door. In one month Sr. M. Elizabeth, who was in charge of helping the poor, was able to provide three hundred families with articles of every kind. Sr. M. Rafaela was the mission Sister. She had been in the Italian convents for a long time and so she was able to learn the Spanish language in a few weeks. God rewarded her labors and sacrifices with His rich blessing.

The furnishing of the house and Chapel caused us a great deal of trouble, such as we had never experienced before. Despite this, everything went well. M. M. Fabiana was indefatigable and made many things for the Chapel herself. She even painted it. On April 7 Bishop Shaw blessed the Chapel, celebrated the first Holy Mass, and to our great joy, reserved the Blessed Sacrament.

In May I returned with Sr. M. Josefa to Milwaukee. After a few weeks, an invitation to open a home called me to St. Catherine's, in the diocese of Toronto, Canada. I went there with Sr. M. Josefa and the Sisters of St. Joseph gave us warm hospitality.

The house which was offered to us was not suitable for our purpose. Since St. Catherine's and the surrounding territory presented a fruitful field of labor, I continued to search for a suitable property. One was found in Merriton about one half hour from St. Catherine's. On a small hill, lapped by rushing waters and covered with trees, I discovered an imposing structure with a large garden and ancient trees, which we bought. It was a charming little spot.

We lived here among people who were Methodists, but, as everywhere else, our association with our neighbors was a friendly one. It did not take long before the most ardent of the Methodist women donated the finest flowers of their garden for our Chapel week after week. Another woman waited for us every morning at the gate of her garden. When we came from Mass we had to pass her place, and she had lettuce and vegetables ready for us. She was a very good woman. One day she told me that she would become a Catholic if she had not promised her dying mother to "remain steadfast in her faith."

I also became acquainted with another elderly lady in a nearby place. She was also a Methodist. She told me that she had had doubts regarding her baptism and then learned that an old man in Hamilton would baptize her. She went to Hamilton, and she had herself baptized. Since doing so she was no longer disturbed about her baptism. It is a pity that these sincerely devout souls are born into the wrong faith and have grown old in it. Of course, they are not necessarily lost, but how much richer they would be in graces if they were children of the Church!

As everywhere else, our Home in Merriton was quickly

filled with children for whom the Sisters cared with tender love. Other Sisters were zealously engaged even as far as Welland in home mission work. Several years later they succeeded in convincing many people (all immigrants) of this place to make their Easter duty. This example made such an impression on the large schismatic parish that they too made their Easter duty in such numbers that their priests came to thank our Sisters for what they had done. From this, one can see the great power of good example.

On June 19, 1914, M. M. Johanna arrived from Bremen with a number of Sisters and postulants. Now that everything was in good order and our Divine Savior had taken up His abode in our cozy little Chapel, I would have liked very much to stay in Merriton. Yet I had to leave this place and with M. M. Johanna, we traveled to East Chicago. It was on this journey that I heard of the outbreak of the war.

We found our house in East Chicago so overcrowded with children that we were forced to enlarge it. If these children did not find shelter there, the fathers would have placed them in the nearby Methodist Home. This was because the Catholic diocesan orphanage was five miles away by train, and the fathers wanted to visit their children more often than was allowed there.

The Sisters and children had prayed one novena after another to Little Saint Therese with the intention of getting a larger Home. Their prayers were answered. The owner of a brickyard, Mr. Kulage, had suffered a severe injury to his leg or foot, and there was grave doubt of his recovery. In his affliction he had recourse to the dear "little Saint" and promised to donate the bricks free of charge in her honor to some charitable cause. Our Sisters became acquainted with this gentleman, and he then promised to donate all the necessary bricks. Other firms were also found willing to donate other materials. The building was begun in August with the approval of the Bishop of Fort Wayne. A good Catholic man, a Swiss, was the builder of this first Home.

Sr. M. Gertrude and her children had obtained their new Home from the Little Saint Therese of the Child Jesus by their prayers, and they were now anxious to move in. Unfortunately, necessity forced us to postpone this day of joy for a whole year. This is what happened. Beginning with December 1912, our professed Sisters had been bringing along some postulants when they came from Europe. There were now nineteen postulants, and their investiture had to take place soon. The only place that had enough room for a novitiate was the new Home in East Chicago. Bishop Alerding gave us permission to open the novitiate there. M. M. Serafica became the novice mistress, and since she had settled in a strange nest with her novices like a cuckoo, the sisters of this novitiate were given the nickname of "cuckoos." The year passed quickly, and the "cuckoos" flew away into various houses, and the "swallow mother," Sr. M. Gertrude, came with her group of children and took joyous possession of her nest.

On January 10, 1915, I heard the words clear and distinct in the quiet of the night, "You have the second Decree." I believed this message, told it to my Sisters, and we all sang a thankful and joyful *Te Deum*. After a few weeks, we received a letter confirming the message: "We have received the second Decree on January 7. All were very happy."

As related above, it was in November 1913 that, at the

urgent request of Bishop Koudelka, I had taken several Sisters to Superior to work among the immigrants. The Sisters labored with visible success and had found many good friends who supported them, so they were in better financial condition than the other Homes. The Bishop had always expressed his satisfaction with the work of the Sisters. In December 1914 he went to Rome. Soon afterward I was shocked to receive a letter from him ordering me to recall the Sisters from Superior, Wisconsin, as soon as possible.

We did not know what had happened, and vainly we tried to discover the reason for this order. To me a bishop's voice was always "God's voice," and I acted accordingly. I ordered the Sisters to leave the place and return to Milwaukee with all their belongings.

On January 15, 1915, Bishop Koudelka, who traveled a great deal, happened to come to Indiana. Since he was very close to our convent, M. M. Johanna and I went to see him. We asked him for the reason for dissolving our convent in Superior. He told us that he had been in Rome, and there the Dominican Fathers had told him that they were very sorry for him having "those" Sisters in his diocese. "They felt very sorry for any bishop who had them in his diocese," he was told.

After the Bishop made his statement M. M. Johanna replied, "Your Excellency came to the right door in Rome."

The Dominicans in Rome have, unfortunately, never been well-disposed toward us. Whatever gave rise to this displeasure, God only knows. But it is remarkable that it was through Fr. Augustine Keller, O.P., that I came to Berlin in 1889, and many times when I was with the Savigny's, I had recourse to him. It was also Father Augustine who gave the first altar for the Home in the Pappelallee. God had permitted this. Of course my frailty furnished the reason for many to regard the work, the Carmel of the Divine Heart of Jesus, to which I had dedicated my life as not being the work of the Lord. I could only excuse the conduct of my opponents whose number was not small. Yet I have never been angry with them. Yes, I believe they were convinced that they were doing a service to God when they tried to destroy the Carmel of the Divine Heart or the St. Joseph's Homes.

No doubt it was this that made Bishop Koudelka report the bad opinion which the Dominicans in Rome had of us to the priests of Lake County, Indiana. For to our deep sorrow we noticed that many of them who were formerly favorable to us, now were completely changed. Now I had to suffer in the New World as I had to suffer in Berlin in 1892. God be thanked for every drop of wormwood. Life passes quickly, and heaven, alas, has no suffering which can be offered to God as a sacrifice of love!

The year of 1915 was a year of suffering for all Europe, actually for the whole world. The following years brought even more suffering. Nevertheless our Carmel succeeded in surviving in the various countries. The German Sisters, however, left England and came to Toronto, Canada. That made it necessary for me to entrust my English boys to Russian and Netherland Sisters who did not know English well enough and at the same time did not understand how to train boys. This pained me very much, but there was little I could do in those days. All I could do was to commend them and everything to the protection of God.

Furthermore, some Germans as well as some Italians who were our friends, in their excitement caused by the war, had persuaded the Superior of Rocca di Papa to leave the convent in all haste with the German Sisters and novices. Only the Italian Sisters, four or five of them, were to stay with the Italian children who numbered over one hundred. The Superior followed the advice and fled with the Sisters to Switzerland and the Netherlands.

This was not enough. One of these over-anxious friends also wrote a letter to Mother M. Alexandra, superior in Cremona, urging her to flee immediately with all the German Sisters. But this brave soul, who had a mother's heart for the boys, went to the Bishop of Cremona with the letter, and the Bishop told her, "This priest is not your superior. If your Mother General recalls you, then you must obey. Furthermore, what about the boys? Do we throw them onto the street? I have no other Sisters for them."

The Bishop had recourse to the government and obtained permission for M. M. Alexandra to remain there undisturbed with her German Sisters. Some of the Sisters also would have gladly stayed in Rocca di Papa, and no doubt would also have received permission from the government to stay if an application had been made in Rome.

The poor, young Italian Sisters who were left behind were not able to take care of the children and preserve religious life. They tried, but their efforts were in vain. It was fortunate that we had only Italian children in our charge. For this reason it happened that we were allowed to remain there, although the Home was confiscated as "German property," and now we had to pay rent. After ten years, it was restored to us.

Like M. M. Alexandria, our younger superiors in Hungary showed courage and endurance when the revolution broke out there. Only an older superior urged the Sisters to pack quickly and flee to Germany. The superiors of the four other convents, however, would not consent to leave. They were determined to remain at their posts at whatever cost and stay with the children, whom they loved tenderly and did not want to hand over to the Communists. They showed that they were true shepherds and not hirelings. The perseverance that they showed, the danger and the suffering that they faced, and the inquisitions to which they were subjected, is all described in the report of their experiences during the revolution which M. M. Clara sent to me in America.

The seed that Bishop Koudelka and some of the priests had sowed against the Carmel of the Divine Heart of Jesus in Indiana, or rather in Lake County, sprang up according to God's will and brought forth a rich harvest of humiliations and trials. We could hardly send our Sisters out on mission work, for then they came in contact with the priests who, in many cases, had ceased to be favorable toward us. The priests even tried to persuade the Sisters to leave the Carmel. Thanks be to God they succeeded only in the case of one Sister, who left secretly with the help of a pastor on July 7, 1915.

July 19 was a real day of suffering for me. Father X., who formerly seemed to be one of our best friends (a German-American), now came from a nearby town and showed himself to be an enemy of the Carmel. In order to get us into his power, he had himself appointed by the Bishop as our "director," and presented himself as such on the aforesaid day. At the first visitation he demanded so many changes and regulations that very little would have been left of Carmel of the Divine Heart of Jesus. The Sacred Congregation had approved our constitutions, and everything had been arranged according to the latest prescriptions of canon law. Our Motherhouse was located near Rome, until the war deprived us of it. After this over- zealous priest had procured and studied the latest book on canon law regarding Congregations and Orders of Women, he did not return for the second visitation.

It was a great grace to be trampled under foot. To this day I am grateful to this priest that I was allowed to be used by him like a "door mat" on that day, and also later at some negotiations where he wanted to be present. Even if the will sends up a joyful *Deo gratias* to heaven, the heart still writhes with pain under the blows.

These were the blows that struck from the outside, but this year also brought us a rich harvest of suffering from within our family. Among the novices there was one very talented Sister who thought she was called by God to do "something great" for Him. She planned to start her own Order, and with her eloquent tongue she tried to win not only novices, but also professed Sisters. She also had a strong aversion against me, as she wrote to me in a long letter in December 1915. Everything I said or did, even every movement of mine, aroused angry resentment in her.

She finally resolved to ask for her dismissal, which was granted. But hardly had she left our convent in East Chicago when she asked for admission in Milwaukee, where I had gone in the meantime. We did not, of course, grant her wish. A priest took interest in her and helped her obtain employment with a family, so she could learn English well enough before she started her own institution. It became especially painful for us when she started asking for approval of her plan not only in other dioceses, but she also turned to bishops of dioceses and archdioceses where we already had houses. In addition, she would write to me incessantly. I felt very sorry for her, and since she was all alone I kept up correspondence with her. Furthermore, I thought perhaps it might even be God's will, and she would do much good with her sisters, since she planned to serve only in the poorest parochial schools. I was always sorry to see so many Franciscans and Dominicans teaching in schools, and no Carmelites teaching. Now she intended to found the "School Sisters of the Carmel."

Around that time I found out that Fr. Soos, the one who made it possible for us to come to Budapest, was now in Canada. I told him of Sr. M. Lucia's plans and received the answer that he would be glad to have her come since he was currently looking for Sisters for his school. Sr. M. Lucia accepted the offer and one of our professed Sisters joined her. As soon as she was settled in Canada, she asked me for more professed Sisters, especially of those who had been in the novitiate with her. According to the enthusiasm with which these had been attached to her at the time, I expected ten or more to follow her. We were resolved to give them full freedom of choice. How great was our surprise and our joy when not even one Sister could be persuaded to leave the Carmel of the Divine Heart of Jesus!

As is often the case, an inordinate attachment had turned into aversion, and therefore, not one of her former adherents was found willing to join her, although I had given them the choice.

Sr. M. Lucia then ascribed their unwillingness to me and conceived even greater bitterness toward me. This was doubly painful to me because I had always been more in favor of her institution than against it. Until the time of her death in 1921, she caused me much pain and trouble by her letters, not only in our American convents, but also those in Europe, where her companions had many friends.

With patience and gratitude I endured this suffering. Yes, it is my vocation to suffer and do penance for holy Mother the Church and for the freedom of the Church as well. Around the whole world she is crowned with thorns. It is only in individual lands that she is bound to the Cross. . . that is, robbed of her freedom.

HAMMOND

We must return to Indiana once more. The Home in East Chicago was for girls, and since we were constantly being asked to take in boys, we received permission from Bishop Alerding to open a second Home in Lake County. After much fruitless searching, M. M. Fabiana and I found a fairly large residence in Hammond, Indiana. This was in August of 1915. M. M. Johanna, M. M. Stefana, and M. M. Fabiana established this Home. I had dedicated it to the Divine Child, and to the great joy of everyone, the Blessed Sacrament was reserved there on Christmas Day.

It hardly had been opened before it was filled with boys of various nationalities. On account of the boundless poverty, building an addition for children could not be started until 1924. This only became possible through the kindness of Fr. Berg, Dr. Weiss, and other benefactors. Mr. Reed (a Methodist), who was a very good builder, was in charge of building this addition. In the Jubilee Year of 1925, a happy crowd of boys marched in with their beloved M. M. Waltrudis, who had worked tirelessly for this project.

In East Chicago, Mr. Riley, president of the Land Company, Mr. Baker, a bank director, and other men and women, had been promoting the building of the main

Home with a Chapel. These individuals were the true friends of the Carmel! They had campaigned for funds and had collected $15,000 for us. The same amount was taken up as a loan. Finally, the contractor, an Irishman, erected the building to the satisfaction of all concerned.

This house was a real blessing for the poor Sisters. We were, and still are, all filled with the most profound gratitude toward these generous benefactors, as well as those who had helped build the Home in Hammond. May the good God reward them a thousandfold in eternity. What they have done for the poorest of the poor God looks upon as done to Him.

The unfavorable attitude toward the Carmel of the Divine Heart of Jesus had also spread to Milwaukee. On January 14, 1916, I went to ask Archbishop Messmer for permission to buy some property in Milwaukee. In answer to my request he said he thought it best if we would leave the diocese.

For a moment I was stunned! I did not have the least inkling that the Archbishop was dissatisfied with us. One can easily imagine, therefore, how I felt! But I remained outwardly calm and said, "Bishop's voice, God's voice!" and agreed to comply with his wish.

Now God came to my aid again with a wonderful dream vision. I saw obstacle after obstacle rise up, but I overcame them all and reached the goal. God also let me see the Motherhouse in exact detail.

Everything came true. For the present I did not follow the request to leave, but went to see a very pious priest in Milwaukee and then also to Monsignor Rainer of St. Francis Seminary. Monsignor Rainer said, "I hope to keep the Sisters for the diocese." He, along with the other priest, succeeded in persuading the Archbishop to revoke his order and permit us to buy a house.

Then began anew an endless search for a house and the collecting of money from the spring of 1916 until October 29 of that year.

CHAPTER FIFTEEN

WAUWATOSA: THE AMERICAN MOTHERHOUSE

The Sisters, realty agents, and friends showed me more than thirty houses in and around Milwaukee. Not one of them really suited our purpose, and none of them looked like the building that I had been shown in my dream.

My confidence did not waver. Divine Providence would guide me to the place chosen by God. In that dream seemingly insurmountable difficulties and a dense darkness surrounded me. Suddenly the darkness dissipated, and it became light. There, standing before the house destined for us, I walked inside. This house had to be located either in the city or in a suburb. Of this I was firmly convinced. With tireless zeal, I continued my search, and God rewarded my trust.

I think it was Saturday, October 28, 1916, when the evening mail brought me one more offering of a house. This came from the suburb of Wauwatosa. On Sunday afternoon I went to this suburb of Milwaukee with Sr. M. Wenzeslawa who knew this area well from her house visits.

The home mentioned in the agent's letter was vacant and therefore locked. However, we saw the sign of an agent on the door of the neighboring house. We rang the bell and were received very kindly by a lady. When I explained the reason for our call, she asked us to wait awhile as she called her husband who was in the neighborhood. After waiting a short time, he appeared, and to my great joy, I learned that he had been born in the Netherlands.

I described the kind of property we were looking for,

and he immediately said with decisiveness, "The neighboring house is nothing for you, but I have a house and garden just as you described. Allow me to get the keys, and I will take you there. The property is no more than a ten minute walk from here."

With amazement I listened to the elderly Protestant gentleman. How could he know what I was looking for? Filled with suspense, I wondered if my good countryman would take me to the building I had seen in my dream.

After a little while, Mr. N. appeared with the keys, and we started out. First we followed the main street, then crossed a bridge over a stream, and finally, climbing gradually, we came to a high spot where a mighty tree stood right in the middle of the walk. Due to its venerable age and unusual beauty, it did not have to yield to the sidewalk, but the cement had been laid around the gnarled giant which was the ornament of the property we were about to inspect.

The gentleman opened the door of the house. I entered and stood in the building that had been before my mind's eye ever since my dream. I saw the same hallway, the same stairs, and doors. Everything appeared exactly as I had seen it.

Naturally I concealed my joy from the agent. On the contrary, I told him that without a much larger garden we would not buy the house. To this he replied, "I will get those two pieces of property next to the garden of this house right away."

Now we went out again on the street. I looked at the neighboring houses. Close by was a large property with a small park and old fir trees and a beautiful, solidly built home with a tower. The whole area pleased me very much.

I asked Mr. N., "Could we get the property with the fir trees also?"

"No," he replied, "the lady demands much too high a price."

Then we agreed that a report on the two pieces of property was to be given to me the next day. At any rate he would have to sell the house for a much lower price, for we could not pay the asking price of $9,500 under any condition.

First of all we asked the pastor of Wauwatosa for his permission to have a house in his parish. This request he gladly granted. Yet, he too found the price of the house too high and said that since he knew the agent well, he would try to get a better bargain.

Our Sisters were overjoyed when we announced to them that we had finally found a suitable property. With a great deal of effort the Sisters had collected more than $4,000 by going from house to house. Now after a long search, the right house had been found, and their efforts were finally rewarded.

The next morning I asked Fr. Peschong, a Luxemburger, who, from the beginning had been our kind friend and counselor, to come and see me. I told him that I had found the property and would like his opinion of it. He arrived within a short time, and, if I remember correctly, he took M. M. Johanna and me to Wauwatosa in his automobile.

After he had carefully inspected the house and property with an expert eye, he shared our joy over this find and said, "You will not find anything better or more suited to your purpose in the whole city." He also donated $1,000 toward the purchase price, and so to our great joy, we now had $5,000.

He also thought that the price, which the agent had reduced from $9,500 to $8,500, would have to be brought down still lower. I therefore asked Mr. Reichert, a businessman and a good friend of the Sisters, to look at the property and to get a lower price, since we had only $5,000. With great suspense we awaited the outcome of his efforts. Finally, on Saturday evening, his message came by telephone, "Have closed the deal for you. Price $6,500. That leaves $1,500 as mortgage, and $5,000 is due when the deed is recorded."

We were filled with great jubilation and joy! Such goodness of God! How our patience had been rewarded.

On February 6, 1917, M. M. Serafica, M. M. Fabiana, and several Sisters began to get the Home ready. It was located at 168 Kavanaugh Place, Wauwatosa. Since we had no money to hire workmen, the Sisters themselves erected the high cloister fence that reached from one street to the other around the whole property.

KENOSHA

In May 1917 we were asked by some ladies to establish a Home in Kenosha, a city not far from Milwaukee and also situated on Lake Michigan. I went to see these ladies, and I was told that a lady, who had recently died, from a German Parish had left $10,000 in her will for a hospital. The ladies wanted us to have this money, but we would have to open a hospital. I was very sorry that I could not accept this offer, since our constitutions expressly excluded the care of the sick and also teaching in schools. However, we would be happy to establish a Home for the aged women and elderly couples of the middle class.

The negotiations dragged on. In addition to this, the Archbishop's approbation had to be obtained, and we already had two houses in Milwaukee. The first Home had been arranged for girls and the one in Wauwatosa for boys.

The ladies themselves had started a movement to establish a Home in Kenosha, and therefore, I asked them to go to the Archbishop and ask for his approval. This they did, and when they returned from the audience with the Archbishop, they were completely stunned. Not only had they not been given permission, but also the Archbishop had told them that we had so many debts that we did not even pay the rent on South Pierce Street. Therefore, he stated, no thought could be given to establish another house.

We were greatly surprised over this misconception, for we had paid the rent of $400 a year regularly, and we had no debts outside the $1,500 on the house in Wauwatosa. After Mrs. Jacobs and Mrs. Sybilla Zeitler heard this, and I had promised them that I would go to the Archbishop myself, they felt reassured and returned to Kenosha. "If it is God's will, we will come to Kenosha," were my parting words.

A few days later we went to the Archbishop with the rent receipts and our account books listing the income and expenditures. These we laid before him. The false statement now became the occasion of our receiving permission to establish a house in Kenosha. His Excellency granted this permission at the end of our audience. The ladies in Kenosha were overjoyed when I brought them the news, but this joy was mixed with the worry of how and where to find a suitable place.

Great efforts were made to find a house, both by us and by our friends in Kenosha, but all was fruitless. Our friends advised us to buy a farm. We agreed to this and paid down $10 on one located near the city. However, the tenant of this farm and his wife could not bear the thought of leaving the place to which they had become attached. We waited patiently for a few weeks, and then we forfeited the $10 and abandoned the idea of buying a farm. The search for a place now began anew. Kenosha is a city of about 30,000 people, and a large house is seldom found vacant. God Himself had chosen a house and property where we were to build a house for Him and establish our first Home for the Aged. In order that I might make no mistake in choosing this place, He again showed it to me beforehand.

In my sleep the Divine Savior appeared to me in the form of a young man. His face was like that in the picture of the "Twelve Year Old Jesus in the Temple," a picture widely seen in the United States. Unfortunately, I do not know the name of the artist, but I saw the glorious, beautiful face only in profile. As I said, I saw Him as a young man, with His hands raised as if in prayer. He walked in the middle between my companion and me with such a rapid stride that He was almost always a step ahead of us. He was beautiful, wondrously beautiful, and He led us from street to street until we reached a stream. Now we went over a bridge and farther along past a bright red gas tank, and then along this street to a house built of red brick where we stopped. I awoke, and the charming vision was gone, but it was still in my mind.

The morning mail brought a letter from Mrs. Zeitler urging me to come to Kenosha at once. A suitable house had been found at last. The purchase had to be made soon because another buyer wanted to acquire it. Mother M. Johanna and I went there directly. We met Mr. Henry, the agent, at the station, picked up Mrs. Zeitler on the way, and started off for the house that was for sale.

I saw the same street through which I had been led in my dream. There, too, was the same stream. We crossed over the bridge, and walking a little father past the big gas tank, we stopped in front of a red brick house. It was just as the Divine Guide had shown to me in the dream!

We inspected the house and came to terms with the owner. Generous Mrs. Zeitler made the down payment and the deal was closed.

The feeling of having been guided by God was so strong in me that I was not able to think clearly, and thus I forgot completely to ask the pastor, who lived across the street, for his approval. After the transaction was finished and we had left the house, I became conscious of my omission. M. M. Johanna and I hastened to the rectory to correct my mistake.

We told the pastor of our plans to open a Home for the Aged in the city. We explained that we had the approbation of the Archbishop, and that we had found a house on Sheridan Road. The house, we mentioned, was almost directly across from the pastor's residence. The residence had belonged to Mr. R. As soon as the pastor heard of our plan, he began to describe the street and the neighborhood as being totally unsuited to our purpose. Poor Mother M. Johanna's face became longer and longer while the pastor condemned our purchase. Thus, when we left, she was completely discouraged. Perhaps I might have been discouraged also had I been in her place. However, to me it was clear that Divine Providence had allowed me to forget about getting the pastor's approval first, and that it had taken a vision to make this purchase possible.

On the way to Mrs. Zeitler's home, we visited the ever

cheerful Mrs. Jacobs. She succeeded in refuting all the objections made by the pastor against the property of Mr. R. As a result, we returned home in the evening in a very happy mood.

On July 26 on the feast of St. Anne, we moved into the house on Sheridan Road. Shortly after, we bought the neighboring house. A few months later we also bought the adjacent property and the corner house as well. Between the second and the corner house there was a plot of land on which we built a small Chapel with the approval of Archbishop Messmer, who later visited our Home on one of his visits to Kenosha. Mr. Lindl, a Norwegian Lutheran, erected the building quickly and tastefully for the sum of $6,000.

The two houses that stood side by side were joined by a covered corridor and arranged for a Home for the Aged. In the corner house, which was the convent, a temporary Chapel was made ready, and on the feast of St. Michael our beloved Savior made His entrance.

My faithful companion and co-foundress, holy poverty, made her presence felt here too. Yet heaven knows no pain of poverty, and therefore, it must be endured gratefully out of love for God and the souls of men during this short life that we each experience here on earth.

SOUTH KENOSHA

One night, before the Feast of the Presentation of Mary on November 21, our dear Lady led me in a dream over fields and meadows to a grove of old trees. She seemed to be about ten years old and was clothed in an extremely delicate, rose-colored robe.

On the same day Mr. Michael Gehl, the uncle of a Milwaukee priest, visited us and offered to sell us his fruit and vegetable farm in South Kenosha. We looked at the farm and then went to see Fr. Malone in whose parish the farm was located. Fr. Malone was not against our buying the farm, and as soon as the neighboring farmers had heard of our plans to settle there, they pleaded with us to buy the property for their sakes. They would help us in every way. They had no more ardent a wish than that a Chapel be built in the neighborhood.

It was very touching when Mr. Gehl, who had been crippled by a fall and was quite elderly, said to us when selling his property, "But please, you will have to take old Michael into the bargain, too!" I gladly promised him that he could remain with us in his little house until he died. This was December 1917, and the very next year we succeeded, with the help of Mr. Gehl, in adding another piece of land with a house located on Bain Road, which was near to the electric railway. This house was made into a convent, and a Chapel as well as a Home for the Aged was added. It housed thirty people.

God blessed the zeal of M. M. Fabiana who did not shirk any sacrifice or effort to make this Home a reality in honor of our dear Lady. What a blessing this peaceful Home and Chapel has become for many dear, elderly people and also our loyal neighbors.

I spent nearly the entire month of December 1917 at Toronto and Merriton, Canada, and returned to Milwaukee before Christmas. On December 22, I set out for San Antonio accompanied by Sr. M. Bernardine. Due to the schedules of the military trains, we arrived in New Orleans at 2 a.m. We were six hours late. At the station a gentleman, who was a member of the Knights of Columbus, came to our assistance and directed us to the hospital of the Vincentian Sisters.

The night nurse immediately opened the door, and Sister Angela gave me the warmest welcome. I will never forget this Sister! How great is charity, the true love of our neighbor! Is it not like the aroma that has come down from the heights of heaven? This Sister's name was Angela or Aloysia, and she was from Ireland.

The next day, December 24, we continued on our journey and were to arrive at San Antonio the next morning by 6 o'clock on December 25. However, at 9 o'clock a. m. there was no sight of the city. Then after 11 o'clock in the mornig, the train finally stopped. M. M. Aloysia and M. M. Serafica welcomed us at the station and took us quickly by auto to St. Mary's Church, where we arrived before the Credo of the Solemn High Mass. We poor travelers were indeed very grateful that we had not been deprived of the Christmas Mass, despite the lateness of the train.

This visit was the occasion of mutual joy, especially for me, because I found the Sisters not only healthy, but also happy and zealous. How touching it was to see them surrounded by more than a hundred of these dark-skinned, charming Mexican children! These children proved once more the great power of love. Sr. M. Gertrude knew how to win the hearts of her charges, and this made her very successful in training them.

During my stay in San Antonio, I was visited by Fr. Muehlsiepen, C.Ss.R., a very zealous priest, who sacrificed himself completely for the Mexican people. His latest work was the establishment of a mission for them just outside the city. It was located on a high piece of land where a large number of refugees had settled. Here they had neither church nor Chapel. He built a church and organized a parish. Later, the Bishop turned his work over to a Mexican priest.

Fr. Muehlsiepen had been the confessor for our Sisters for a long time, and he knew their fruitful work among his beloved Mexicans. In the interest of this young suburban parish, he asked me to establish a second Home there. He would take care of the Bishop's approbation. I was instructed to go there and look over the area and the church but not to forget to inspect the corner house and the property, as this could be purchased without delay.

This proposal was very welcomed by me, not only on account of the Mexicans, but more so on account of the Sisters who lived in very confined quarters on a low piece of land on San Saba Street. This property was small and there were many children living there. The dwellings of the poor Mexicans surrounded us. For Germans, Texas is unbearably hot. San Antonio has almost tropical heat. Palms are the shade trees of the streets and plazas. Cacti, large and small, grow like weeds. Roses bloom throughout the winter.

Soon we drove out to the mission. This was built in a charming, picturesque country! The mission church and the proposed plot were located on an elevation, but wherever one looked, hills rose into the sky. There were religious institutions built on some of the hills. On the next hill was the convent of the Good Shepherd Sisters. The nearness of the Gulf of Mexico as well as the hilly region are the reasons why a gentle breeze is always blowing, making the climate more tolerable than the inland areas.

After seeing all of this, we were in favor of a new foundation. Fr. Muehlsiepen was pleased with our decision and immediately obtained the Bishop's approval. The corner property was bought, and as soon as the owner vacated the house, it was made into a temporary little convent with room for four or five Sisters. The best room was made into a small sanctuary for our Divine Savior. The Sisters had to be content with this small convent for almost five years until Sr. M. Josepha, with her usual energy and zeal, managed to collect $15,000 for a Children's Home. This Home was built with the approval of Bishop Drossaerts (a Netherlander) next to the first house. The solemn dedication took place, I believe, in 1924, and was performed by the Bishop himself. I have never seen this new building because I had to leave the United States in 1920.

In March of 1918, if my memory serves me correctly, I returned to the North with Sr. M. Rosa. After traveling a day and a night, we ran into a blizzard such as I had heard and read about but had never experienced. Slowly and ceaselessly the snow fell. The train battled its way through the storm, but finally its strength seemed to be exhausted. During the storm that night, the locomotive stood still for hours. Toward morning it crept along slowly, and finally we reached Chicago. The train could not enter the station because the snow was several feet deep. Our traveling companions struggled to get to the station with the greatest effort. We had to struggle likewise until a friendly official led us through some covered sheds to the station. Yet we knew not how to proceed further or where to go. No train was running, and there were no streetcars or other vehicles. The streets were covered with several feet of snow, and it continued to fall without end.

There was nothing to do but to look for the nearest hospital which could be reached by the elevated train, but we were unsure how to get that far. I could not find a firm footing as the snow was so slippery. Then an army officer and a policeman took pity on us and led us to the elevated train, and in a little while we were at the hospital. Sadly, no angel in the form of a Sister received us here as on Christmas day in New Orleans!

The next morning the trains were running again, and we rode as far as Hammond. Here we had to walk for an hour since no streetcars were running. Luckily the many workers had already made a path in the snow, and so we finally reached our convent. However, it was walled off toward the street by six feet of snow, and in some places the snow had drifted even higher. The neighbors had tunneled a path through the wall of snow. We followed this and at last, after traveling three or four days, found ourselves happily in the midst of our dear Sisters. I think M. M. Stefana was superior at that time in Hammond. After a night's rest, we went on to East Chicago for a short visit. We then returned to St. Raphael's Home on South Pierce Street, Milwaukee. This Home was surrounded by an even higher wall of snow than was in Hammond, but an opening had been made in it. In the meantime, the snow had stopped falling. In Milwaukee the snow was not carried away as it is done in Berlin; this was left to the sun, which gradually melts away even such large masses of snow as we had seen.

Before I visited the Sisters in Kenosha, I surprised M. M. Johanna and the Sisters in Wauwatosa, where I was very anxious to buy the property with the fir trees and the house with the tower. To my great joy, Divine Providence had now smoothed the way to acquire this beautiful property for our Carmel. My plan was to build a Chapel and an oratory between the two houses. At that time, unfortunately, the money for this was still lacking.

In Kenosha I found the elderly people happy and contented. Yes, they thought that they had found a heaven on
earth. The Sisters made every effort to brighten their
lives, and the same was true of our confessor, Father
Augustine (a Netherlander), a Carmelite, whom the elderly people dearly loved. He knew how to get along with
them as few people do.

One day during our evening recreation, I was called to
the telephone. M. M. Johanna of Wauwatosa was on the
phone and told me that a priest from La Crosse was coming on the evening train. I passed this information along
to the Sisters.

"Oh, Mother," said Sr. M. Fabiana, "that is not a priest
from La Crosse, but the old lady from Holy Cross church
whom the Vincentians are sending." I doubted this
because I heard "La Crosse" clearly and distinctly. However they did not believe me, and so I let them keep their
opinion. Sr. M. Theodora asked me whether she would be
permitted to stay up and wait because the next train did
not arrive until 11 p.m. I agreed, and Sister then warmed
up the bed for the dear old mother and waited until midnight, but in vain.

During our morning reading, the doorbell rang at about
9 o'clock. A priest from La Crosse was there, wishing to
speak to me. After I had greeted him, he said that he had
intended to come the evening before, but the train had
been too late, and he waited until the morning to come.
The purpose of his visit was the establishment of a house
in his parish in the southwestern part of the state of Wisconsin. He spoke of a small place with no factories. It
did not seem to be the right kind of mission field for us. I
declined therefore to accept this offer, but the good
Father pleaded so earnestly that I could not help but

promise him to look at the place and the house that he had ready for us.

I said nothing to the Sisters of this proposal, but I wrote or telephoned M. M. Johanna in Milwaukee, asking her to bring another Sister and come to Kenosha. After her arrival, she agreed to go with me to Fr. Ambauen (the priest from La Crosse), and soon we were on our way. I believe we arrived at the site toward evening, and we immediately saw that neither the locality nor the little house was suitable for our Carmel. To please the elderly pastor, we went to see the Bishop of La Crosse. He received us with great kindness and told us that he would like to have us in his diocese, but that the parish of Fr. Ambauen was not the place for us and our type of work. However, we might find something more suitable in Reedsburg. A lady had offered her property for a convent; perhaps we would like to look at it. We stopped in Reedsburg on our way back to Milwaukee, as it was on the same railroad line. The lady welcomed us and was very friendly, but after all we had seen and heard, this offer seemed to be no more acceptable than the one of Fr. Ambauen. After a few hours waiting, we rode back to Wauwatosa.

It was about midnight when we awoke the Sisters and surprised them, for they had no idea of our trip. They thought that since the next day was Sunday, M. M. Johanna, the superior, had suddenly returned.

ST. JOSEPH'S HOME OF THE DIVINE HEART

The next morning after Mass M. M. Johanna asked me to greet the Guardian of St. Francis Monastery in Milwaukee. He had said Mass in our Chapel in place of the regular Father, so I went to greet him.

After a brief greeting, he asked me how things were going in the Home for the Aged in Kenosha. I was happy to be able to say that all was well, and then he proposed that we open a Home in Milwaukee for elderly people of the middle class since there was no Catholic institution of that kind in the city. Some elderly people had saved a little money but not enough to keep a servant to look after them when they could no longer care for themselves. I knew that such a Home was needed in Milwaukee, but we were unsure how to obtain the Archbishop's approval. I avoiding thinking of the issue.

I spoke to Father Guardian of my fears, and he replied, "The St. Vincent de Paul men will get the Archbishop's approval." I expressed my doubts about finding a suitable place. "I can mention two very suitable places right now," he answered.

"But where will we get the money?" I asked.

"I will give you the address of a family who will give you the money."

Now I was defeated and had to accept the addresses of the two houses as well as the wealthy family. I promised not only to look at the properties but also to report to him right away, since the two houses were only a few minutes' walk from the monastery.

That afternoon I asked M. M. Johanna to accompany me on my inspection tour of the house on Galena Street which had been recommended to me by Father Guardian. After a long ride on the streetcar, we found it without trouble. As soon as I saw this imposing, elegant residence I turned away and said, "That is no St. Joseph's Home. We will look at the other place, which has been a hospital and will be much more plain."

We now searched for the other house, but Father Guardian had not mentioned the name of the street. He had only described the house, saying it was only a few minutes walk from Galena Street and could easily be found and recognized. For more than a half-hour we walked from block to block, occasionally asking people, but to no avail. We could not find the house. Suddenly, to our great surprise, we were again in front of the corner house on Galena Street. Now I remembered the Villa on Maglodi Street in Budapest from which I also had turned away at first only to have Divine Providence lead me there again. I had been struck by this fact and, as such, then rented the dwelling. Later it was bought and made into a Home for the Divine Friend of children and became, in truth, a source of blessing not only for the children but also for the people of the neighborhood.

All my thoughts from the past returned to me. I suggested to M. M. Johanna that we speak to the owner of the house and look at the property. We rang the bell, a lady appeared, and asked us the purpose of the visit. I replied that the Guardian of the Capuchin Monastery had given us this address, and recommended it as a Home for the Aged, and that we understood that the property was for sale. The lady told us to come again the next day, when we would be able to inspect the house and the property.

We returned at the appointed time and were received very graciously by Mrs. Schroeder and her brother. They took us through the entire residence, and I had to admire its beauty, for everything was in the most tasteful color and style. While walking through the rooms, the house appeared to me like a paradise for the elderly people who had toiled all their lives and now, with the help of their savings, could enjoy a peaceful, carefree evening of life here and prepare themselves for the journey into eternity.

The cost was $22,000. It had cost $50,000 to build the house, and fifteen years ago it had been furnished with elegance and luxury for $30,000.

I told Mrs. Schroeder that we were totally without means and would have to borrow the money. We could pay $2,000 down at the most and then make an annual payment of $500, with interest on the remaining debt. Both she and her brother were satisfied with this offer, but we could not make a binding agreement until we had obtained the approval from the Archbishop.

Mrs. Schroeder, a Lutheran, now told us that she had often seen the Capuchin Fathers walk by, and likewise a group of colored children with the Sisters from Father Stephen's orphanage. This had led her to offer the house to Father Stephen as he had a very small house at the time. He had been to see the place with the Archbishop, but the latter had said, "This is not the place for a Home for your colored children, Father Stephen; it is more suitable as a Home for ladies."

Mrs. Schroeder added, "The Archbishop, therefore, thought even then that our residence would be a suitable place for such a Home. No doubt he will be in favor of it now."

We reported the results of our visit to Father Guardian who was visibly pleased with our willingness to accept his proposal. He spoke to the members of the Vincent de Paul Society about the results of our talk with Mrs. Schroeder, and these men obtained the approval of the Archbishop. All this was completed on May 2, 1918.

In the meantime we had obtained the $10,000 from the family mentioned by Father Guardian. Just then I needed only $2,000 as a down payment on Galena Street. At last we could now buy the property with the tower and the fir trees on Kavanaugh Place. This was the property which I had always wanted to buy. The owner was satisfied with the first payment of $5,000, and the home became ours. To my great joy we could take possession at once, and I immediately ordered the necessary changes. Originally the home had belonged to an Italian General and was beautifully and solidly built. It became not only our convent, but later served as our provincial house, for since 1923 our fourteen houses in the United States and in Canada formed a separate province. The first house had been converted into a Home for boys, and between the two houses we built a Chapel with an oratory, under which a refectory was arranged for the Sisters.

After receiving the Archbishop's approval, we again went to see Mrs. Schroeder to make the final business arrangements. This time she showed us the two adjacent houses, each with twelve rooms, a large stable, and a garden, all of which was part of the property and included in the sale. Now my joy was complete, for now we could have a Chapel with an oratory and connect it to the corner house, which was to be the Home for the Aged.

Without delay I now began to remodel the one house for a Chapel and Sisters' quarters because it was vacant. Mrs. Schroeder was not leaving the corner residence before July 1. I continued to live in Wauwatosa and rode almost every morning at about 6 o'clock with Sr. M. Agatha to Galena Street. We bought milk and bread on the way, then we opened the house for the workmen and went to the nearby Slovenian church for Mass and Holy Communion. Whenever my presence was not needed in the house, we made the necessary purchases for all the items needed for the Chapel, the convent, and for the housing of more than fifty elderly people who were yet to be selected. This meant much walking and riding.

We must never forget the generosity of Mrs. Schroeder. When she left the residence at the appointed time, she not only donated precious rugs, drapes, and the furnishings of the dining room and the library, but also a complete electric washer and dryer, and even a gas range. May the good God reward her and her family for all the charity she has done for us. The whole property could be regarded more as a gift, for she could have sold the large residence at any time for $35,000, and the two adjoining houses and stables for $22,000.

The Divine Heart had selected this family home for His dwelling and had guided everyone and everything in such a wonderful way that I gave the Home the name of St. Joseph's Home of the Divine Heart.

Hardly were some of the rooms furnished when the first elderly ladies entered. From week to week it became more evident how much such a Home was needed in Milwaukee.

Our joy and that of the dear elderly people was complete when the Blessed Sacrament was reserved in the Chapel on August 18, 1918. Divine Providence had visibly chosen Father Guardian of the Capuchins as the instrument of this foundation. I, therefore, asked the Archbishop to allow him to bless the Chapel. This request was granted, and Father Guardian blessed the Chapel as well as the Sisters' oratory and celebrated the first Mass in the small but very devout Chapel. Afterward the whole house was blessed. Oh, that was a feast day of joy! The eyes of everyone were shining with gratitude and happiness!

From my heart I thank the good God for granting me the

grace of establishing Homes for the Aged. It had been a dream that I had cherished since April 1891. How many souls are thereby won for the Divine Heart, even in the eleventh hour! And how many prepare themselves here, where they are so near to God. Here they are so much better prepared for the end in a much better manner than they could have experienced in the everyday world.

God is good, wondrously good and merciful; let us praise Him for all eternity!

ST. JOSEPH'S HOME OF ST. RAPHAEL, SOUTH PIERCE STREET

Now I must return to the first foundation of the Carmel of the Divine Heart of Jesus in America. We had moved into this Home on the eve of the Presentation which was November 20, 1912. By summer of 1918 the number of children had increased to such an extent that there was not a corner in the attic in which beds could not be found, and which did not serve as sleeping quarters for the Sisters or the children.

Dear M. M. Felicitas of the Holy Cross was superior. She was filled with compassion for the poor Sisters and children who had to sleep in the attic rooms in the terrible summer heat, and she, therefore, ardently wished for another house. In this great need, felt by everyone in the house, she made a novena to our Lady before the Feast of the Assumption on August 15. This novena was made with all the children, big and little, and by the Sisters as well.

During the novena a priest begged the Sisters to take five children whose mother had just died and whose father, a working man, was at his wit's end. The father had to go to work and could not possibly leave his children alone.

Mother M. Felicitas called me by phone, told me of this sad case, and urged me to come. I followed her wish, and she immediately begged me to find another home for these children. She could not refuse to take the children but would be forced to do so. She herself could hardly stand the heat in the house. It was a sixty year old frame building and stood on an elevation all by itself.

I thought and thought and prayed for help, and finally I told her to call Mr. N. and tell him that I was with her at South Pierce Street and wished him to come and see me that evening if possible. He promised to pay a visit. This good gentleman was one of our "helpers in need." It is impossible to give an account of the many occasions on which he had helped me while I was in Milwaukee. God alone knows of these incidences and may He reward Mr. N. for all he has done for us!

It did not take long for our "helper in need" to appear. I told him about the troubles of Sr. M. Felicitas, the lack of space, and the terrible heat. I continued, "Mr. N., you surely know of a house for us."

"No, there are none to be had because there is no construction going on. It is very hard to get workers, and even if you can get them, who would pay the high wages?"

"But, Mr. N., surely there must be some old vacant residence, just give it a little thought."

This was followed by a deep silence! I did not disturb him but waited. Suddenly he exclaimed, "That's right! I know of an old residence, and it is vacant! We can go there right away! Come along!" He ran to get his auto ready, and I went to call Sr. M. Felicitas to come along. I told her that Mr. N. was going to show us a large, vacant house.

In a few minutes we were speeding along. One can imagine how excited we were! We did not have far to go, for this residence was near Grand Avenue. This house was far different from the one on South Pierce Street. It was built massively, was three stories high, and had large rooms with space enough for fifty children on the first two floors. One story could be used for the convent of the Sisters, and the garage could be remodeled into a Chapel.

We were overjoyed, and Mr. N. thought we could take possession of the property right away at the cost of perhaps $10,000 to $12,000 and with only a small down payment. He said that he would get in touch with the owner, who lived in Chicago, as soon as possible.

It can easily be imagined what joy and jubilation the news aroused in the Sisters and children! All were convinced that our Blessed Lady had heard our novena.

The Archbishop gave his approval to our moving. The property was bought, and the remodeling began. I gave the contract to the same architect who had done the work in Wauwatosa and Galena Street, as he had done the work so well and at such a reasonable cost.

The work did not go as fast as the Sisters and the children had wished, but the prospect of escaping from the heat in the near future made it more bearable. After eight weeks we gradually began to move into the new home.

It gave special pleasure that Father Augustine, the Carmelite who said Mass on South Pierce Street every day, wanted to sing a High Mass for the last time. M. M. Felitias told me that there would be a Mass at St. Raphael's on October 30. Naturally I went there, for this day was a memorable anniversary for me. Nobody knew this, so I celebrated it with God and my dear saints, whom I asked to praise and thank God with me for all the graces granted to me in that hour.

It was on October 30, 1888, that I became a child of the Church and for a long time I had wished to celebrate this day with a High Mass, and, without anyone being aware of it, my dear Heavenly Mother fulfilled my wish. How often are not the secret wishes of her children fulfilled! Would that all men were children of this most loving and caring Mother and praise and love her as such. I regard everyone, no matter what class, race, or nationality, who does not have the Mother of God as his Mother, as being a motherless orphan. All these individuals are, in truth, poor orphans, and if they do not recognize this now, the hour will come when they will agree with me. By that time, however, it will be too late, as this faithful Mother can no longer help them.

Not long after our St. Joseph's family left the house on South Pierce Street, a fire broke out in the home during the night. Probably some sparks which the wind often carried from the nearby foundry had fallen on the tarpaper roof of the connecting walk or the addition and set the building on fire. The former children's sleeping quarters and the stairs leading to them were destroyed by the fire. The children hardly would have been saved had they still been there. We were completely shaken by this disaster, but thankful at the same time to God's fatherly love which had saved us from a terrible misfortune.

The building of the Chapel in Wauwatosa was again entirely the work of Divine Providence, and hence I cannot pass it over in silence. Father A. was the indirect cause. It must have been in the summer of 1918, shortly

WAUWATOSA: THE AMERICAN MOTHERHOUSE

after we moved to the Home of the Divine Heart on Galena Street, when Father A. came to us one day with the
intention of becoming our house chaplain some time
later. Wauwatosa pleased him very much. The deep shade
of the streets, the dark green of the lawns, the beautiful
flowers in front of the houses and, above all, our location
on a hill, made Wauwatosa a truly charming place. He
also liked our property and planned to rent, or perhaps
buy, a home nearby where he could live with his sister.
While I was leading him through the garden with the fir
trees, I told him of my ardent wish to build a Chapel
there, and I expressed my deep regret about not being
able to get the money. He replied simply, "I will lend you
the necessary money."

The next day M. M. Johanna and I went to the Archbishop to ask him if we could have Father A. as our chaplain. We met the Archbishop while he was on his way to
the streetcar and could speak to him for only a few minutes while walking with him. He had to catch a train and
did not have any time to spare. So we walked about a
hundred steps to the car line with him, and I told him
about Father A. Surprised, the Archbishop said, "Has he
been to see you?" I quickly added that Father A. liked
Wauwatosa very much and was willing to lend us the
money to build a Chapel, and then I asked the Archbishop for his approval of this plan. Since he knew that Father
A. was wealthy, he gave his permission, and we returned
home with happy hearts.

We immediately contacted the architect and asked him
to come as soon as possible, as we wanted to build a
Chapel between the two houses and in this way connect
them. He did not make us wait long, and I soon went over
the plans with him. The refectory and the kitchen were to

be on the lower floor above the Chapel. The sacristy was to be on the one side and the grille on the other. Finally, behind that would be constructed a large oratory, connected directly with the convent by a corridor.

On February 2, 1919, the dedication took place with a solemn High Mass in the new Chapel. The joy and thankfulness of the Sisters was very great, but mine was less so because the corridor had not been built.

DETROIT

For a number of years Fr. H. Kaufmann had made efforts to have the Carmel of the Divine Heart of Jesus admitted into the Diocese of Detroit, Michigan. Until now all efforts had been in vain because the very aged Bishop, John S. Foley, would not permit any new Orders of sisters into his diocese. The Bishop himself had said that to me in 1912.

In January of 1918, God called him to eternity, and his successor was Most Rev. Michael J. Gallagher. Amid the rejoicing of the whole diocese, especially the priests and religious, His Excellency took possession of his See in July 1918.

In the fall of the same year, I was asked by a priest to establish a house there. After an exchange of letters, I finally agreed to meet him for consultation. Some relatives of Fr. Kaufmann very hospitably received us. The latter assured us that we would obtain the permission of the Bishop. In the meantime, another difficulty had arisen, and that was the great lack of housing prevalent since the war. Fr. Kaufmann, however, promised to look for a residence or some other property.

Naturally, I first wanted to obtain the Bishop's permission. We asked for an audience, and when the time arrived, we were received very kindly. After giving an account of our work in the parishes and for the poor children, we were given the long-awaited approval. Happy in spirit and also strengthened in our confidence by the Bishop's blessing, we returned home on February 7, 1919.

Now we patiently waited for Fr. Kaufmann to find us a house. Finally, in April, a letter came with the happy news that Fr. Kaufmann had found a place and that we were to come and have a look at it.

How disappointed we were when we saw the property. It was a small residence without a garden. No, this house was completely unsuitable for our purposes. With deep regret for having made a fruitless journey, we returned, I believe, to East Chicago that same evening.

Weeks passed, and we heard nothing from the Kaufmann family who were our only acquaintances in Detroit. No doubt it was impossible to find a place. Despite this difficulty, I did not want to give up this foundation which would mean, perhaps, the salvation of many souls. Besides, we had the Bishop's permission.

Trusting in our Blessed Lady, I set out again for Michigan with Sr. M. Zita. This time we traveled without being asked to come. The Dominican Sisters of the Perpetual Adoration gave us a friendly welcome, but soon our Blessed Mother led me to St. Mary's Church, and to Fr. Wuest, superior of the Holy Spirit Fathers who were at that church. I told him why we had come to Detroit and asked him to find us lodging, if possible, with some lady here in the center of the city. I also asked for addresses of real estate agents. He immediately went to the phone and notified several agents that we were looking for a large house. He also inquired about lodging for us.

A few days later he had located a dear, elderly lady who had a room for us. To our great joy, this lady lived only a short distance from the Italian church, around which a colony of Italians had formed.

We took lodging next day with good old Mrs. Schulz, but the street on which her house stood was extremely noisy, and our room was so hot that we found it difficult to sleep. This noise and this heat were a source of torture for me night after night for six long weeks. Every foundation demands its own sacrifices, and the more difficulties there are to be endured and overcome, the more blessed will be the foundation. I had often experienced this, and so I bore all the sufferings and hardships with gratitude toward God. My companion, Sr. M. Zita, slept so well that neither the noise nor the heat bothered her. That was a great consolation to me.

The agents were busy trying to find a place for us. We were shown one house after another. First we had been told that there was none to be had. Then, within a few weeks, a dozen were offered to us, but not one of them was suitable. I was looking for two houses, side by side, which could be connected. One house would be for a Home for the Aged, and the other for the convent and Chapel. We were so busy finding and inspecting houses offered to us that the days just flew by. Thus, we found no time to make other visits. This led Mrs. Spoo, one of our first acquaintances, to assume that we had returned to Milwaukee. This lady, a widow, was waiting impatiently for the opening of a Home for ladies. We had become acquainted with her through Fr. Wuest and had told her of our fruitless search for a suitable property. She, therefore, asked an agent she knew to make inquiries, and this broker finally succeeded in locating a suitable piece of property. She wrote this information in a letter which she sent to me in Milwaukee thinking that I had returned there. From there the letter was forwarded to me in Detroit.

In the meantime a large residence had been found. Although it did not suit me much, we had nevertheless begun negotiating with the owner, because Fr. Kaufmann was in favor of it. The transaction was not completed because I considered the price too high.

One night during that time, I saw a house very clearly in my sleep. The vision of the windows, the outside steps, and the peculiar roof was so clear that I could have drawn it when I awakened. I was firmly convinced that this dream came from God, and that this was the house He had chosen for this foundation. Praying and questioning, I turned to His Divine Majesty, "How can I find this house in this city, among so many thousands of houses?"

Like always we went to Mass at St. Mary's that morning, and we hardly had returned when I received Mrs. Spoo's letter from Milwaukee which recommended a certain Mr. Hahn, who knew of a very suitable house for us. We immediately telephoned Mr. Hahn and asked him to show us the house as soon as possible. After a short while, he picked us up with his auto and took us to Leland Street.

I was so immersed in my dream that I did not enter the house when we got there but walked across the street to view it from there. I looked up and saw what my dream had shown me: the steps, the roof, color of the house. I saw everything in the smallest detail. Yes, that was the house that Divine Providence had shown me!

The admiration and the thankfulness which filled my heart at the moment defies description! It is God's work, the Carmel of the Divine Heart of Jesus. My task was only to seek and do God's will as long as I was able to serve as His instrument!

This house was a double or two family house, very well constructed and preserved. On both sides were houses that I immediately thought could be purchased in addition to the one we were shown.

I thanked Mr. Hahn and told him that I first had to consult the pastor in whose parish this house was located, and that I also had to obtain the permission of the Bishop to buy the property.

The pastor, Fr. Tennes, knew the house well, since a number of Catholics lived close by. Like us, he also found the residence very suitable for a home for the aged. I then asked him to show the house to the Bishop, which he promised to do as soon as possible.

After one or two days we went to see Fr. Tennes again. He told us that he had taken the Bishop in his auto to Leland Street and that the Bishop had said, "You cannot find a better and more suitable property in the whole city."

Now the negotiations for the property began. Naturally I was again without money. Yet I had this idea: either I begin with money, or with God and His blessing. I have always started all foundations without money but with God's blessing. So far God has always furnished the necessary money. The same happened here.

The property belonged to a good Lutheran Mecklenburg family. The noble gentleman even donated $500 toward the Home. Nevertheless, the one house was not enough, for one cannot support a home for the aged if it does not house at least thirty people. In a few months we succeeded with the help of Mr. Hahn to buy three more houses. Now it was our task to connect these five buildings.

My Divine Master again came to my aid and gave me the idea for the remodeling and the additions. Finally, a place was found where the Chapel could be built, and this was done very tastefully by a Polish architect. To this Chapel was joined a little convent for the Sisters.

On July 26, 1919, on the Feast of St. Anne, we two Sisters moved into the new Carmel, which I dedicated to the Divine Heart: "St. Joseph's Home of the Divine Heart." A few days later, M. M. Felicitas, Sr. M. Afra, and Sr. M. Josefa and other Sisters came to help us. We now set to work with great zeal getting everything ready. The urgent pleas to be admitted soon, not only from Mrs. Spoo but from other women as well, forced us to hurry with the work. Some of the dear, elderly people were able to enter the home in August. In the beginning of September, the rooms of the first house were all occupied. We could not admit any others until the houses were connected.

The Bishop did us the great honor of coming in person to celebrate the first Mass and reserve the Blessed Sacrament in the small room that served as a temporary Chapel. Only on the prior evening had we found out that His Excellency was coming, and, as such, were unable to make any preparations at all.

Trusting in the help of our dear Lady, we had gone to Detroit in May, and our trust in her motherly protection was not misplaced, as the history of this foundation shows. In thanksgiving I chose September 8, 1919, as the greatest feast day for this house. For on this day, the Feast of the Birth of our dear Lady, the Chapel was dedicated and the Blessed Sacrament reserved.

This day, September 8, was also a special anniversary for our Bishop because five years before, on this feast of the Mother of God, he had been consecrated Bishop.

What a blessing it was for Diocese of Detroit to have such a Bishop filled with wisdom, holy zeal, and a real love for souls! Born in Ireland, he began his studies in France, and when he had to leave that country, he continued his studies in Innsbruck.

When we were with him for a while after breakfast, he told us a story of his younger days.

The two young priests who had been with him were smoking, but he did not smoke. When I expressed my surprise, he told us that one time when he went to confession as a young man, he was nauseated by a strong smell of tobacco. This made such an impression on him at the time that he resolved never to smoke, and he has kept this promise unbroken.

This is a mark of strong character, and the Church of God needs such characters, but unfortunately, how few strong characters there are nowadays! Are not most people slaves to some passion? What else is it but slavery if I am in the power of some habit that I cannot resist?

Is it not slavery if I cannot live without a cigar, a pipe, or tobacco? Is it any different if I cannot live without the enjoyment of wine, beer, or such other beverages? Is it any different if I allow myself to be so taken with the reading of novels, or with gambling or dangerous friendships, that I neglect my duties? Is not all of this a form of slavery?

Who can count the many kinds of chains with which the enemy of souls enslaves mankind? Should not every sensible, thinking person break such chains and cast them from himself? The breaking of these chains would be more becoming of a good Christian whose soul could then be consecrated to God!

How much salt has lost its savor! How ripe the harvest

and how few the laborers! Taking the illustration of our Divine Savior, what has caused the salt to lose its savor? Is it not, in so many cases, one of these passions, chains, or addictions?

Why is there such a lack of harvesters? Why the same complaint everywhere, "The harvest is ripe, but the laborers are lacking"? Why? Because a large proportion of the souls called by God to His service are bound by the chains of slavery!

Such an example, such a manly deed in the years of youth (I believe His Excellency was then fifteen years old) makes a lasting impression. I often think of this Prince of the Church with admiration and reverent love and wish to do much for this diocese. Unfortunately, this has not been possible in the measure I desired, until now. Eternal thanks to the good God that with and through prayer one can work everywhere, quietly and secretly, for the salvation and sanctification of souls. I firmly believe that this can be accomplished even from the greatest distance across the ocean. The power of prayer is omniscient.

The Bishop had no idea that he had given his permission for a Home that God Himself had chosen. Since then, a dear family had formed there around the Divine Heart hidden in the Tabernacle, and often this family finds itself in suppliant prayer in the Chapel.

Old age has something wonderfully attractive when kindness and peace shine forth from the eyes of the dear, elderly people, and a gentle smile plays on their lips!

It has been a great joy and satisfaction to me that I was able to establish this Home for the Aged. A Home, and not an institution, is what it should be. It should be a Home for elderly women and couples, in which they can spend a quiet evening of life, lighted up by peace and warmed by love! It also must be a Home where, when the elderly have closed their eyes and passed into eternity, they are remembered with love and prayers.

Yes, all the convents and Homes of the Carmel of the Divine Heart of Jesus should be such abodes of peace and love.

ST. CHARLES, MISSOURI

Since I described the beginnings of all American establishments I must not leave St. Charles unmentioned, especially since it is the last Carmel of the Divine Heart that I was privileged to call into life in the United States.

While traveling to San Antonio, we passed through St. Louis, and I became acquainted with this metropolis in the state of Missouri. On that occasion we wandered through some of the poorest sections of the city, and I received the impression that here would be a rich mission field for us.

Ever since that time I had a secret wish to go to St. Louis. Yet only now, after four years, did I have the opportunity. This was due to a Nun of the Carmelite monastery. This Nun assailed us with letters urging us to establish a Home in St. Louis. In August 1919, she wrote that she had found a lady who wanted to donate her property for a convent.

Finally I grew weary of these letters and turned to Father Irenaeus, O.C.D., of Milwaukee. I wrote to him asking him to advise me what he thought of the matter and what course of action I should take. He advised me to see the Archbishop of St. Louis and also to look into the situation of establishing a convent.

Following his advice, dear M. M. Benedicta and I left for St. Louis on Sept 19, 1919. We arrived in the morning and after we had secured lodgings for ourselves for that night in St. Anthony's Hospital of the Franciscan Sisters, we went without losing any time to the monastery of the Carmelite Nuns. After getting the details of the offer of the property and of the conditions attached to it, we saw immediately that this was nothing for the Carmel of the Divine Heart of Jesus. Yielding to the urgent pleas of the Nun, we took the address of the residence and went to inspect it. It was not even necessary to go inside. Its location, all by itself in the woods and far from any contact, made it entirely unsuitable for our purpose.

Although the affair that had brought us to St. Louis was thus settled, we nevertheless asked for an audience with Archbishop John J. Glennon. Luckily, we found him at home and were very kindly received by him.

The plans of the Carmelite Nuns were well known to the Archbishop, and he was not surprised that we had turned down the offer. I told him about our Homes for the Aged and asked his permission to open such a Home near St. Louis.

As in Milwaukee, so also here, there was a need for a Home for elderly people of the middle class. This moved the Archbishop to grant his permission, and we were given the names of three or four suburbs among which we could choose the location for a Home.

I thanked the Archbishop heartily, for it was indeed a great joy to have my wish fulfilled. It was also a great delight to be given permission to plant the Carmel of the Divine Heart in the Archdiocese of St. Louis and under the protection of the kind and benevolent Archbishop. Such permission was a wonderful grace for me as I was now in the eleventh hour of my sojourn in America. I saw in this foundation only a small beginning. I hoped that here, as in Wisconsin, one establishment after another would arise. I especially desired that the house mission work in St. Louis would flourish. Unfortunately, my wish has not been fulfilled in the past five years. Nevertheless, it is, at present, uncertain what will develop out of the Carmel of the Divine Heart of Jesus in St. Louis.

I must now go back to September 20, 1919. Divine Providence led us to St. Charles where Monsignor Willmes had been pastor of the German parish for forty years. He took us under his wing, as did Fr. Winkelmann. Through his efforts, we found a beauiful piece of property with a double house. Our search took us only a few hours. The home belonged to a French family but was rented out. The negotiations for buying the property were begun. Everything went quickly as in a dream, and so we were back in Kenosha on September 21. After this, however, we had to practice patience for about a half year, until the physician, who occupied the larger house with his family, and the other families had vacated the two premises.

Finally, in the month of St. Joseph, we were able to take possession and go to work. On the evening of March 8, Sr. M. Petronilla and I went from Chicago to St. Louis. While frigid weather still reigned in Michigan and Wisconsin, sunshine and balmy spring air greeted us in St. Louis. St Charles, located on a hill near St. Louis, is a charming little place. Ancient trees shade the streets. The summer is very hot. Our massively built houses lay in a garden that had fruit trees as well as shade trees.

We arrived early and entered the empty house which had no water or gas connections. Many helping hands were found to assist us in getting the house in order within a few hours. An Englishman and an Alsatian were especially helpful.

Great was the surprise of Mother M. Felicitas and Sr. M. Theodora when they arrived, not like we did in glorious spring weather, but with thunder and lightning. There on March 10, they found us quite well established.

We continued to work busily. Two more Sisters came to help us. The unavoidable remodeling and additions and, above all, a temporary Chapel were undertaken immediately. Monsignor Willmes blessed the Chapel on May 3. The Blessed Sacrament was reserved during the following High Mass. Monsignor Willmes was just as happy as we were, and according to his advice, the building of a permanent Chapel was begun on May 8. Sadly, I was no longer in America to witness its dedication.

My days in America were numbered. I appointed Mother M. Felicitas as superior and went on May 31 to San Antonio with Sr. M. Josefa. We had a nice trip and arrived there on June 2. I led my companion to the little Home on the hill on Nebraska Street and installed her as superior.

I was able to enjoy the zeal and the spirit of sacrifice of my dear Sisters for only a month when the first hour of parting struck, to be followed by ten more. What heart-wrenching grief this was for me!

FAREWELL TO AMERICA

Mother M. Francis had come to call for me. We then returned to St. Charles, where I was happy to see the new Chapel already under roof. After a painful parting, we went to Kenosha, South Kenosha, and Milwaukee, where I visited my dear ones in all three of the convents. Then we traveled to Hammond and East Chicago. At each location the same sorrow and pain greeted me. How great my love for my Sisters was shown by the deep grief which the parting from each caused me. I dare not even think of it, for even now my eyes fill with tears!

How great is that holy love that binds religious together! It is this love that makes the life in the Order a paradise despite all sacrifices, hardships, and privations. Also the love of the Divine Savior, Who, hidden in the most Holy Sacrament, draws us around Him like a magnet and fills us with tender love for Him and for one another!

At this fountain of love, the most Holy Sacrament, our souls are refreshed and enkindled more and more with the fire of divine love. That love never rests but ever sends forth new flames that consume itself in works of charity toward others!

After we had visited our Sisters in Detroit, Toronto, and St. Catherine's and had made our farewells, we traveled in company with Sr. M. Johanna and Sr. M. Afra to New York by way of Buffalo. We arrived there on Sunday. We were very anxious to get to Mass, and so we went directly to the Cathedral. To our great surprise it was filled with the devout faithful. There was standing room only. Near the entrance, but off to the side, we still found standing room. After a few minutes, an usher came to us and whispered to me that as soon as the sermon was over he would lead us to some seats. The sermon was over in a little while and the usher appeared again, motioning for us to follow him. Unsuspecting, we followed him, and were amazed at what transpired. Opening a way for us, he walked down the middle aisle. We poor Sisters followed him to the communion rail, where he had placed some chairs for us.

At first I was horrified. Accustomed as I am to attending Mass hidden behind the altar in the oratory, it is always a great sacrifice for me if I have to attend Mass in a church (especially on a Sunday) while traveling or when establishing a convent. Now we occupied a very prominent place!

As soon as I reconciled myself to the situation which could not be changed, and raised my eyes to adore the Divine Savior in the Most Blessed Sacrament, I noticed that an unusual celebration was taking place. Cardinal N. and a number of Bishops were present in the Cathedral. A glorious and magnificent High Mass was sung. I was raised up in spirit and filled with gratitude for this disposition of Divine Providence that allowed me to assist at a Pontifical High Mass as I was about to depart from my dear America. We learned later that the Archbishop from Melbourne, Australia, was on a visit to the Cardinal of New York and was present at Mass.

On the Feast (July 21) and under the protection of the holy Prophet Elijah, whose large image stands near the Confession in St. Peter's in Rome and bears the inscription, "Father of all Carmelites," our steamer left New York. We had left our faithful companions and through them had sent our last farewells to all our dear ones in America.

When we previously had traveled to New York or Hoboken, our journey had started at Naples and led us past the coast of Spain and Africa. Now, the return journey took us past the coast of England and France. It was an indescribably beautiful trip, but unfortunately the days passed too quickly! Bright sunshine made the foaming waves glitter and sparkle, and when evening came, the setting sun dipped the waves in gold. This work of the

Creator was intoxicatingly beautiful. We had hardly made two thirds of the journey when the sea gulls appeared, and the closer we came to the coast, the larger the numbers of gulls that fluttered and soared about the ship. At times such a beautiful view offered itself that it cannot be described. When the ocean took on its deep blue color, the hundreds of white Sea Gulls fluttered about, and then, as if on command, suddenly swooped down and settled on the dark blue surface of the water. It seemed as if, for a minute, the ocean had become a mirror of the star-studded heaven.

I say so much about the sea with its wondrous beauty, but my real admiration is directed to the Creator of this boundless ocean, the most glorious of His works. It was this admiration of God's creation that inspired the singer of the Old Testament, the royal Prophet, to the most elated love of God and made him praise the Creator in his psalms. In a similar way, nature, the wondrous beauty of God's creation, has inflamed me to love and praise God since the days of my youth.

We were not only favored by good weather, our spiritual nature was also well provided for. As passengers we had a bishop and five priests on the ship. Every day we had several Masses and could receive Holy Communion. On Sunday the Bishop said Mass for the first class. For us in second class, a Paulist Father said Mass and preached in English. An Oblate Father said Mass for the third class and preached in their language for the many German passengers on board.

The sermon of the Paulist Father fit our sojourn on the ocean, far from the world. "Yes, far from the world," this is how all children of God ought to live, not only when on the ocean, but also in the midst of the turmoil of the world! He repeatedly said, "We must be on the alert for the voice of God, so we can hear it and learn His will to be able to do it."

He himself, the son of a Protestant preacher, had secured the peace and quiet of his soul and had thus been able to hear God's voice and heed it. He became a Catholic, a priest of the Paulist Fathers. He had found peace in the Church and joy in his holy vocation. That was clear to everyone who came in contact with him.

This priest belonged to the fortunate ones who had found the "buried treasure" and bought the field. That is, those who have joined the Church and had done so without delay.

I called him blessed and also all those souls who have found and who still find this "Treasure." Blessed also are those who with the grace of God, and with courage and confidence, give everything they possess to purchase this field and become children of Holy Mother Church! They will never regret it, no matter what the price, and no matter how great the sacrifice!

CHAPTER SIXTEEN

HOME AGAIN

We landed in Rotterdam on July 31. To my great surprise and joy our oldest Mothers awaited our arrival. After a most hearty greeting, we went immediately to Haarlem, where Mother M. Francis and Mother M. Gabriel had founded a St. Joseph's Home during my absence. They also had established homes in Leiden and Amsterdam. One house after another was visited. We arrived in Sittard on August 4.

The first week proved a very difficult one. I think I was in dire need of rest, for on the ship I could sleep very little. No one suspected how miserable I felt. With great longing, I remembered the Carmel of the Divine Heart of Jesus in America and all my dear Mothers and Sisters. Now the ocean separated me from them, who had lived and worked with me in such close association.

On August 11, Mother M. Francis and I went to Paderborn by way of Cologne. Bishop Klein received us with great kindness. During the audience he spoke about us taking over the old Dominican convent in Halberstadt which had been built in 1227 and had been suppressed by Napoleon at the beginning of the nineteenth century. We went to Halberstadt on the same day. Father Iseke gave us hospitable lodging for eight to ten days. On August 21, we were assigned some rooms in the convent and moved in. The convent had undergone many changes. For a time it had been used for military barracks, then as a prison, and finally three manufacturers had taken over the rooms for their purposes. To the great discomfort of the Sisters, one of them was still occupying one part of the building.

With patience, however, everything will end, and so, too, the terrible results of the war from which millions are suffering.

To the honor of God and in thanksgiving for the wonderful protection that the Carmel of the Diving Heart of Jesus had experienced in these grievous war years, we began the remodeling of the convent with courage and hope. With the visible blessing of God, Sr. M. Theresia Dolorosa, with tireless zeal, carried out all the plans of remodeling. Unfortunately, it took some time before a temporary Chapel could be furnished and the Blessed Sacrament reserved. Our first mission work in Halberstadt consisted of alleviating the suffering of the poor. Women and children besieged our door day after day, and thanks to my dear Americans we were able to lighten their suffering, for we had been sent milk, flour, and other items, from America. Thus we could fill the baskets of the poor every morning.

It was touching when some poor woman would approach and shyly say in a low voice, "I am a Protestant. Do they also get something here?"

"My dear woman," was my answer, "we do not inquire about anyone's religion. We want to help all the needy ones as much as we can." With a full basket such a woman would then return from the convent of St. Gertrude to her home where a group of children and an unemployed husband were waiting, wondering whether they would receive assistance from the Sisters even if they were Protestants.

After a few weeks, M. M. Gabriela and I journeyed to Berlin-Charlottenburg. I was grateful for not finding any Sisters who were really ill, although all of them were suffering from the years of privation and strain caused by the war. There were very few Sisters who did not have a father or a brother who had not been in the field or in the terrible trenches, and yet not one Sister was actually ill. The Sisters in Berlin, who numbered over one hundred in the four convents, needed better food and a change of air. I immediately began to send some of them to Vechta and later to Halberstadt. I have always regarded it as my main duty to look after the health of the Sisters. I am convinced that good health is the basis for progress in the spiritual life. It is also absolutely indispensable for the fulfillment of one's duties and especially for the work of training children. How can a tired, nervous Sister act with patience and reasonableness? Again and again her over-strained nerves will put patience, kindness, and reason to flight, and nothing remains for the poor creature but remorse and regrets!

Our St. Joseph's Homes had been considerably enlarged, except the one located in Charlottenburg. The great need for housing the poor children made the purchase of the neighboring houses necessary. Only poor Charlottenburg still had as its entrance the same old barn or stable door that had horrified me when I first saw it back in 1905. This time I was determined to get rid of it, and our good architect found an old, but attractive door. I bought the door and had it placed there as a worthy entrance to our convent of the Most Holy Trinity.

My next stop was in Frankfurt on the Oder, which can be reached from Berlin in an hour by railway. This Home also came into being during my travels in the United States. So much had been written to me about the "beautiful Home" that I was greatly disappointed when I saw it. It was an ill-starred foundation, such as those in Leiden and Amsterdam. Any remodeling or improvements were entirely impossible. The poorly constructed house could not be made into a convent or a Home for children. I, therefore, told the superior to search for another building, and in the meantime, I went to Danzig where dear M. Maria Magdalena of the Five Holy Wounds had bought a suitable property. Unfortunately, the sad conditions prevented her from making arrangements for a convent and a Chapel. Large barracks were set up for the children, and two to three hundred of them from the poorest section of the city now spent the day there and received the necessary food, clothing, and above all, loving care and training. The dwelling of our Savior caused me great pain. It was a tiny room without any adornment. It was only on my second visit there that I was able to arrange for a worthy Chapel and an oratory.

To my great joy and admiration, the Carmel of the Divine Heart had made astonishing progress in Germany. This was accomplished despite the war, its hardships, and privations. All the Mothers and Sisters who were aided by the numerous "Friends of the Poor Children" had accomplished wonders.

Even my long cherished wish, to have a convent in the Archdiocese of Cologne, had been granted by Divine Providence. M. M. Brigitta had founded a St. Joseph's Home with a Chapel and oratory in Dusseldorf, and the Home was already crowded with children.

In January 1921, I visited Halberstadt once more. One day an agent came and offered me some chairs from a hotel that were for sale. I asked him if the hotel were for sale too. "Yes," he said, "and very cheap."

"How many rooms has it, and what is the price?" I asked.

His answer was satisfactory, and after thinking for a

while, I requested him to show me the hotel.

We arrived there a few minutes later, for it was not far from our convent of St. Gertrude. The agent led me through many rooms and finally to the dining room. The gentleman then opened the door to a huge recreation room. As soon as I entered it, this large room changed in my mind, or fancy, to a beautiful Chapel! Here in the middle of the city it could become a Sacred Heart Chapel and a Home for the Aged. That would be wonderful! That is what I thought and planned in those few moments. I am not one to merely plan, and so we started the negotiations for the purchase of the hotel. An architèct was consulted about closing off one wing of the large building for the Sisters and installing a stairway. The emblems of the hotel that were etched into the glass also had to be removed. I had a vision of the Sacred Heart made in colored glass for the Chapel door, and eventually the coat of arms of the Carmel of the Divine Heart of Jesus was placed in the window over the entrance of the Home.

Mother M. Brigitta later undertook the remodeling and furnishing of the Sacred Heart Convent and the Home for the Aged. At this time she traveled with me by way of Berlin to Frankfurt, where the superior had written to me that she had located a house.

This place, too, was absolutely unsuited for the Carmel. I stayed there a few days and began to search for a house myself. By telephone I asked one agent after another whether a larger house could be obtained, but all my efforts were fruitless. The agents all said that no house was to be had at the present time.

I now began to look for a restaurant. However, one was too far from the city, and the others were too small. Not one suited me. At last we were on Leipziger Street. We had just left a restaurant and had walked a short distance when I saw an elderly man standing on the sidewalk. I went up to him, greeted him, and asked whether there was another restaurant in this neighborhood. "Yes," he said, "a little farther on." We followed his direction, and I found all that I was looking for: a restaurant with a large dining room, and next to it a residence. Of course, we did not go in, for if the owners see that "Sisters" want to buy, the price goes up considerably.

After returning home I immediately asked Mr. N., a Lutheran agent in whom I had the fullest confidence, to buy the restaurant for us. To the owner, a war invalid, the offer to buy his restaurant came entirely unexpectedly. The offer was welcomed by him just the same because he was still suffering from the effects of his injury and could not stand the noise and clamor of the many guests for any length of time. In a little while, the purchase was made under favorable terms.

I was happy that now a beautiful public Chapel could be opened in Frankfurt for a few hundred visitors. There was also space available for a Home and a day nursery for poor children. Next to the Chapel a small convent was furnished for the Sisters. God alone knows how much blessing flows and will flow from this foundation in the future!

For years the urgent need had been felt to have a place near Berlin where the Sisters and the children could find recreation. Our Mothers had made many efforts in this regard but without success. I had an ardent wish to provide such a place for the Sisters, as well as the children, who needed a rest. We needed a location where they could be renewed in body and soul.

After my return from Frankfurt I asked Mr. Bunning,

our always-accommodating architect, to place an advertisement under his name seeking a restaurant with a garden. He was kind enough to do this, and I think hardly ten days had passed when he submitted the offers he had received and made a report. Among all these offers that of Birkenwerder seemed the most suitable.

We got ready without delay to go with him to Birkenwerder. This find was really one that filled my heart with joy and gratitude, for this place is truly God's gift to the Carmel in Berlin.

Besides the restaurant and garden with the beautiful trees, we were able to acquire several plots of land over the next few years. The government did us the great favor of granting us about twenty acres of the adjacent pinewoods.

The dining room of the restaurant was remodeled into a temporary Chapel, and soon the first Mass was celebrated and the Blessed Sacrament reserved. In 1924 an addition was begun to house a Chapel and a home for children.

St. Joseph's Home in Birkenwerder has not only become a place of recreation, but a real vacation spot for the four hundred or more children in Berlin who spend their short or longer vacations here in turns, one time the boys and then the girls. All day long they play in the woods, which is enclosed by a high cloister wall. The hilly terrain of the woods and the many kinds of berries growing there increase the enjoyment of the children.

After these external affairs had been taken care of or set in motion, I began the main task of the restoration of the novitiate. The most important duty in the Order is the training of its new members. The Order does not depend on scientific training, on which, perhaps, the greatest weight is laid today. The Order concentrates on the training in religious life, on the practice of virtues (especially of humility and charity), and on self-sacrificing love for one's neighbor, on which depends the existence of an Order.

After M. Maria Magdalena, on the urgent advice of several priests and also of the Vicar-General of Frascati, had left Rocca di Papa with the novices, and after the Italian government had confiscated our convent, Rocca di Papa was given up as our novitiate house. In place of this one novitiate, five temporary novitiate houses had been established (with the approbation of the respective Bishops) in the various countries during the war. This took place during the time I had spent in America.

Now, in 1920 over one hundred postulants were waiting to be invested, but finding room for them was a major concern. All our houses were filled with poor children.

In this great need I asked the architect to take me to Spandau where I wanted to look at the barracks which were still for sale. We bought several of them that could be used for our purpose. One of them was set up in the convent grounds at Charlottenburg and served as a refectory. The superiors of the various Homes took some of the children into their own places, and the upper story was then remodeled. Thus we gained sufficient room, and, to the great joy of all, the investiture took place in Charlottenburg on July 16, 1921.

I now had a great longing to visit my dear ones whom I had not seen for nine years in the former Austrian countries. Prior to this, I did not want to leave Germany before I had found a place for a novitiate. At this time, however, there was nothing to hold me back, and I started on my journey in the fall of 1920 with M. Gabriela.

Whoever had not made a journey in Europe in those days has no conception of the conditions that prevailed. We had indeed read about them in America, but this journey taught me the great difference between reading about the traveling conditions and experiencing them! The seats, formerly upholstered in the railway coaches, were now in rags. The windows were without glass and were often boarded over, and worse, there was no illumination in the coaches. As soon as night came, one had to sit in pitch darkness with complete strangers. After the first experience of this kind, we always carried a small candlestick and some candles and matches with us. When the darkness started to become frightening, we placed a burning candle on the floor. The pleasing expressions of our fellow travelers showed how welcome this light was, even though it was weak.

Despite the strong draft in the coaches and the bothersome checking of passports and visas and the customs inspections, all of which often took hours, we arrived in Vienna safe and sound. However, we had discovered that during the time that I had been in America our convent had been transferred.

District XXI, Floridsdorf, can certainly be called the worst Communist suburb of Vienna. Anyone who walked through the streets could convince himself of that. One looked in vain for an expression of contentment. Hatred and bitterness were stamped on the faces of the older people, and frightening dissoluteness appeared on the faces of the younger inhabitants.

Indeed, these were poor people who had been allowed to sink so low! No wonder that thousands of Austrians emigrated to America! Unfortunately, all efforts to arouse them to new religious life there were also in vain.

We had left the streetcar in the main square and then asked one person after another for Toellergasse but to no avail. Some did not answer, and some turned away as if they had not understood us. One could see plainly that they would not give any information to us "Sisters." Finally one woman, who did not look too trustworthy either, seemed to take pity on us and showed us the way. Yet, after wandering about for half an hour, it became plain that she had given us the wrong directions. We walked around for more than an hour before we found our convent.

I was amazed when I saw the next day what had become of our little St. Bernard's convent! I saw an imposing convent and Home with gardens and playgrounds! This was surely a wonderful blessing of God, especially during those awful war years! May God reward the noble benefactors who bought this house for the Carmel of the Divine Heart of Jesus. May God not only reward them but their children, and their children's children a thousand-fold!

More than one hundred charming Viennese children had found a loving home there. It is unfortunate, however, that we can do nothing for the many children who grow up on the streets and suffer bodily and spiritual ruin, because we do not have room. The large rooms that would have been suitable for this purpose must now be used as a Chapel and oratory.

The building of a Chapel, which, I believe, I have already mentioned, had been started by a very devout gentleman, a count. Sadly, he could not continue the project for lack of funds. We were very anxious to open a "day care" for several hundred children, but we could not do this before the new Chapel was built.

I was very happy to see that the Sisters had again undertaken house visits and that they had already won many souls for the Divine Heart.

I was sorry to see that the second St. Joseph's Home in Vienna, in District XI, Ebersdorf, had not made any progress. There was much to be done before it could become a Carmel of the Divine Heart.

At that time, I believe, I was also in Moedling. The Mothers wanted to buy an old convent with a beautiful garden. This was done at a later date.

After a short stay we went on to Croatia, now known as Yugoslavia. Here we had a long wait at one of the larger railway stations. One could no longer speak of trains being on time, for the change in schedules sometimes meant hours of waiting. We had to spend this time in wooden sheds, and at times we waited in the open. We simply had to stand in all kinds of weather and wait for our turn. Woe to those who were told, "Get over there; your visa is not in order," or were otherwise detained. That happened to us one time and caused us a great hardship, but the people seemed to have a soft spot for Sisters and showed them kindness. This I have often found to be true not only among Christians and Jews but also with Moslems.

Evening came and we found ourselves alone in a large, second class waiting room. When we heard the train moving into the station, a wild, hundred-voiced cacophony arose. The thought that a riot or revolution was taking place flashed through my mind. Never in our lives had we heard anything like this. The tumult lasted a long time, and then quieted down. Now I ventured to leave the waiting room and asked the official the reason for the riot. It was neither a riot nor anything of the like. Apparently there had been an election at Klagenfurt, and these men had arrived here in a drunken state after performing their civil duty, and they were informed that they could not get transportation before morning.

This answer calmed us, and we waited patiently without fear for the train for Agram. Finally the time arrived and an official led us outside, climbed into a coach, and showed us the way with his lantern. We followed him and found one coach after another filled with men who were sleeping! The officials had solved their transportation problem by locking the whole drunken crowd in the empty train where they could sleep off their drunkenness. Efforts to waken them from their stupor were unsuccessful. There was nothing for the other passengers and us to do but to have patience.

After waiting seven hours, another train pulled in and we finally were able to depart. The long delay caused us to arrive at Agram in the evening, and after waiting for the trolley, it was almost eleven o'clock before we reached our destination. Here we stood helpless in the dark, unable to make ourselves understood, since we did not know one word of Croatian.

There were two officials with a lantern standing in the station. They could evidently see where we wanted to go by our religious habit, but I said, "Leskovac." They talked together for a while, no doubt debating what should be done about us. Then one of them handed the lantern to the other, and the latter motioned for us to follow him.

That was an unforgettable experience. We had no idea that our convent was on a hill. I could not see a thing, so my climbing was more of a constant stumbling. My companion, dear M. M. Gabriela, could at least see the trees when the light of the lantern shown on them. Here, as on the entire journey, she was my second guardian angel, or rather, an angel in human form.

As with our other travels, this wandering finally came to an end. Our faithful guide stopped, cast his lantern light on a house, found the door bell, and rang it. It did not take long before dear M. M. Eleanor appeared, simply amazed to see us at the convent door after midnight! Her hearty welcome made us very quickly forget the hardships of the journey. First of all we greeted our Divine Savior in the Blessed Sacrament and thanked Him that we had at last, after all of our fright, terror, and darkness, happily and safely reached the Carmel of the Divine Heart of Jesus in Croatia.

M. Maria Theresia of St. Peter must herself describe the history of the founding of this Carmel. She was my faithful traveling companion of 1897. While I was in America, I had sent her to Agram to get the approbation of Archbishop Bauer for a foundation in Agram. She not only obtained his approbation, but he became a generous protector of the Carmel.

The fortunes of this St. Joseph's Home were like most of the others. It had been watered with hardships and sufferings of all kinds. We hope now that we have found and bought a house in 1924 in Agram, that the Carmel of the Divine Heart will also flourish in Croatia. God always crowns patience and perseverance with His blessing. A glorious harvest field awaits us here. The Croatians are very charitable, and the ladies of Agram are unusually helpful and generous. A children's Home in which several hundred children will find love and care and be trained to become good Christian citizens will be built there soon.

I do not remember whether we stayed there for two or three weeks. The sad day of parting arrived, and we had to leave our Sisters and their wonderful boys and depart from Leskovac, which we had come to love. From Agram we then set out for Budapest.

Again it was a journey that demanded much patience. There were inspections at the Hungarian Border that lasted for hours. This delay made us reach Budapest late in the evening, just before the last car had left for Ujpest. Unfortunately, we had not heard that new routes had been laid out, and so it happened that we were entirely lost when we arrived at the end of the line. There, as everywhere else, the street lighting was very poor as a result of the war. Here and there was a lantern that gave a little light, but, generally, the houses were all dark. I was completely at a loss and did not know what we should do. Suddenly we heard footsteps and two big men stood before us. Unafraid, I asked them about our convent. They knew where it was and told us to follow them, for they were going that way. I was unsure what to do, but trusting in our holy Father St. Joseph we followed them. Finally their way parted from ours, but before leaving us, they gave us directions on how to reach our destination.

Their intentions were good, but it was dark, and we saw no streets or anything recognizable at all! We now began to wander around and look for the fence of the convent. Still we had no success. Finally we saw a light in a house. Dear M. M. Gabriela knocked on the lighted window and a man appeared, and she asked him for directions. He spoke German, knew our convent, and described the way to reach it. Again we began the search, but again without success, for it was just too dark. Filled with anxiety and worry, we kept on walking in silence. Suddenly M. M.

Gabriela cried out, "We are at the river!"

"Then we are on the bank of the Danube!" I added, terrified.

We had lost our way completely! What were we to do? Asking God for help, we turned from the Danube, our hearts quaking with fear. After a while we again heard footsteps. I called out, asking for help. When we came nearer we saw a young man and a young woman who said that they knew our Chapel and very kindly led us home. For this we shall be eternally grateful to them. The next day we found out they were brother and sister. In the meantime midnight had passed, and it took some trouble to awaken the Sisters from their deep sleep. After our patience had been tried for the last time, the door opened to us poor, tired, and scared wanderers. The love and joy and warmth with which we were received by our dear Hungarians, who appeared one after the other, helped us to quickly forget the hardship we had endured.

During the next days we visited all our dear ones in the four foundations in and near Budapest. Everywhere there was the same mutual joy of reunion.

We were filled with admiration but also with deep compassion when the Mothers and Sisters related their experiences during the revolution. One could almost imagine it to have been the French Revolution at the end of the eighteenth century, so full of terror and fear were these months for Priests, Sisters, and loyal Catholics.

Just as in France, so the persecuted Priests wandered about in Hungary and Croatia looking for refuge. Some sought and found sanctuary, often for months, in the Carmel of the Divine Heart of Jesus. In return, the Sisters had the good fortune of having Holy Mass frequently. Of course, the Priests came in disguise. Whenever the superiors of the four convents wanted to meet for mutual consultation, they too had to wear disguises. God be thanked who protected them so wonderfully and gave them courage and wisdom in their many and long inquisitions.

Aside from St. Lawrence, where another house had been bought and occupied in my absence, and the restoration of the Chapel in Ujpest, all the convents were waiting for much- needed enlargements. The great need of the many children, victims of the most bitter poverty and misery, had filled all the St. Joseph's Homes to overcrowded conditions.

The convent in Gyon had been added to the others. This beautiful property was the gift of Countess Vay de Vaya. Her son, Bishop Vay de Vaya, had been generous enough to carry out the wish of his dying mother and not only turn over this property to the Carmel but also to build a children's Home and a Chapel in connection with the manor. About eighty to one hundred poor children have now found a home in Gyon, and since the Catholic Church was quite far from there, our Chapel was able to serve the neighbors as a parish church for the time being.

Since my beloved Hungary was only a stopping place on my tour of the convents, we again set out on our journey after an affectionate farewell. We passed through Vienna and went on to Switzerland. Joy and sorrow awaited us there, too. After a long delay at the border, we arrived late at Dietikon on a rainy evening. A kind lady told us simply to continue down the street, and we would find St. Joseph's Home. She stated that a wall surrounded the garden. The good woman did not consider that we would be unable to distinguish a wall in the darkness that enveloped us. Luckily we had brought matches with us. From time to time we lit one, and with the help of this meager illumination M. M. Gabriela at last discovered the wall, the steps, the door, and the bell. We were indeed very happy to be with our loved ones again, and they did everything to make us comfortable.

After a short visit we rode to Hermetschwil, Altstaetten, and Wildhaus. I do not remember the order in which I visited them. The Carmel had made great progress in Switzerland. M. M. Brigitta had bought a house in Wildhaus, and the Bishop had donated a stately residence in Altstaetten. M. M. Brigitta had made a Boys' Home of the former, and M. Maria Magdalena a Girls' Home of the latter.

It was fortunate that the Swiss Government, like the Netherlands and the North countries, had not let itself be drawn into the war of 1914. Having been spared this great calamity, all these countries were very generous in their missions of mercy, without regard to religious creed. The Carmel of the Divine Heart of Jesus owes much to the generous, noble benefactors of these countries that the Sisters and children did not have to suffer undernourishment to any great degree, and, certainly, never to the point of exhaustion. With the exception of one Sister who contracted a fatal disease, all the Sisters and the children were able to maintain their health.

Soon the hour of parting struck here too, as our Sisters in Italy had been waiting for a long time for our visit. The first stop was Cremona. Here we found a great deal of misery due to the war. The poor Sisters really suffered much. They lacked everything, especially coal. Hence, the poor people had neither gas nor wood either for cooking or for heating. Sawdust was burning, or rather smoldering, under the large pots which held the food for eighty merry Italian boys who filled the house to the rafters. The poor kitchen Sister was enveloped in smoke, and this smoke spiced all the food of the Sisters as well as that of the children.

The Sisters truly lived a life of sacrifice. Hardly anybody sent alms to Italy. Nothing was left for them but to suffer patiently, and this they did for a number of years. The German Sisters did everything for love of the poor Italian children, whose fathers were perhaps fighting the Sisters' fathers or brothers on the battlefield.

Full of sorrow and pity we left Cremona, our dear Sisters and their flock of boys, and hurried on to our last stop, Rocca di Papa in Rome.

God be thanked that the building had remained the same, dear, old convent! "Yes, you have fared the best of all in Rocca di Papa," I was told by a Roman gentleman. After witnessing what had happened to other foreign religious, we knew that he was correct. The convent had indeed been confiscated, but the Sisters and the children were allowed to stay there upon payment of rent.

After a short stay in Rocca di Papa and Rome, we returned to the North. We celebrated Christmas of 1920 in Halberstadt, where the Sisters set up a temporary Chapel. Our Divine Savior made His entrance there in the Holy Night to our very great Christmas joy.

I spent the entire year of 1921 traveling. Again I visited almost all the of European convents, and endeavored, by counsel and deed to repair the harm done by the war and my long absence.

To my great joy I found in all our St. Joseph's Homes how wonderfully our holy Father St. Joseph had protected and helped us.

Monsignor Jahnel always worried when he saw the poverty of the Homes, but for my part I loved this poverty and wished to preserve it as the foundation of my work. For on this foundation rises the walls of humility and trust in God.

Did not the Divine Savior say, "Be not solicitous, therefore saying: What shall we eat, or what shall we drink, or wherewith shall we be clothed?" (Mt. 6:28) As our holy Mother St. Teresa of Jesus tells us to strive only for perfection, we shall never lack the necessities of life.

With firm confidence in the "Divine promise" and under the protection of our holy Father St. Joseph, I have founded, with hardly any worldly means, not only one home for poor children, but under the guidance of Divine Providence, I went from city to city, from country to country, and have been privileged to establish many convents and St. Joseph's Homes.

The care for the purchase of the property and for the building, beginning with the first Home in Berlin, I have always left to the Divine Child. The care for the support of the ever-growing family of Carmel, I placed in the hands of our Father St. Joseph.

It is not as if I had done nothing to procure the necessary means. On the contrary, I worked all day, and in the first years, many a night as well to obtain alms or to gain friends and benefactors for the work. I also did this later when the Sisters joined me. The Divine Savior rewarded my trust in His promise, and has blessed our efforts, and heard our prayers. He heard hundreds of times the prayers that we laid in His Divine Heart for the intentions of our kind benefactors. This all-merciful Heart leaves unrewarded no cup given in His name to the poor.

The foundation of the work, holy poverty, has proved itself gloriously in the past thirty-four years. This also includes the terrible years of the war and the revolution.

In the same manner, the walls that rise from this foundation (humility and trust in God) have proven themselves. As long as these walls stand firm, the blessing of the Divine Child and the protection of our holy Father St. Joseph will never fail the Carmel of the Divine Heart of Jesus.

If, however, in this edifice, humility, trust in God, and poverty, should ever be wanting, then the blessing of God will also be wanting, and the splendid edifice will fall into ruins. Therefore, all Mothers and Sisters must watch carefully that no breach is made in the walls of this foundation.

What a sorrow it would be for the Heart of God, for our dear Lady of Mt. Carmel, and for our beloved St. Mother Teresa of Jesus if the Carmel of the Divine Heart of Jesus, founded by Himself in His great love, should ever perish.

Fidelity is the means of preserving Religious Orders. An Order in which all members are faithful in observing the Rule, the Constitutions, and customs, not only faithful in great things, and in general, in the little and littlest thing, not "faithful one time," and "unfaithful three times" - but always and perseveringly faithful - such an Order cannot perish.

Every Order that has come to ruin has done so only through the unfaithfulness of its individual members. One unfaithful member is like a decayed fruit that soon infects others. Gradually, then, a whole religious family is thereby ruined. In place of zeal and fidelity will be found unfaithfulness, lukewarmness, and discontent. These inevitably lead to ruin and to the abyss!

During these long, hard years, the special blessing of the Divine Friend of children rested visibly on the Carmel of the Divine Heart of Jesus with its St. Joseph's Homes.

Each one is a "Home for the Homeless."

In the Carmel the souls entrusted to us are cared for and loved. In every child we love the Divine Child, and this sincere love affects the heart of the child, just as the sun affects the tender, growing plants. Without the sun the young plants wither and die, and, likewise, the soul of every child withers without love. There is hardly a task more important and of more grave consequences than the training of children and the education of youth.

To spoil children is harmful, yet even more harmful is too great severity, for this makes the heart bitter.

To educate children without religion is a crime committed against young souls which long for God. Nevertheless, it is worse to go to extremes in training children to piety and to torture them with too lengthy and too many prayers. People who have grown up without religion often find the way to faith and to the Divine Heart more easily with God's grace than those who were forced to excessive piety, because then religion had been made repugnant to them.

MUNICH

It took twenty years to gain Bavaria for the Carmel of the Divine Heart of Jesus.

When finally the approbation for the founding of the Carmel of the Divine Heart in Munich had been obtained, we could not find a house which suited our purpose. We had been in Munich several times, but due to the shortage of housing at that time, it was impossible to find one.

In the meantime, Fr. Gorbach, in his zeal and love for the welfare of young men, had built a small house for them, Then in June 1921, we were asked to take over this

Home that was located in Milbertshofen, District 46 of Munich. Although we could not accept this offer, M. M. Gabriela and I again set out for Munich in the hope of finding a suitable property.

We arrived in Munich on June 28 and were given hospitality by the Sisters with whom we went to 5 o'clock Mass on the Feast of St. Peter. Having taken breakfast at the convent of these Sisters, we rode to Milbertshofen.

When we reached this suburb and left the streetcar, we saw neither a church nor anyone whom we could ask to receive direction, so we inquired at one of the nearby houses. A friendly woman opened the door, and we asked about the way to the church. Instead of giving us the information she told her daughter, who was about ten years old, to take us there.

On the way I asked the little one if there were any restaurants out this way.

"Oh, yes," she answered.

"Have they large gardens?"

"Yes," she replied, "there are restaurants with large gardens."

That was enough information for me. Now I knew what I wanted to know.

We met the pastor in front of the church and told him why we had come. He then introduced us to a St. Vincent de Paul man, who was to take us to the young men's Home after the High Mass, since Fr. Gorbach was in Munich at the time.

As soon as High Mass was over, we started out with our guide. After about twenty minutes we reached the Home which was still under construction. The time had passed quickly because our guide, like all men with whom we had come in contact during those years, spoke in a very interesting way about his war experiences. A closer inspection of the house was not needed. We could see from a distance that it was not suited for our purpose.

I, therefore, asked our guide to take us to a restaurant with a large garden, since this would suit us much better. He willingly obliged, and after about seven minutes, we walked into a garden attached to a restaurant. The owner appeared very quickly, and after I told him that we were looking for a restaurant with a large garden for a Home for children, he replied, "My neighbor, Mrs. N. wants to sell her restaurant that rests on six acres of property." We thanked him for the information and went to see Mrs. N., who was evidently happy to know that we were ready to buy her house and grounds if the price were acceptable. She had been looking for a buyer for a long time but without success. She was glad, therefore, to let us have the property for a reasonable price.

The restaurant had originally been a small, princely hunting lodge. It was a place that not only needed repairs, but the upper story would have to be remodeled so that at least eight Sisters could be housed there. The dining room would have to be made into a temporary Chapel. There was no room for children, so I looked around again for some barracks. The builder, who had undertaken the remodeling of the house, took me to an airfield where excellent barracks were available for sale. I bought those that were best suited for our purpose. After they had been set up and plastered, about two hundred children could be kept there during the day, or school children could spend their free time there. The Sisters did everything they could to care for these poor, undernourished children and to clothe them properly. Many a child came to them on a cold winter morning with a raw turnip in his hand that the mother had given him for breakfast.

Our dear Sisters and our benefactors in other countries cannot imagine the misery the Sisters encountered on their house visits. One must have seen the poverty and misery with one's own eyes, otherwise it would not seem possible. Only a prolonged war could have produced such terrible results.

The charitable gifts that the Sisters received from Auxiliary Bishop Buchberger and other generous benefactors enabled them to help the most needy families. After the physical needs had been relieved to some extent, the Sisters also endeavored to help these poor people in their spiritual need. Unfortunately, their misery had not taught them to pray but made them cast religion aside. It did not take long, however, and new life was awakened in many of these families. The children became merry and happy, and soon they began to sing and to pray. From one Sunday to another, more and more parents accompanied their children to church, and many also received the sacraments again and regained happiness and contentment.

THE MOTHERHOUSE TRANSFERRED TO SITTARD

In the fall of 1921, I left Charlottenburg for good and went to Vienna. Because our convent in Rocca di Papa had been confiscated, the Carmel of the Divine Heart of Jesus was now, after thirty years, once more without a Motherhouse!

All my prayers were, therefore, directed to one end: to learn the will of God regarding a Motherhouse. I searched for a property in Bavaria that would be suitable, but I found none.

While I was living in this uncertainty at St. Joseph's Home of St. Bernard, God let me see in a dream a peculiarly formed unusual tree. It stood in a garden in a corner formed by two brick walls. Along the one wall there were bushes, and along the other there was a path bordered by a number of violet and yellow crocuses. They were in bloom.

I awoke and knew without any doubt that this tree was to be the sign pointing to the convent that God had chosen. Again and again I sent prayerful sighs to God asking, "How can I find this tree?"

It seemed to me that it was December 8, 1921, when Divine Providence directed my thoughts to Sittard with the idea of choosing this convent for a Motherhouse. I kept this plan in my heart until several of my oldest companions came to visit me in January of 1922. On January 18, our thanksgiving feast of St. Teresa, I submitted this plan to them. All agreed enthusiastically that we were to choose the cradle of the Carmel of the Divine Heart of Jesus, our first convent in Sittard, as Motherhouse and Generalate.

The Superior of Sittard at that time, M. M. Francis, was then commissioned to ask Bishop Schrijnen of Roermond for permission to transfer our Motherhouse from Rocca di Papa to Sittard. The Bishop gave permission to the greatest joy of all.

In the beginning of March 1922, M. M. Alexandra, M. M. Fabiana, and I left Vienna and made our headquarters in Sittard.

After some time I happened to be walking in the adjacent garden bought by M. M. Gabriela, that was separated from the original property by a wall. Slowly, absorbed in thought, I was walking along when, to my great amazement, I suddenly saw that peculiar, unusually formed tree that God had let me see in my dream. Drawing near, I saw the corner, formed by the walls, and the path, and a number of yellow and violet crocuses blooming in the very place in which I had seen them.

I was overcome with joy and happiness. Now I was sure that Sittard was the Motherhouse chosen or designated by God. I no longer hesitated to ask the Bishop of Roermond to petition the Sacred Congregation of Regulars for permission to transfer our Motherhouse from Rocca di Papa to Sittard, in the Province of Limburg, Netherland. A few months later we received the permission from the Holy Congregation in Rome.

Divine Providence continued to guide this work and make known to me that here in Sittard would be the postulate and a flourishing juniorate, but no novitiate!

I then began the building of the postulate, but as soon as this was available it had to be used as a Chapel and oratory, because the old Chapel and oratory had become entirely too small.

In the course of years enough candidates who had passed the State Examinations came to Carmel. Thus, my ardent wish will be fulfilled that the order itself can give the Sisters all the education and training proper to the times and necessary for their work. Divine Providence had furnished the needed teaching personnel. Another difficulty was the shortage of space. After so many years, I was now in the same situation as in the beginning in the Pappelallee. There was not enough money. The additions were not sufficient one way or the other.

Nevertheless, the Carmel of the Divine Heart of Jesus was not my work, so again I turned in this need to my Divine Lord and Master. I had never prayed for help in vain, and this time, as often before, God again enlightened me in my sleep.

I saw the front and the wing extending to the south. The front of the convent appeared to me in exact detail even with the elevation before the entrance. I walked in my dream down the steps to the door of the side wing that lay below.

It was God's decree that enabled us to continue building. I had said nothing to the architect about the little elevation or the front of the building. I was amazed when he submitted the plans to me, and they agreed perfectly with the picture of the building I had carried in my mind.

On the recommendation of Bishop Schrijnen, the Sacred Congregation in Rome granted us permission to take up a loan. On the feast of St. Lawrence on August 10, 1923, the solemnity of the laying of the corner stone took place. This was performed by Monsignor D. Claessens.

In 1903 it was this saint and martyr, St. Lawrence, deeply venerated by me, who had led me to Cardinal Satolli during the novena made to him before his feast and thereby to Rocca di Papa. Now again he had helped me to get a new Motherhouse through his powerful intercession.

Monsignor D. Claessens, the long-time friend of our convent, conducted the solemnity and preached an eloquent sermon that enthused every one. During the celebration, dear M. Maria Magdalena of the Five Holy Wounds and Sr. M. Constantia arrived from Vienna. That, naturally, heightened our festive joy.

The Motherhouse was blessed in 1924 by Dean Thijssen, who also preached a sermon that filled us all with gratitude toward God and praise of His Fatherly kindness.

Our Blessed Lady had led us to Sittard in 1898 and led us back again in 1906 after a period of trial. She had always shown herself as the Mother and Protectress of the Carmel of the Divine Heart of Jesus, and she will remain the Mother and Protectress as long as every convent and every religious family glorifies God and edifies the world by the "odor of Carmel."

The Carmel in Palestine was called "God's garden of spices" because the most precious aromatic herbs grew on its heights. The "Carmel of the Divine Heart" should become and remain, in truth, "God's garden of spices." Here all virtues shall be practiced with holy zeal, and the aroma of these virtues, manifested by the works of self-sacrificing charity, will not only edify and delight our fellow men but will also win them for the Heart of God.

I have, therefore, endeavored every day with renewed zeal to gain God's pleasure and to give joy to His Heart. Unfortunately, despite all efforts, I did not get beyond good will, desires, and wishes. I trust that God, who once sent His angels with the glad tidings, "Peace on earth to men of good will," shall, in His boundless mercy and goodness, also regard my "good will." Countless times He has not only forgiven and remedied my faults, sins, and perversities, but despite the great unworthiness of His instrument, He has showered His Blessing on the Carmel of the Divine Heart of Jesus.

It is the task of all Carmelites of the Divine Heart to ensure this blessing for the Carmel of the Divine Heart for all times. Yes, it is the task of every individual Mother and Sister of the presently living generation, as well as all following generations, to maintain His Blessings until the end of time. It must be the desire of all, "to suffer and to work, to sacrifice oneself," for Holy Church, for the salvation of souls, and for the spread of the kingdom of God on earth!

Every Carmelite of the Divine Heart of Jesus must be a holocaust victim of love!

All my life I regarded it as a great grace to be able to work and suffer for God's kingdom, the salvation of souls, and the freedom of the Church. Soon I will no longer be able to do this. I hope instead that I will be able to implore grace and blessing at the throne of God, not only for my beloved family of the Carmel with its missions, its children, its dear elderly people, and generous benefactors, but also for the souls that hover in danger, and for all the poor of all nations and countries of the world!

Yes, to be able to dry tears, to heal wounds of souls from the heights of heaven—that is my most ardent desire! Yet not my will, but Thine be done, my Lord and my God!

July 2, 1925

EPILOGUE

THE LAST YEARS – OUR GRATITUDE

*Who shall find a valiant woman—Strength and
beauty are her clothing...She has opened her
mouth to wisdom, and the law of clemency is on
her tongue, She has looked well in the paths of her
house. (Prov. 31:10. 25-27)*

Mother Mary Teresa has reported the story of her life
until the year of 1925. She completed her notes exactly on
July 2, the feast day commemorating the foundation of
her work (1891), to the glory of the Holy Trinity.

Since the Motherhouse had been moved from Rocca di
Papa to Sittard, the Foundress took up her permanent
residence in this convent. The times when she had to lend
a hand always and everywhere, the restless years of
founding convents and Homes now belonged to the past.
She could have spent the eve of her life in well-deserved
peace, but she remained faithful to her motto, "Wait for
the Lord with courage, be stouthearted and wait for the
Lord" (Ps. 27, 14). From Sittard she gave instructions for
the foundations of convents and Homes in Leipzig-
Engelsdorf, Leipzig-Leutzsch, Offenbach on the Main,
Hoheneck near Stuttgart, Lehmen on the Mosel,
Eschweiler near Aachen, and also more in Hungary. She
directed the Carmel of the Divine Heart of Jesus from Sittard with wisdom, energy, and an all-embracing love until
the end of her days, when she was unable to do so any
longer. Even at that time, there were worries of all kinds
and many sufferings, but there were also times of happiness. In the community of her Sisters there was a famil-

iar, happy, cheerful atmosphere. The death of a Sister was not only painful for her but sometimes also a source of quiet joy. On those occasions, Mother Mary Teresa realized that God had completed His work with the Sister and had accepted her at an early time in life as an entire sacrifice. This was especially the case with Sr. M. Teresa of the Holy Trinity, a Netherland Sister, who had died in America at the age of 28, after enduring her suffering heroically.

When the Congregation was finally approved by Pope Pius XI, it was a time of very great joy for Mother and her Sisters. On May 9, 1910, the rule of the Congregation of the Carmelites of the Divine Heart of Jesus had received the Decretum Laudis from Pope Pius X. On January 7, 1915, the Constitutions were approved on a trial basis by Pope Benedict XV for seven years. Because the foundation continued to flourish and to produce a rich harvest of blessing, Pope Pius XI gave the final approbation to her and her Congregation on May 12, 1930. The rule of the Order of the Blessed Virgin Mary of Mount Carmel determines the spiritual direction and is observed according to their own Constitutions.

Mother Mary Teresa's desire to lead people in misery to God and to reconcile them to Him, "to win souls for the Divine Heart," had not decreased over the years. Now that she had obtained ecclesiastical approbation for the Carmel of the Divine Heart of Jesus, this "hunger and thirst" made her say, "Now I once more want to taste all the sufferings of my life."

It did not take long until her pleading was fulfilled. The Motherhouse was plunged into great need. The growth of her Carmel had partially been due to the unending troubles of World War I, the consequences of the war, and the worldwide economic crisis. Misery and sorrow were overwhelming, and even she could hardly think of any advice or help. That caused her many humiliations, but her trust in God remained unshaken. "God has allowed this last trial, and He knows how to turn the dark cloud into bright sunshine at the given hour." She was also confident that once she was in heaven, she could be of more help.

The Foundress had tried to adapt to the social demands of her time and environment. Thus, the foundations of the Carmel of the Divine Heart of Jesus were started mostly in urban and industrial regions or in their vicinities. She had started her work in Berlin where she had dared not only to found children's Homes but a new branch of Carmel. Looking at just one aspect of her work, the promotion of Catholic life (a great diaspora) in Berlin around 1890, would be worth a special study. As a young professor, Archbishop Pisani had been introduced to Mother Mary Teresa in 1900 through L. Werthmann, founder of the German Caritas Society in Berlin. Among other things, the Archbishop testifies, "To her I owe the foundation of the Italian mission and of our Italian workers' office in Berlin, first in Pappelallee and later in Charlottenburg."

The journal "Caritas am Werk" writes in October 1938, "It has to be mentioned that the first Catholic Kindergarten in Berlin has been founded by Mother Mary Teresa."

In a letter from July 12, 1891, she describes the situation in Berlin as follows: "You may have often heard of the misery of the Church in Berlin, my dear. Hearing it or experiencing it makes a big difference. Up to now, you have heard about it, while I have experienced it. Hundreds of Catholics are being lost by the Church each year, and hundreds of souls are facing eternal ruin. Why? It is not malice, nor an evil will in most cases, but a luke-warmness and laziness among Catholics caused by the situation of the Church. Berlin has almost as many Catholics as Cologne, and these 150,000 Catholics are divided up in four parishes. Now, imagine these parishes, each one of which is probably bigger in area than entire Cologne. Do you still wonder why the people forget the Church? Often they have been living here for years without knowing where a Catholic Church or priest can be found. Up to now, I have been wandering through this endless ocean of houses by myself. After the experiences and successes that the grace of God has granted me, the thought and the hope arose in me as to whether the Savior could not choose workers and send them to me for this great mission work."

It was around 1896 when she wrote, "No era has offered a woman such great holy work like this country and like today's social conditions."

In the last years of her life, she remained completely open to the great need of mankind for the Church. She especially suffered because of the increasing crisis of the Church in Germany and saw a great storm gathering over all Europe. In 1934 she wrote to a Sister, "The times are inexpressibly grave, but the gravest times are yet to come for Europe. Nothing will happen to the Carmel of the Divine Heart of Jesus, unless it becomes forgetful of observance." On May 2, 1935, she wrote, "God be praised that the misery awakens new life and zeal in the two denominations daily more and more." Every evening one of the Sisters read aloud from the Maasboten, so that all would be moved to pray and make sacrifices on behalf of the Church throughout the world.

When meeting this tall, slender Sister who approached everyone with a quiet dignity and whose fine, brown eyes could glow so warmly, one felt that there was something unusual about this woman. Here was one who had her sights fixed on one essential issue and who carried the law of God in her heart. Yet, perhaps few surmise that she was a great woman of prayer and penance, and that she could be so childlike and merry in her association with others.

She was, indeed, a woman of prayer. That was her very being; it was her at-one-ment with God. From the very beginning she had grasped the truth that it was not enough merely to work for God and for His kingdom. In all the years of toil and labor, of trials and tribulations and disappointments, and, indeed, to the very end of her life, the one great need of her heart was to immerse herself in God. This made it possible for her to hold converse with the Savior in the Tabernacle for hours at a time. She lived what is regarded as the core of the original Rule of Carmel: "Ponder the Lord's law day and night and keep watch at prayer."

To prayer she joined the spirit of penance and atonement. She was completely consumed with the thought to offer herself as a sacrifice to God for the salvation of souls. She, therefore, accepted all sufferings with joyful love and was always severe and rigorous with herself, seeking to mortify herself to the very end of her life. "I have but one wish," she wrote to one of her daughters, "to suffer as much as possible for this short while. It does not matter what kind of suffering, as long as it is suffering. From my heart, I bless and thank all who have caused me to suffer. To suffer for God is the only joy which heaven does not have."

On her second visit to Rome she was forced for a time to be content with bread, coffee, and some fruit. After the distressing financial situation had been relieved, she desired, as an act of penance and out of love for God, to restrict herself for the future to this very meager fare. Her confessor readily gave her the necessary permission to abstain thereafter from all foods that were cooked. She kept this resolution for thirty years, with the exception of a few occasions during her illness when the physician ordered otherwise. When she took her meals with the Sisters, she ate only dry bread, fruit and milk, or tea. Nevertheless, she was always concerned that the Sisters had sufficient and nourishing food.

If a good spirit is to reign in a religious community, there must be punctuality, fidelity in small matters, and silence in the Convent. Mother Mary Teresa insisted on these principles with unwavering firmness. She could do this because she, herself, gave the best example to her Sisters. One never heard her raise her voice unduly, and even when she had to give a correction, she did so with a calm, quiet voice. "Every day we have to learn to weigh our words more and more," she said, "that is, think first, and then speak!" Of utmost importantance to her was sisterly love. In the last days of her life, her one great concern was to bequeath this spirit of true, heartfelt sisterly love to her daughters.

She was always conscious of the grave responsibility resting on those who were burdened with the guidance of others. "What will happen to a tree if it does not get into the hands of a good gardener, and if its dead wood is not pruned in time? It will never bear good and plentiful fruit. God will demand an account of us for every soul entrusted to our care." She was keenly conscious of her own responsibility and sought, therefore, to guard her charges with motherly care and with an unswerving insistence on the practice of virtue. Her one aim was to help them make progress in the spiritual life. The time she spent at Lindenburg and her contacts with all kinds of people for many years had given her a deep knowledge of human nature. All of her actions were motivated by this ruling principle: "If a community is to be a fruitful garden of God, then the first principle is to have a personal love for every Sister!"

She had a mother's solicitude and concern about the well-being of each individual Sister, even those at a great distance. This was especially true regarding the sick. "How can they leave me without news so long!" she sighed at times when she had heard of a Sister being sick in one of the other convents. "Dear Mother" was the name given her by all her daughters, and she was, in truth, a mother to all and the soul of the whole religious family.

The spirit that Mother Mary Teresa wished to instill into her Sisters can be seen from some of the following maxims that she wrote:

"Every daughter of Carmel has the sacred duty to practice charity. St. Paul said, 'Charity is patient and is kind; charity does not envy, is not pretentious, is not puffed up, is not ambitious, is not self-seeking, and is not provoked. Charity thinks no evil and bears with all things. So there abide faith, hope, and charity, these three, and the greatest of these is charity.'"(1 Cor, 13:4 ff).

"See God in all, serve God in all, love God in all!"

"A true Carmelite of the Divine Heart of Jesus should come down from the heights of Carmel to grief laden, peaceless humanity like an angel of peace and comfort."

"For religious especially there is only one way: that of self-denial."

"A religious who always observes the vow of obedience is always accompanied by the blessing of God."

"A silent soul is a recollected soul and will soon come to close union with God."

"In the Carmel of the Divine Heart of Jesus everything should show of poverty but also of spotless cleanliness."

"To possess the Rule avails very little if one does not endeavor to acquire its spirit."

"The interior law of loving God and our neighbor, which the Holy Spirit imprints on the hearts of men, is more effective in the fulfillment of our calling than all external laws."

"Every Carmelite should be a victim of love."

"Who, besides God, can render a true judgment of a soul? This judgment demands: knowledge of the natural aptitudes, of inherited qualities, of family conditions, and the like. Weighing all these things in the light of grace makes every harsh judgment impossible."

"Each kind of soil demands a special care and study, and so also does each child. A wise and faithful educator will, therefore, first study each child. She will punish very seldom and never punish in anger or out of irritation."

"The Sisters should always be filled with gladness and love and be cheerful and friendly in their dealings with others."

"In a sound body, so it is said, will be found a sound mind. Therefore, care must be taken of the health and normal growth of a child if his education is to be successful."

"No superior has the right to abolish the family system

as it has been established in the St. Joseph's Homes and approved by the highest authorities. It is essential to this system to have small groups of children in each division. This is absolutely the first requisite."

"It is harmful to spoil the children, but it is still more harmful to use too great severity, for this embitters the hearts."

"It is a crime to educate children without religion, a crime committed against their souls which long for God. However, it is much worse to train children to exaggerated piety, to torment them with too many and too lengthy prayers. People who have grown up without any religion more easily find the faith with God's grace than those who were trained in false piety, because religion had been made repugnant to them."

"Blessed are the meek, for they shall possess the earth. This "earth" are the souls of men."

"The Sacred Heart of Jesus, which God in His infinite, Fatherly love has given to men, is and always will be an inexhaustible treasure for us. From this Heart we always want to draw love to give to our Sisters and to others."

HER HOLY DEATH

All that God does is good.
Always praise and glorify God!
(Words of Mother Mary Teresa.)

The new religious family of Carmel of the Divine Heart of Jesus had chosen the poverty of Bethlehem and Nazareth for its inheritance. In order that food and shelter be not wanting for the various works of charity, the saintly Foundress and her daughters relied on the fatherly solicitude of good St. Joseph. Mother Mary Teresa also relied on the kindness and generosity of good people, whose generous alms helped to support the work of Carmel (although there were occasional larger donations). If, despite the generosity of benefactors, there was still privation and want, the Sisters endeavored to supply what was necessary by harder work and self-denial.

In 1938 the last year of the life of the Foundress had come, and the loss of bodily vigor made it felt more and more. "Oh," she exclaimed, "the Holy Father is right. Old age alone is a sickness! No one knows how hard it is if one cannot do the things one would like! Help me to pray for patience!" From week to week this cross became heavier for this active, energetic woman. Added to this burden was the financial distress of Sittard, and she saw no way of relieving it. "I see no way out of this," she would say, "but when I am home, I will be able to help."

The Sister infirmarian in the Motherhouse in Sittard at that time was Sr. M. Pia (later the third Mother General from 1957 to 1970). She, who was almost in constant attendance to Mother Mary Teresa during her last illness, gives a vivid picture of the saintly Foundress in the fol-

366

lowing brief account.

"A heavy fall on the edge of her kneeling bench in her cell made dear Mother afraid to climb the steps alone, so I was allowed to accompany her every evening. Arriving at her cell, she took the glass of holy water in her left hand and raising the right hand in blessing, made a large cross in all directions. Her eyes were raised to heaven. If one of the Sisters was sick, she was given a special blessing. As long as dear Mother could raise her hand, she never omitted this evening blessing. During the blessing I was unconsciously forced to my knees. Two months before her death she said, 'Soon I will be in heaven; then I will come every evening to bless you all.'

"On New Year's Day 1938, dear Mother said a number of times, 'We cannot pray and sacrifice enough! Say that again and again to the dear Sisters. The good God needs works of atonement!' And somewhat later, 'Whether I am going to die this year is not altogether clear to me, but this is my last year.' I begged dear Mother to stay with us. She replied, 'Do not begrudge me the beautiful heaven! I yearn for it so much! And yet I thank the good God for every day and especially for every night. In heaven we are not allowed to suffer any more. Just think of what that means!'

"On the Sacred Heart Friday dear Mother was very miserable. Yet, she prayed for two full hours before the Blessed Sacrament. Twice I tried to get her to leave, but she continued to pray. Afterward she excused herself, 'Forgive me, I could not help myself. That the Church must suffer so much makes me really ill.' Before the Benediction service in the afternoon she suffered a spell of weakness, and from that time on she never fully recovered. Her condition would change constantly. She promised over and over to spare herself and did so when she could not do otherwise. She did everything possible to care for the health of others, but she had no consideration for herself. Severe neuralgic pains in the head tortured her at times during the day and night. Nothing seemed to help. The physician had been dismissed with thanks. She suffered horribly from these pains, but she always said, 'What is this compared to the great sufferings of the Church!'

"The cheerful disposition of dear Mother helped her to surmount all the difficulties caused by the changes in her condition. But the greatest help was her unremitting readiness to suffer, as well as her interest and concern for the needs of the times. She often prayed for hours in the Chapel or in her cell. The good God sent her a new affliction. She almost completely lost her sight. She then asked to have the Gospel read to her every day, as well as the most important events in the news.

"Loneliness was a heavy burden. She also experienced agonizing hours of complete inner abandonment, so much so that she exclaimed at one time, 'Oh, what the dear Savior must have suffered! When we suffer, there is someone to help us, yet, to be abandoned by God and man, only infamy and outrages abound. It is horrible!'

"In July her walk began to become unsteady. Nevertheless she continued to make the genuflection with both knees and bowed to the floor before Holy Communion. On August 2, on the children's feast day in the St. Joseph's Homes, she was very ill. In the course of the morning she was somewhat better, and then she spoke of the love for children and of mutual love among the Sisters. With her hands folded in her lap, and her eyes turned to another world, she said, 'O love! We always think of ourselves first. We do not consider that mutual love is the greatest and strictest commandment of our Savior. We all have faults, and I most of all. And that is good! It is only if we are conscious of our own shortcomings that we know how others feel! . . . I am at the end of my life, and I feel that my work is done. I am no longer needed. I am firmly convinced that all the sacrifices were necessary. But one thing I know, if the Holy Rule is not observed as it was given, really and truly according to the spirit, all blessings will vanish. Some superiors esteem observance above charity, but that is not our spirit. Love comes first!' When dear Mother spoke that way, one could only listen. Then she would say in conclusion, 'Isn't that true?'

"After August 23 she was no longer able to go to Mass. 'Oh,' she exclaimed, 'how cruel it is to rob the poor people of the Mass! One can bear anything if he has offered himself completely with the Savior in the morning. My greatest sacrifice is to have to go so often without Holy Communion.' But she could not be persuaded to take something before receiving the Sacrament. 'If you struggled for this great happiness as I had to,' she said, 'you would understand.'

"Until the very last dear Mother wanted punctuality to be observed. At a quarter to eight she got ready to go to her cell so that I would not be late for Compline which began at eight o'clock. At times she would indulge in a merry jest; in fact, she never lost her cheerful spirit during her entire illness.

"On September 7, at about three thirty in the morning, she said clearly and distinctly, 'Sr. M. Pia, have you a drop of water?' But she was sleeping and had spoken in a dream. She then woke up and said, 'Forgive me; now I have disturbed you again!' She was seized by a convul-

sion. Her eyes began to roll and then remained fixed
toward the left. At five o'clock she received the Sacrament of the Sick. When she was able to speak again, her
first words were to ask for the relic cross which had
accompanied her on all her journeys and had stood on
her desk until now. From this moment, she had it constantly near her, kissing it often with great tenderness,
until the time of her blessed death.

"In the evening dear Mother lay there deeply absorbed
in thought. Suddenly she raised her finger and said slowly, stressing every word, 'All—that—God—does—is—
good! Always—praise—and—glorify—God!' It was like
the last glow of the setting sun, the final word of solace,
and the last admonition to us before her departure from
this earth. The next morning I was able to tell her that the
Holy Father had sent her his blessing. 'Oh, thanks,
thanks; that is wonderful!'

"A complaint never escaped her lips. She never forgot
the 'thank you,' 'please,' or 'forgive me.' She felt distressed when we sacrificed a night's rest for her, yet, she
often had attacks of extreme fear at night, and then she
would plead, 'Please stay with me! You will not leave me
alone, will you? When I have gone home, I will see to it
that you will have your night's rest for a whole year!' (She
kept this promise to the letter. Though there are always
sick and aged Sisters in the Motherhouse, not one of them
needed my attention at night during the following year.)

"During the night she had but one thought, 'I must go
home. . . home to the Father! Let me go home!' On the
feast of the Sorrowful Mother, her favorite feast, she
could not receive Holy Communion any longer. The next
day all the Mothers and Sisters were allowed to see their
Mother once more. She lay there quietly on her straw

sack and straw pillow (she could not be persuaded to use a feather pillow). A rosary was in her right hand, and the relic cross tightly clasped in her left.

"The evening of September 19 arrived. Silent grief lay on the faces of all. I continued to prompt prayers to dear Mother. At half past two in the morning of September 20, a sudden change set in. Her breathing became slower and slower, and quietly a tear ran down from her half-closed eyes.

"Our good, dear Mother had gone home to her Heavenly Father. Her features were resplendent with a look of happiness, and in her passing she had assumed a youthful appearance. Lying on her death bed, clothed in the holy habit and the white Carmel mantle, she was a picture of ineffable happiness and most profound peace."

MOTHER, WE THANK THEE!

On September 20, 1938, in her eighty-fourth year, God took His faithful servant to Himself. A long and unusually rich life had reached its end, and a great heart ceased to beat when Mother Mary Teresa of St. Joseph went home to her God. Many, very many people had crossed her life's path. Some, not a small number, were reserved, distrustful, or even hostile; others were filled with sympathy for her work and were generous in their assistance. In this book we have met many of these generous people. Some are people whose names have already become history, especially Church history. One of them, Blessed Bernhard Lichtenberg, a provost of St. Hedwig's parish in Berlin, should be especially mentioned here, as he died in 1943 while being transported to the Dachau concentration camp. At the death of the Foundress in September

1938, he wrote, "If you take a look from the little house in the courtyard of the St. Joseph's Home in Pappelallee to the fifty-eight convents of the Carmel in the Old and New World, another world opens up. It is a world in which the Foundress and first General Superior was a Mother to over 1000 Sisters and 10,000 forsaken children. The former pastor of the Sacred Heart Parish in Charlottenburg knows what the Carmel, and, especially, what the Sacred Heart Parish in Charlottenburg owes to the Foundress. What a life, blessed by God to the highest degree! Gratias agamus Domino Deo Nostro! We mourn with Carmel and rejoice in deepest admiration of the blessed mother."

> With grateful devotion,
> Father Lichtenberg

Whatever joy or sorrow her sensitive heart had to experience served but one purpose: to make known to her the will of God, who tries His chosen ones as gold in a furnace. Holiness does not consist in the one act of surrender to God, but in the courageous perseverance in virtue, in the faithful and steadfast doing of the will of God despite all difficulties, even in the face of apparent outward failure. God again chose the weak to confound the strong.

Mother Mary Teresa now rests in the peaceful cemetery of the Carmel of the Divine Heart of Jesus in Sittard, Netherlands. Reverence and love often lead her daughters to her hallowed grave that bears the inscription:

"MOTHER, WE THANK THEE!
MOTHER, WE FOLLOW THEE!"

These words express the desire and holy commitment of her daughters to continue to work in the spirit of their Foundress for the honor of God and the good of souls. Not only do her own daughters visit her grave, even strangers find their way to this sacred spot. They are guided by their veneration, gratitude, or desire to recommend their concerns and misery to this great and noble woman.

After a decade, the heavy financial burden was lifted from the Motherhouse. The Congregation had survived the second severe war without lasting damage. Not one Sister suffered any harm during the war. All this may be ascribed to the intercession of our dear Mother Foundress.

To rescue souls and to bring them to the Divine Heart was the purpose for which Mother Mary Teresa lived, sacrificed, and suffered. This is why she founded the Carmel of the Divine Heart of Jesus. She gave special attention to the children who were physically neglected or who were growing up in a morally corrupt environment, isolated from God and the Church. Indeed, it was already during her youth that she became aware of the misery of these children, and this instilled within her the desire to build a Home for those who had no home. She emphatically impressed on her Sisters that they should first and foremost be mothers to these children and not teachers or nurses. They should be mothers who will sacrifice everything for their children.

This was the reason she did not want the Congregation to do other works of charity. Taking care of orphaned or neglected children should in no way be of secondary importance. Therefore, no schools or hospitals were established. Caring for the elderly was a quietly cherished ideal, and it became a reality when the first "Home for the Aged" was established in America. Here also, her goal was the salvation of souls.

Mother Mary Teresa's daily prayer:

> *O Lord, I vow to you poverty, chastity, and obedience—*
> *To devote my entire self for the salvation of souls—*
> *To the deepest annihilation of self—*
> *To perfect conformity to Your Divine Will—*
> *And to strive to reach the highest love of God and neighbor.*
> *O Lord let this chain of love forever bind me to your Sacred Heart, and in this life let me be a child of my Heavenly Mother.*

After the death of the Foundress, the Carmel of the Divine Heart of Jesus expanded even farther. Its foundations are in Germany, Austria, Switzerland, the Netherlands, Italy, Croatia, Canada, Nicaragua, Brazil, Venezuela, and the United States. Carmelites of the Divine Heart of Jesus are also living in Hungary.

Some months after the death of the Foundress, her hand-written autobiography was found in the archives of the Motherhouse, as her successor, Mother M. Katharina of St. Jude Thaddeus (second Superior General 1939-1957), testified. After Bishop Lemmens of Roermond and his vicar general Dr. Feron had read the autobiography, they urged her to publish it. The Bishop, who had personally known the Foundress and had supported the Congregation in the years of poverty, wished to open the process of her beatification himself. On February 2, 1953, the informative process for the beatification of Mother Mary Teresa of St. Joseph was solemnly opened by Bishop W. Lemmens.

The informative process was completed in 1957.

In 1972, the writings of the Servant of God were approved. Mother Mary Teresa had written over 3,000 letters which were all included in the process. We do not know the number of letters that cannot be found. She wrote, "Not that I had done nothing to procure the necessary means. On the contrary, I worked all day, and in the first years, many a night to obtain alms or to gain friends and benefactors for our work."

Reading the biography of Maria Teresa Tauscher has already given comfort to many, who have to struggle with difficulties and sufferings themselves. Her great gratitude can show us that we can be much happier in life if we know how to be grateful to God for everything. She gave to her Carmel the practice of closing each day with the *"Te Deum."*

Once again, it is the living faith that our times need above all. It is that faith which can move mountains. May she implore this faith for each of us!

*   *   *   *   *   *   *

In her introduction to the first English translation of the Autobiography, Mother M. Katharina of St. Jude Thaddeus, our second Mother General, notes, "Mother Mary Teresa of St. Joseph had a great love for America. When she returned to Europe in 1920, she took some earth from the American soil, and this was to be strewn on her grave. She also expressed the wish to be buried in a habit which she had brought from America."

THE WORLD
FROM WHICH
SHE CAME

Memorial to Mary Tauscher
Foundress of the Carmel, D.C.J.

by
Dr. Eckhard Tauscher

(Translated from the German)

It was only after the death of his relative, Mary Tauscher, Mother Mary Teresa of St. Joseph, that Dr. Eckhard Tauscher became acquainted with the Sisters of the Congregation that she had founded. From then on he showed great interest in her and her work. His grandfather was the youngest brother of Hermann Tauscher, the father of dear Mother Foundress. His grandmother also was from the Tauscher family. "Aunt Mary" was thus a cousin of his parents. He, like no other, is qualified to trace the family history of our Foundress and to show its spiritual and cultural background.

For a better understanding let the following be said: not only were the father and grandfather of the Foundress Protestant Pastors, but there was also a whole line of ministers, sons-in-law, grandsons, and great-grandsons among the descendants of the grandfather. The father of Dr. Eckhard Tauscher was also a Pastor. He was stationed for about thirty years at the Parish of Gusow, which was the last assignment of Mother Foundress' father. Thus he himself knows very well the atmosphere of a Lutheran-Evangelical Parsonage of those days.

Hermann Tauscher, the father of the Foundress, was born at Wellersdorf on August 15, 1825. He was Deacon at the Friedenskirche (Church of Peace) in Potsdam from 1852 to 1854, Pastor at Sandow from 1854 to 1862, First Pastor and Superintendent at Arnswalde from 1862 to 1865, Founder and First Pastor of St. Luke in Berlin from 1865 to 1882, and Pastor at Gusow from 1882 to 1897. He died in Berlin on October 31, 1902.

The grandfather, Johann Traugott Leberecht Tauscher, was born in Plossig on February 5, 1799. He died on September 3, 1881, in Zettemin. He was Pastor in Wellersdorf from 1824, in Woxfelde from 1844, and in Zettemin from

1848.

Eckhard Tauscher was in contact with the Motherhouse of the Carmelite Sisters D.C.J. and with Bishop Lemmens of Roermond at the time of the Information Process for the Beatification of the Servant of God, Mother Mary Teresa of St. Joseph. Shortly after the death of his wife, he came to Sittard for the Christmas holidays in 1971. As an "outsider," yet as a brother in Christ, he tries in the following pages to approach the mystery of God in the life of his Aunt Mary but then halts in reverence before it.

What he says about Sittard, the Sisters, and the spirit of the Motherhouse holds good for all the other Homes where the Foundress' word becomes an ever new challenge to be a "Home for the Homeless."

The Carmelite Sisters of the Divine Heart of Jesus

Sittard

May 1973

Traugott Franz Eckhard
Tauscher

THE POWERS OF GOODNESS IN SITTARD
(In gratitude)

At the Central Depot in Cologne on a weekday in the beginning of January, the waving hand of the young religious in the brown habit disappears in the crowd of waving kerchiefs. I too draw in my handkerchief. Now, back to my home, the lonely place from which the sun vanished. I return into the emptiness of my life from which all meaning, all purpose, and (in fact) all was taken. For love is all.

> "Was sind dieses Lebens Gueter?
> Eine Hand
> Voller Sand,
> Kummer der Gemueter…"

>> What are the treasures of this life?
>> A hand
>> Full of sand,
>> Grief of mind…

Of the goods (perhaps not in abundance) of this life, I have sufficient to live free from care. But that is not important. A person who is needed by others, and who may care for others, lives. A man from whom that has been taken continues to exist, but he walks as through a mist. That man's only hope is that out of this mist, some day soon that final piece of sod will emerge which means peace to him.

Cologne is behind us now. The train is speeding southward carrying with it into the darkness an aged man to whom God has said, "NO." Or was it God? And if it were

God, was it a "NO"? These are questions he cannot answer himself. These questions are useless to be asked by a lonely man on the way to his grave because who would seek from him an answer? Thus, he silences all questioning within him.

> "Man sagt, er sei jetzt weise,
> doch wer so spricht, der irrt,
> es schweigt in jedem Greise,
> was ihm begegnen wird.
>
> Wo alle um ihn sprechen,
> sinnt er dem Einen nach.
> Gott wird sie unterbrechen,
> wie er ihn unterbrach."

> They say that he is wise,
> but who thinks so, is wrong,
> the aged man in silence awaits
> what the future holds for him.
>
> Where men raise noisy discussions
> he muses about his loss.
> God will interrupt them
> as He has interrupted him.

Christmas was approaching when the tragedy occurred with the uprooting winds rending my life. "A fugitive and a wanderer shall you be on the earth."

There are still some good people in our times. These are people who want to help you or divert you. From far and near there came invitations from relatives and acquaintances. However, they have their life's work, and they need each other. Among them my life's emptiness would have been unbearable during these days of the feast of the love of God, during which time others find happiness and peace. Therefore, I sought flight. . . nothing but flight! But whither should I flee? Perhaps I should seek the lonely, of course, or those who live in the same state of perdition. Hermann Hesse has felt what the lonely feel:

> "Voll von Freunden war mir die Welt,
> Als noch mein Leben licht war,
> Nun, da der Nebel faellt,
> Ist keiner mehr sichtbar.
>
> Wahrlich, keiner ist weise,
> Der nicht das Dunkel kennt,
> Das unentrinnbar und leise
> Von Allem uns trennt..."

> Many a friend I called my own
> When my life was steeped in light.
> Now that I am feeble and mourn
> There is no one in sight.
>
> No one truly wise can be
> Who has not darkness known
> Which quietly, inescapably,
> Parts us and leaves us alone...

I would have found them, these lonesome people. There are, no doubt, legions of them in the world. But in that hour when I went out to look for them, and when I made the first contact, there came a letter from Holland. The General Motherhouse of the Carmelite Sisters of the Divine Heart of Jesus, the Congregation founded by a convert aunt of mine about ninety years ago, invited me to spend the Christmas days there in a Home for the Aged, an annex to the Motherhouse. In less than five minutes my decision was made. Here was offered me the aim of my flight, not promising to make me forget, nor to console me, but to give me quiet and rest, peace in a foreign country with people whom I respect without understanding them, and whose life I esteem without comprehending it. Can anything better happen to an old man, who sees no purpose to his life, than to live in an environment of pious people with a piety strange to him? There it will not be noticed that I no longer can pray, for I would have to do it with words unfamiliar to me. No one would expect that of me.

I had planned to stay one week in Sittard, but it turned into three. This was not because from the first night on I could sleep again, not because I could live in quiet, not because I was left in peace, but because I was sheltered in a silent goodness.

Last night we sat together once more, the Sisters in their religious garb and in their midst I, a "layman," a Protestant, and the son of a Lutheran pastor. They sang their joyful, yes, really joyful hymns. Towards the end I was asked for my favorite song in such an evening hour. And so we sang together Paul Gerhardt's evening song:

> "...
> Mein Augen stehn verdrossen,
> im Nu sind die geschlossen.
> Wo bleibt dann Leib und Seel'?
> Nimm sie zu deinen Gnaden,
> sei gut fuer allen Schaden,
> Du Aug' und Waechter Israel.
>
> Breit aus die Fluegel beide,
> o Jesu, meine Freude,
> und nimm dein Kuechlein ein!
> Will Satan mich verschlingen,
> so lass die Engel singen:

Dies Kind soll unverletzet sein."

Mine eyes with weariness have drooped,
Soon will they be closed.
Where then shall body and soul dwell?
Take them in Your grace,
All blemish to efface,
You watch and guard of Israel.

Spread out Your wings,
Oh Jesus, my joy,
And let me hide in Thee!
In that dread hour
When Satan seeks to devour, let angels sing:
This child unharmed shall be.

Shortly before we parted, my eyes wandered once more
to the picture of the Foundress of this Congregation. She
had known this song by heart. She prayed it as a child at
mother's knee as all the Tauscher children have prayed it.
This was the song "Spread out Your wings." She sang it
often together with her father, the Lutheran Superintendent, her mother, and her sisters. Now she looks down
on us from the picture. The kindness in her eyes betrays
neither the penance she has practised all her life, nor the
difficulties and persecutions which she overcame from
the outset of her work. The average person would have
given up. Giving up was not her style, and not, at least, at
that time, the style of the Tauschers. A humble heart, an
outcast from home and family, filled with charity, a pious
woman's heart against a Cardinal. . . these phrases could
be the heading over this woman's first steps in the foundation of her work. No, not "her" work. She would not
sanction it when one would speak of "her" work. It was
God's work, and she was the instrument. Therefore, the

little heart, and not the great Prince Bishop and Cardinal, was victorious! If we knew nothing else of the life of Mary Teresa Tauscher we could already understand why the Bishop of Roermond of that time found her worthy of the honor of the altars when he introduced the Information Process for her beatification. Yet this man had probably no idea of the whole story of the church-political background of events.

Neither does one suspect that behind the kind eyes that looked down on me there in Sittard that there was something of a readiness to fight and a refusal to surrender. But I, the last in line of this Tauscher family of pastors, recognize (and not without pride) in the beginnings of the work of this woman (whose religious beliefs I do not share) that confession of faith "EVEN THEN will I trust," without which no religion is true. "EVEN THEN I abide with You. EVEN THEN You are the consolation and the portion of my heart." For one hundred and fifty years the Tauschers have been victorious through their conviction of deep faith in spite of contradiction. The grandfather of this woman was against secular authority, the father was against theological liberalism and public opinion, and the cousin, as successor to her father, was against the Church authority. Was all that coincidence? I do not think so! Yet maybe I first had to go to Sittard to experience among her spiritual daughters the faith active in charity in order to find it worth consideration and to retrace it in history.

In 1824 King Friedrich Wilhelm III of Prussia, interested in theological questions, intended to unite the Congregations of the Reformed and the Lutheran Church into one National Church, thus forming a "Union" of both denominations. As one of the prerequisites, therefore, he had a Ritual, acceptable to both Churches, composed from an outline he had drawn up.

In the same year, 1824, the grandfather of the Foundress of the Carmelite Sisters of the Divine Heart (which on March 19, 1973 celebrated the seventy-fifth anniversary of the foundation of their Motherhouse in Sittard) became Pastor of the Lutheran Congregation in Wellersdorf in the Lausitz. From the beginning he was doubtful about the new Ritual mainly because of the changes in the Lutheran celebration of the Lord's Supper in favor of the Reformed Church. At first he kept these doubts to himself, since the King left the introduction of the new Ritual up to the free decision of the Congregations. However, as many of the Lutheran Congregations adhered to their former ritual, or as Tauscher in Wellersdorf accepted only minor changes in the celebration of the Divine Worship, it was obvious that this optional way would not lead to the "Union" desired by the King. So in the year of 1834, by order of His Majesty the King's Cabinet, the introduction of the new Ritual became obligatory.

Now on the feast of the Trinity of 1834, Pastor Johann Traugott Leberecht Tauscher, who was determined to fight for the cause, went to the pulpit and announced to the Congregation the King's order. He proposed that they come in the morning of the following Sunday for the unchanged, complete Liturgy for High Feasts, and arrive in the afternoon for the new, abridged Liturgy, both of which he would conduct each Sunday. He further added, "In giving this information to a Christian Congregation, I wish to ask you that everyone recommend beforehand this intention to God in prayer so that the Holy Spirit may guide us to do what is right."

After attending both Services, the Congregation in one accord opposed the new Ritual. Tauscher then reported this to the King's Consistory on June 27, 1834, concluding with these words: "I therefore believe that in complying with the unanimous decision of my Congregation to retain the former order of worship, the Lutheran Rite, I act according to my conscience and the duties of my office."

The news that the Wellersdorf Congregation would retain the old Lutheran order of worship, and not accept the new Ritual, struck like a bomb in Lausitz. Sunday after Sunday people came from far and near in order to be able to celebrate the Lord's Supper in the Lutheran way. They brought their children to be baptized, and asked Tauscher to enroll their children in Confirmation classes to have them confirmed by him, the "orthodox believer." They arrived for the Sunday Services on Saturday afternoons from distances up to twelve Prussian miles (about 56 miles). In those days there was no public transportation.

At first nothing happened because Tauscher did not baptize any child of another parish for which he did not have the "Dimissoriale," the written consent of the Pastor of whose Parish the family belonged. This was a procedure permitted by Church law, but the Authorities looked with great displeasure upon these pilgrimages to Wellersdorf.

One day two children from the vicinity of Breslau were brought to him for Baptism without the Dimissoriale. Tauscher refused to baptize them. The parents laid the children on the table before him saying, "Reverend Pastor, we have brought these children to you from a distance of 112 miles with great difficulty and much expense. We were confident that you, as Pastor of the

Lutheran Church, would help and assist your persecuted fellow believers. Here they are, the poor little creatures! Would you want us to take them back unbaptized? If they should die on the way, or if need be, we ourselves had to baptize them and then had to go to prison for being unable to pay the fine for it, would your conscience be at peace? Would you, a Lutheran Pastor, refuse us with these poor children?" Of course, Tauscher baptized the children.

Finally the Royal Government had a claim against him. On his thirty-sixth birthday, February 5, 1835, he received a summons to appear in court. His wife and children (his oldest son, Traugott Hermann, the father of the Foundress, was then ten years old) sang in answer to the government notification the following stanza of the hymn:

"Warum sollt' ich mich denn graemen?
Hab ich doch
Christus noch,
Wer will mir den nehmen?
Wer will mir den Himmel rauben,
Den mir schon
Gottes Sohn
Beigelegt im Glauben?"

Why should I dejected be?
Have I not
Christ for my lot?
Who will take Him from me?
Who will deprive me of Heaven,
Which God's Son
For me has won,
Through faith to me 'tis given?

The Sunday before he had to appear at the Court of

Sorau, Johann Traugott Leberecht Tauscher mounted the pulpit once more, probably for the last time, as he told his weeping Congregation. The next day he confirmed the children from the neighboring parishes, and the following day those of his own Congregation. Communion Services for six hundred people lasted from 9:30 a.m. until 2:00 p.m. The hearing by the Royal Commission took place the next day. Tauscher refused to introduce the new Ritual into his Congregation, therefore he was suspended.

The following Sunday the Superintendent of the Union preached, but he stood before empty pews. The fathers in Wellersdorf assembled their families in their homes with their doors locked for fear of the police. There they knelt and prayed for their Pastor. Then the Superintendent of the Union, at that time a Royal Official with corresponding faculties, made a great mistake. Enraged by the boycott of his sermon, he ordered the Congregation and the Elders to appear for interrogation as to why they did not come to church. The people asked by what law they were bound to go to church. The Union Superintendent had no answer. They then remarked that there were many people in Sorau who seldom went to church, and some never, among them were the aristocrats with whom the Superintendent associated. Why did he not also interrogate them? The Superintendent tried to evade this painful situation by explaining theologically that there was no essential difference between the Lutheran and the Reformed teaching of the Lord's Supper. But the farmers of Nether-Lausitz knew better. "This is my Body..." or "This signifies my Body...", there should be no difference? The Superintendent had to let the people go.

The church in Wellersdorf, before which the police stood guard to hinder the Parishioners and the suspended Pastor from entering except at the time of Sunday Services conducted by the Union Minister, remained empty. The children to be baptized were taken to a seventy-seven year old Pastor at Reinswalde who baptized them according to the old Lutheran Rite without the Dimissoriale, which Tauscher had no faculty to give. Because of his advanced years, the authorities did not interfere. The dead were buried with the tolling of bells and singing of hymns but without a Minister. Once when a farmer on his deathbed forbade the presence of the Union Pastor at his funeral, the attendance was exceptionally large. All the mourners knelt at the grave (an act not common in Lutheran Congregations) and prayed aloud the "Our Father."

But this passive resistance could not remain for long. Shortly after the suspension of their Pastor, the Congregation petitioned the King: "Your Majesty, will you not have pity on us, and in your fatherly mercy graciously permit us to retain our old Ritual. Return to us the Pastor of our souls and let us continue to exist as a Lutheran Congregation in the National Church." Urged by the Congregation, Tauscher also made an application, "Your Royal Highness, deign to permit us to continue quietly and undisturbed with the practice of our old ritual within the National Church."

Waiting in vain for an answer, the Congregation sent a delegation to Berlin. After much pleading, they obtained from the Royal Consistory the permission to continue in their Lutheran faith and administration of the Sacraments, and they were recognized as a Congregation of the National Church but spiritually independent of the Union. This was the only case at that time that a Pastor with his

Congregation had procured from the King the acknowledgement of the old Rite, independent of the Union, and at the same time the affiliation with the National Church. In the Seven Books of Prussian Church History" (Volume II, page 336, Berlin 1859) this is recorded as follows: "We consider Tauscher the only one of the suspended Pastors of that time who has followed the simple way prescribed in the Gospel, 'If your gift is ministry, then use it in ministering!' (Rom. 12:7)."

Why do I relate a story which happened about a hundred and fifty years ago, the denominational facts of which interest no one today? Important to me were the children of the Confirmation class whom the Wellersdorf farmers boarded for months just for a "God reward you" in order that they would be instructed in the faith of their fathers. Also I am thinking of the two unbaptized children placed on the table before Tauscher and who were thereby on his conscience.

About fifty-five years after these events had taken place, the first children who were also spiritually deprived found a "Home for the Homeless" in Pappelallee in East Berlin with the granddaughter of this man, who, in his own way and according to his belief, fought for the Kingdom of God.

One day in the dining room of the Gusow Parsonage (it must have been toward the end of the First World War), a visitor turned the conversation to "the Catholic Mary," as Aunt Mary was called by the family as far as her existence was known. Her name was not to be mentioned in the presence of the children. "Just imagine," the visitor told me, "she was expelled from Prussia because she had rented a house in Berlin, went on the streets, and lured the Protestant children to her, making them Catholics!"

My father, a strict Lutheran like the grandfather of the Nun and successor in office to her father in Gusow, listened. "Naturally, that is all nonsense," he said. "But if it were so, don't you think that it was better that Mary made the children Catholic, as you say, than to let them die in the gutter?" Embarrassed silence followed for minutes. Perhaps most of the readers of these lines do not see an inner parallel between Wellersdorf of 1835 and Pappelallee of 1891. I do see it, perhaps, because of the ecumenical perspective, which broadens our view these days.

Aunt Mary was a witness to her father's deep faith, overcoming hatred and opposition in his attitude of "EVEN THEN will I trust," and has honored it in the memoirs of her life. These are mainly the years from 1869 to 1881, during which Hermann Tauscher was Editor of the "Evangelical Church News." This paper "attacked," as the Church Historian Press from Erlangen says, "like a chained watchdog everything that seemed to discredit the Lutheran Church, and did not halt even before the Royal Prussian Union." By this medium of communication, but more so by personal public controversy, by being insulted as the "Zealot Tauscher," he fought for the preservation of the fundamental truths of Christendom against the theology of liberalism, and even exposed himself to the personal hatred of the Prussian Crown Princess of those days. Years later when the Crown Prince, the father of the last German Emperor, once met his former classmate from the Gymnasium of the Grey Cloister in Berlin, Traugott Julius Tauscher, the brother of Hermann, was wanting to introduce him to the Crown Princess. She turned aside saying, "Tauscher! Oh, all you Tauschers are as black as night!" Nevertheless, Traugott

Hermann Tauscher remained firm. He became President of the Pastoral Conference of Berlin. In 1873 he was co-founder of the so called "August Conference" which included all "orthodox" Lutheran theologians in Prussia. In 1877 he founded the "Home Mission of Berlin" together with the renowned Court Chaplain, Adolf Stoecker, who enjoyed the special benevolence of Prince Wilhelm, later Emperor Wilhelm II, and who made a very deep impression on Aunt Mary when she met him in her parent's home in Berlin. This Home Mission is still working with God's blessing today.

In the Prussian National Church of those days, there was hardly any leader or important personage besides Counts and Lords of the Prussian nobility whom the Foundress of the Carmelite Sisters of the Divine Heart of Jesus had not met. This was so especially during the years of 1874 to 1878 after the death of her mother. She not only was in charge of the household but also of Parish activities. Certainly, mental and spiritual incentives were not wanting to her in those days, for many of the gentlemen remained for dinner, and according to Lutheran tradition, conversation at the table in this leading circle of the Berlin Parsonage was an essential part of the discussions on special church and political problems.

On one occasion a guest turned the conversation to the dogma of the Infallibility with the remark, "How is it possible that a man can declare himself [to be] infallible?" Then, the not yet twenty year old Mary responded, "It is not meant that way, but 'ex cathedra' means the same as when the high priest of the Jews was prophesying only in his capacity as high priest." There followed an embarrassed silence. Of course there was not one of the theologians present who did not know this, yet it seemed ridiculous to be told so by a young girl!

The most important guest at the Tauscher Parsonage was probably the aforementioned Court Chaplain Stoecker. Dr. Cremer, a leading theologian of that time, said about him, "No one can preach the Gospel as Stoecker. None of us can compare with him. He is the only man in Berlin who can really preach." No wonder that Aunt Mary went often to his services in the Berlin Cathedral and told him that she had much to thank him for. After she had become a Catholic, she visited Stoecker in the interest of her "homeless" children of Berlin. It is interesting for us to know that she did this not on her own (although she personally knew Stoecker), but on the advice of a Catholic Priest. Interesting, also, is what Stoecker told the convert daughter of his friend and co-worker on parting, "I am glad that you have found peace." These were unusual words, if one thinks back eighty years when there was no thought of an ecumenical movement. These were words of deep human understanding which Mary had never heard before, nor would hear again from members of church circles which she had left, including her own father who, in spite of all his renown, could not step over his own shadow. Indeed, these were words of unusual tolerance from a Protestant leader of that time!

The peace of that day which Miss Tauscher had found (as Stoecker saw it) was found by all her associates and followers. Today it is found by all in Sittard who desire it, "Peace I bequeath to you, my own peace I give you, a peace the world cannot give; this is my gift to you. Do not let your hearts be troubled or afraid." (John 14:27).

Wellersdorf, Woxfelde, and Zettemin, as long as Johann Traugott Leberecht Tauscher was in office, kept the old

Lutheran Rite in essential points, especially in the administration of the Sacrament of the Altar amid the "Evangelical National Church of the Old Prussian Union" which allowed theological liberalism. His son-in-law, his successor in Zettemin, followed his example. It was the same with Sandow, Arnswalde, the Berlin Congregation of St. Luke, and Gusow while Traugott Hermann Tauscher was in charge. In Gusow this order of Divine Service was practised until 1936 when the last of the Tauscher Pastors had to retire because of a severe eye defect. Since then, these Parishes have become an arid land and continue to become even more arid.

In the years between 1920 and 1930 this last Lutheran Pastor of the Tauschers suffered an attack against his administration and against the faith of his Congregation by the Countess, the Protectress of the Church, which was supported by the Consistory, the official Authority of the Church. He was offered the office of Superintendent if he would submit. This was also the wish of the General Superintendent (Head Minister of a Diocese). "Tell the Reverend General Superintendent that here in Gusow I am the Bishop!" my father answered the Representative of the Consistory. He, in turn, angrily replied that Traugott Johannes Tauscher should not imagine that the official Authority of the Church would not be able to break the resistance of a single Pastor. Like a thunder bolt my father's fist struck the table, "And if Consistory Councillors are raining from the sky, Dr. X., no one of them will make me waiver in my convictions, and I have my Congregation behind me as ninety years ago the old Wellersdorfers stood behind my grandfather!" The Representative of the Union returned to Berlin, and nothing ever transpired.

Eberhard Bethge wrote the first biography about his friend Dietrich Bonhoeffer, the best-known Protestant Theologian Martyr of the Third Reich, entitled, "Resistance and Surrender." The words "Powers of Goodness" which I used in the heading of this meditation are words of this Martyr of Jesus Christ, which were written in one of his darkest hours. Through the person of their Foundress, the Powers of Goodness in Sittard are also the fruit of resistance and surrender. That is why I spoke of the resistance that the three Tauscher Pastors of the past hundred and fifty years have performed for their faith. This picture is completed, however, only through the resistance of the daughter of the second one, the convert to Catholicism. For here, this resistance is perfected, and that means it becomes victorious through obedience.

To describe this "way of resistance in obedience" would be the subject of a biography about the Foundress of the Carmelite Sisters, D.C.J., because her autobiography gives only a few indications, at least in the beginnings of this obedience. That is, in my opinion, the most essential, and the most decisive part. Her opposition towards her father is hardly mentioned in her autobiography. This opposition, which no doubt lasted for many years, is no surprise considering the two strong characters of father and child with opposing convictions clashing in the narrow family circle. On the contrary, we find a profusion of words of recognition for his positive religious attitudes and willingness to defend his faith. We have no details, but we know that until her final departure from home she was an obedient daughter to her stern father and, at the same time, she remained true to her religious convictions. When speaking of her own life, it was done with great modesty and almost secrecy. For example, the time between 1874 and 1879 must have been of importance for her spiritual development. At this time she presided over her father's parsonage in Berlin and took part in conversations with prominent Protestant Theologians and the faithful of the Brandenburg Nobility. Of this period in her life we find but one sentence: "Hardly twenty years of age, I had to manage the household." Of the time in Gusow there is strictly speaking only this, "I benefited greatly from the solitude and quietness of the country; we lived a truly happy life in this isolated village." She did not mention that the Church Protector, Count Richard Clemens (titled "illustrious") of Schoenburg-Glauchau, rode on horseback to inspect his estate and almost daily stopped at the Parsonage where current civil, church, and political questions were discussed. There is no word that she herself with her parents often used to be guests at the Castle, and there was scarcely one family of High Nobility with whom she was not acquainted, not to mention those of the gentry from the surrounding areas. Neither does she speak of the connections with the Officers' Corps of the Prussian Army which was opened for her by her step-mother who was of the nobility. This corps included her "cousin" Erich Ludendorff who later became General Quartermaster in the First World War and often was a guest in Gusow. I know only from one of her first companions that she had prayed for this once so-renowned General after he had renounced his faith, and she told this confidant, who was already near the throne of God, that he was "saved" by the grace of God.

Besides all this, she was a beautiful woman. Her picture in the religious habit reveals this even after decades. She was not only refined and intelligent, she intellectually surpassed all women of her rank and surrounding. I do not know whether it is true (as the old people of Gusow had told me when I was a child) that a Count had asked for her hand in marriage. However, she could have married well, could have played any role, and could have been the center of an illustrious society. She was never proud, arrogant, or vain. I would consider it a miracle that with the importance of her position and situation that she went the way she did. Today we can trace that to Sittard.

About this we know little or nothing. Everything that she herself had written about her religious inclinations, her early aversion to Lutheranism (to which her mother, whom she loved above all, and her "dear little" grandmother adhered without reserve), and all that she said about her approach to Catholic circles, and about her conversion does not, at least to an outsider, explain sufficiently this step, nor what she afterwards did. There must have been spiritual powers at work which a person, guided by them, cannot explain, and before which an outsider stands amazed. When she became a Catholic on October 30, 1888, she prayed the Tridentine Creed of 1564, which is in the form of an oath and accentuates the Dogmas and the Sacraments denied by the Reformers. Soon after the Council of Trent had opened, at which this Creed was composed, Luther died. Had he lived to see the reform decrees of this Council on the formation of the Clergy and against the abuses in the Church which he had protested, the division never would have occurred. The movement which he had started, but did not want to be named after him, developed after his death in directions of which he would not have approved. Nevertheless, this is said only on the sideline as an explanation for my view that in this conversion and way of life there was more involved than the rejection of exterior forms and practices and the "soberness" of the Reformed Church. No biography, if it were written in these days, could say anything about it. Perhaps had it been started sooner, one could have gathered more information about human relations and attitudes. I first met the Carmelite Sisters at the end of April 1943 in Berlin at the funeral of the youngest sister of the Foundress. At that time there were people who had known her and were still living in Gusow and in St. Luke's, Berlin. From the relatives who had grown up with her more details could have been obtained. Yet, was that essential?

Looking back over the last decades before the turn of the century and thinking of the so-called "good" society and its life style, one can clearly see that this woman was an exception. Something has already been mentioned. Mary Tauscher grew up in a Church which emphasized authority. Its controlling power, the upper class, adhered to the Throne just as closely, if not more so, as to the Altar for whom the one without the other could hardly be imagined. For the ladies of this society, it was a time of patriotic associations and benefit bazaars. This was about the only way that the worker, the lower class, was assisted. In contrast, however, this woman stood apart from such associations in dispensing charity and mercy. She went to the poor and homeless children; she was not satisfied by merely giving alms and Christmas parties. To know this is sufficient for me, for the fruits of this life have, after eighty years, ripened and nourish today the lonely and the homeless.

What happened after this woman had made up her mind to join the Catholic Church can be explained. Here too we have the working in deep faith in spite of difficulties and persecutions; "EVEN THEN will I trust." Here too a person renders resistance, not a resistance in disobedience, but a resistance through continuous obedience, through untiring willingness to suffer, and a resistance through loyalty. That she does not depart from what she believes to be the truth shows her to be a true daughter of her father. Yet as she continues on her way she surpasses both him and her grandfather. The founding of a new Congregation, which she does not undertake by herself because she considers it to be the Will of God, is forbidden her. By the command of the Prelate, the Blessed Sacrament is consumed. Nonetheless, she continues not in another Order, as she had been advised, but alone, destitute herself for the destitute, homeless herself for the homeless. She believes it is God's Will and that God is with her. Therefore, a Cardinal gains nothing by going against her. Perhaps in those days of "Raging Waters of Affliction," as she herself called them, she remembered the verse of a hymn she sang as a child:

"Die Sach' ist Dein, Herr Jesu Christ,
Die Sach' an der wir steh'n,
Und Weil es Deine Sache ist,
Kann sie nicht untergeh'n."

The cause is Yours, Lord Jesus Christ,
The cause for which we stand,
And because it is Your cause
It shall not go a-strand.

Victorious was not the Cardinal, Prince-Bishop of Breslau, victorious was not the Prelate of St. Hedwig, Berlin, victorious was not Reverend Alesch, nor victorious was

Father S. Victorious was the little, the poor, the rejected daughter of the Superintendent of Gusow in the Mark. However, she would not want to hear that, for she believed the Will of God was victorious.

During the peaceful hours which I was privileged to spend in Sittard, we spoke much of Aunt Mary and her way. I remembered then a conversation that I had had with an older cousin of mine who was a Pastor and also a nephew of Aunt Mary. He knew nothing of her except that her name was Mary and that she had become a Catholic. I told him of Cardinal Kopp's refusal to let Aunt Mary found a new congregation. At first he would not believe me, as he stated, "It is impossible that this wise Church leader should have committed such folly! Nothing greater could have happened to the Catholic Church in the Capitol of the Reich than that the convert daughter of a royal Prussian Lutheran Superintendent wanted to found a Catholic Congregation of Sisters!" But it was neither folly nor short-sightedness. It was, if I see the connections correctly, a thoroughly prudent political decision of the Church. By way of explanation we may say that the Cardinal had sufficient knowledge not only of Hermann Tauscher's activities in the seventies in Berlin, but also of his connections, through which Stoecker's Christian Social Party reached into the Reichstag and to the Throne with the aid of his friend, the Royal Court Chaplain Rudolf Koegel. The *Kultukampf* (Bismark's struggle with Catholicism) had ended only a little more than ten years before. If now the oldest daughter of the co-founder of the Home Mission in Berlin, as a Religious of an already existing Order, would have used a branch of the work which her father had begun in the Catholic field, the State and the Public would not have opposed it. If, however, she intended to start a new Congregation for this purpose, it would have aroused the Christian Social Party to action or, at least, a sharp anti-Catholic propaganda could have been expected from the political and the Protestant-theological Liberalism. Obviously, the Cardinal did not want to expose to danger either the relatively small Catholic population in Berlin or the Catholic Church in Prussia. This might have been the considerations of the Archbishop of Breslau. Yet Mary Tauscher could not have known this. As a Catholic she obeyed the command of her Bishop. What he could not command was her belief that God had given her this work to do, and in this belief she conquered.

Before the bombs of the Second World War destroyed almost all family remembrances, we had at home two thick photo albums with family pictures. Among them were several of Aunt Mary and her sisters. They all had a certain family resemblance. It is said that being in constant contact with another person is supposed to produce a similarity with that person. I do not know if that is true, but the first time we visited the Motherhouse in Sittard we saw a Sister who looked just like Aunt Mary in her younger years. She was delighted when I told her so. However, there were "interior" similarities of greater importance. Ten weeks after the death of my wife, the Sisters of Sittard called me from my "homelessness" to their home. There I spent several weeks. I was greeted, among others, by the (then) Vicar General with a warmness which cannot be acquired by study because it comes from faith that expresses itself in love (Gal. 5:6). I was told that the Sister had suffered from a severe illness, and, therefore, I could see her only occasionally. On the morning of my departure she came with the other Sisters to the car and, shaking my hand she said, "If you cannot cope with your loneliness, come again; you are always welcome." Kindness radiated from her eyes. It was a warming love, which seeing a stranger's need, forgot her own misery. When I returned in less than a year, she had departed this life. One of her last sayings, reported by the General Superior to the Sisters all over the world was, "It is beautiful to live with Christ, but more beautiful still to die with Him." She was a witness to love in life and a witness to faith in dying! "Our faith is the victory that has overcome the world," writes St. John the Apostle in his first letter. Not will overcome, nor shall overcome, but has overcome! How many Christians through the centuries have heard these words and have learned to suffer and experience the truth of them? In Sittard a religious woman, a Carmelite, summarizes the experience of the Beloved Disciple, which he expressed at the end of his long life, as her experience in her own words. Thus living and dying by the faith of her Foundress, she has given a testimony to this Foundress who shines as a beautiful gem in her crown. On my next visit to Sittard for which the departed had invited me, I could but stand at her grave. I understood then that standing at a grave can be a grateful joy, and that also was for me a blessing of the "Powers of Goodness" in Sittard.

The last time I was in Sittard, some of the Sisters visited their Home in Frankfurt on the Oder, and from there the village of Sandow in Sternberger Land across the Oder, which is now in Poland. When the Sisters returned, the accounts they brought with them turned back the pages of time in my memory to the childhood and youth of Aunt Mary. She was born in Sandow on historical ground, so to say, not far from Kunersdorf where in the year 1759, the great Prussian King, victory already in sight, underestimated his opponent, lost the battle, half of the army, and almost his own life. Mary was six years old when her father was promoted to superintendent and assigned to St. Mary's Church in Arnswalde. At thirty-seven years of age he must have been the youngest Church superintendent in the country. Here he stayed only three years and then was transferred to Berlin where he was stationed for sixteen years. This was the time when he proved himself true as he opposed those who denied the fundamental truths of the Christian faith. His oldest daughter was conscious of his struggle in those most difficult years, respected his attitude, and considered it just. Why she did not continue with him on his way, why she not only gave up her family but also left the Church of her fathers, of which she, as a daughter of such an important representative, could have been proud, we do not know. My father once said something similar to this, "For this woman of strong faith, prudent and of great initiative, there was no place in the Evangelical Church of those days." That is certainly true. Nevertheless, even though there had been a place, without her Sittard would not be. Without her, the "Powers of Goodness" for the security of the many lonely and homeless would neither be there nor in the many other Homes that exist today still breathing her spirit. That should silence our query. It should suffice us to conclude from the way she went and which, according to the words of Bishop Wilhelm of Roermond, made her "the greatest and most remarkable woman of this century," that she, in her deep faith, in spite of persecution ("EVEN THEN will I trust"), stood just as firm as her Lutheran ancestors, and was just as unflinching in obedience to the faith as they. That her resistance against the rejection of her faith was not a negative rebellion but a positive one again demonstrated nothing but obedience. In this obedience, resulting for her in great need and suffering, she remained steadfast to the last. Yet for those of us who stand "outside," that too is not the deciding factor. The deciding factor is that this spirit, this faith proven in obedience, was and is effective beyond her grave. Perhaps, to understand this, one must have passed through the very depth of true suffering, and to have been burdened to the limit of one's endurance with failures, mistakes, and faults, abandoned by love.

The Disciple John tells the story of how Jesus called Phillip to follow Him, and how the latter in turn told Nathanael that he had found the Messiah, namely "Jesus, Son of Joseph of Nazareth."

"Can anything good come out of Nazareth?" answered Nathanael.

But Phillip insisted, "Come and see" (John 1:45).

Sittard, too, is but an insignificant Nazareth, and to find the Savior of the World there or in any other part of the world depends on the intensity of the search. But the breathing of His Spirit can be felt there by the brokenhearted and those who are crushed in spirit (Psalm 34:19). He experiences, if he is rightly disposed, some of the faith which is active in charity, which suffers in obedience, and is obedient in suffering. These are the invisible "Powers of Goodness" which draw out of the depths into security as the already mentioned Christian Martyr of our time has confessed in faith:

"Von guten Maechten wunderbar geborgen,
erwarten wir getrost was kommen mag.
Gott ist mit uns am Abend und am Morgen

Und ganz gewiss an jedem neuen Tag."

By the powers of goodness wonderfully borne,
We calmly await what may come our way.
God is with us at evening and at morn,
And He will be with us each new day.

Prelate D. Dr. Th. Schnitzler
Pastor at Sts. Apostles   Cologne, July 5, 1973

Venerable Sisters:
XXXI
Many thanks for your kindness in sending me your booklets and papers!

It is, indeed, a long time since I have read anything so beautiful as Dr. Tauscher's writing on your Foundress. I admire the literary quality of the composition, its plaintive poesy and inner piety and the pious touch of which is not repelling but rather attractive. The scholarly general historical view and the convincing integration of the person of your Foundress into this milieu is admirable. The attempt to explain the rejective attitude of Prince Bishop Kopp is an alluring and significant apology, although I believe that German Hierarchy of that time is not completely to be absolved from a certain hostility against Religious Orders. The aspect of life all through the family and personal history is magnificent. The way Dr. Tauscher presents the uniform life from grandfather to grandchild is complete. Besides, it was urgently needed that the heritage which lay hidden in the Foundress be set forth. Once again we are standing with admiration before the cultural strength of the East German Protestant parsonage.
I wish to congratulate Dr. Tauscher on his writing which is "deserving of the Nobel Prize." I congratulate the Sisters on this portrait of their Foundress which belongs in the hands of each Sister and especially in the hands of the Roman Administrators for the Beatification Process.
God bless you!

Yours in Christ,
Dr. Th. Schnitzler